# THE STATE OF THE LANGUAGE

# THE STATE
# OF THE LANGUAGE

*English Observed*

BY

# PHILIP HOWARD

New York
OXFORD UNIVERSITY PRESS
1985

*Egeriae*

First published in Great Britain in 1984
by Hamish Hamilton Ltd
Garden House 57–59 Long Acre London WC2E 9JZ

First published in the United States in 1985
by Oxford University Press, Inc.
200 Madison Avenue, New York, New York 10016

Copyright © 1984 by Philip Howard

ISBN 0–19–520467–0

Filmset by Wyvern Typesetting Ltd, Bristol
Printed and bound in Great Britain by
Richard Clay (The Chaucer Press) Ltd, Bungay, Suffolk

# CONTENTS

# INTRODUCTION

'In his whole life man achieves nothing so great and so wonderful as what he achieved when he learnt to talk.' Ascribed to 'a Danish philosopher' in Otto Jesperson, *Language*, V, 1922

'Language is not an abstract construction of the learned, or of dictionary-makers, but is something arising out of the work, needs, ties, joys, affections, tastes, of long generations of humanity, and has its bases broad and low, close to the ground.' Walt Whitman, *Slang in America*, 1885

Let us not give in to the delusion of the middle-aged that the world is going to the dogs. They have been spreading the delusion since records were kept, from ancient Nestor looking back wistfully to the golden heroes who were slain in front of Troy, adding, as a pathetic postscript to the list, his own dear son, to Harold Macmillan reminiscing about the golden *douceur de la vie* before the First World War came and ruined everything; from Hesiod, moaning that he was born in this brutal Iron Age, in which men work and suffer continually, to Ronald Reagan looking back through rose-coloured shades at an imaginary America, where men were men, and respected the flag, and grandma and grandpa could sit safely on the stoop in their rocking-chairs without being mugged; from Juvenal to his latest successors as satirists, satire having always found it persuasive to compare the present unfavourably with what has gone before.

The world has been going to the dogs since time began, if you care to look at it that way, dear boy. *Il faut rire avant d'être heureux, de peur de mourir sans avoir ri*. The robust and sensible course is to get on with the business of living, which lasts for a short enough time in any case.

Quite recently the Cassandras and associated worriers have found something new to worry about. They suggest that it is not just the world, and civilization as we know it, that are going to the dogs; but specifically that the English language is falling to bits. This is not an original worry. It comes in waves. Swift reckoned that English was going to the dogs. So did Dr Johnson, who started his *Diction-ary* to stop the rot in the English language, 'which, while it was employed in the cultivation of every species of literature, has itself been hitherto neglected, suffered to spread, under the direction of chance, into wild exuberance, resigned to the tyranny of time and fashion, and exposed to the corruptions of ignorance, and caprices of innovation.'

It is curious, and perhaps significant, that previous periods of revolution in English do not seem to have felt such gloomy apprehensions. When the inflexions of Old English started to wither after the Norman Conquest, when the regional dialects of Middle English started to coalesce, when the new world produced the exuberant fireworks display of new language exemplified by Shakespeare, not a whisper of gloom about the state of the language is recorded for us. Perhaps the Cassandras who felt their language was going to the dogs could not write; and the clerks who could write recognized that language was made for man, not man for language.

The recent wave of worry about the state of the English language has been rolling for about twenty years. It manifests itself in a proliferation of societies for the preservation of pure English, and regular columns in the press largely concerned with verbal error. Disgusted, Tunbridge Wells, and thousands like him or her, write, purple with indignation, to the BBC to protest about alleged solecisms and mispronunciations. The House of Lords has devoted several debates to the subject of the decay of English, during which noble and eloquent voices were raised against the use of such vogue words as *ongoing*, *relevant*, and *viable*.

Disgusted, Tunbridge Wells, and other worriers never stop to ask when English was in its golden age, from which it has declined so disastrously. If you ask them, they tend to reply that it was when they were at school, and were taught old-fashioned English grammar and spelling, and whacked when they got things wrong. The taboo that one must never split an infinitive, and the belief that it is terribly important to know how to spell *eschscholtzia*, are imprinted indelibly in their memories – or some other part of their bodies.

When all else fails, doom-watchers of English do what the desperate and incensed have done as a last resort for the past two centuries: they write a letter to *The Times*.

That was partly how I got into this game. I drew the short straw of having to deal with letters to the editor complaining about the language. Their volume and vehemence are alarming. Their subjects range from the most piddling misprint to the full Doomsday statement that the Death of English and the End of the World are nigh. Probably the most popular topic for complaint, year in, year out, is alleged mispronunciation by news-readers and other regular broadcasters. It is gratifying that people should choose to write to *The Times* about such matters, but not a lot that *The Times* can do about them.

There is a touching belief about that *The Times* is, or at any rate used to be, the guardian of the Queen's English. It is said that before the war any reader who found a misprint in *The Times* and sent it in was paid a shilling: poppycock and folklore. *The Times* has always had misprints. There was the famous one in which a disgruntled compositor altered the account of Queen Victoria opening the Menai Bridge, so that the phrase, 'The Queen then passed over the Bridge', represented Her as doing something far less proper. Folklore, too, I am afraid. Victoria was not there for the opening of the bridge; and diligent search cannot trace so improper a misprint when she visited it two years later. However, I have seen the issue in which a Parliamentary Reporter who had been sacked said goodbye with a bang by inserting, 'The Prime Minister then said he felt like a fuck', at intervals through his final report. We printed it, and caused a sensation to our High Victorian readers. If *The Times* had ever paid a shilling for every misprint, it would have gone out of business within a year.

I regret to say that the popular opinion that *The Times* always wrote the Queen's English well is also more romantic than historical. The Queen herself would not have the vexing rag in the palace. Of course, it published William Howard Russell, George Borrow, and many other vivid journalists. But the cure for admiring the English of *The Times* as the golden standard from which we epigoni have decayed is to read the old issues. The language is often turgid, pretentious, meaningless, and full of solecisms.

For a time I was overwhelmed by the tide of angry letters, and almost succumbed to the delusion that English was decadent, if not terminally ill. Then I took a more robust view, and started writing an occasional column entitled 'New Words for Old'. It was one of the first language columns in the newspapers created by the anxiety of readers on the subject. To write such a column is to give a daily hostage to fortune: old hands in Fleet Street advise that one should write a column about gardening, or ice dancing, or any other daft subject under the sun; but never about correct usage. For as soon as your copy has a misprint or a solecism in it, as is bound to happen in the hurly-burly of daily journalism, you will have twenty gloating letters saying, 'Ya, Boo; Physician heal thyself,' to answer. And I am two-and-twenty, and oh, 'tis true, 'tis true.

Nevertheless, such letters from worriers and gloaters have to be answered. I tend to reply that they must remember that *The Times* contains as many words as three novels of average length; that we do not start writing them until after lunch, and they must be aware of the popular (though exaggerated) reputation of journalists' lunches; that we have the whole mighty paper written, printed, and delivered to their breakfast tables in Exeter or St Andrews on the following morning; that it is a daily miracle of industry and many technologies; and that they must not be surprised if the result displays occasional misprints and other imperfections. It would be a miracle if it did not.

Should we, like Dr Pangloss, dismiss all such worries about the state of the language as mass hysteria, and fly the flag that all is for the best in the best of all possible languages? That might be a bit complacent. It might also be untrue. Language develops to meet the needs of those who use it. It has no independent power to flourish or decay apart from those who speak and write it. The English language is alive and well in the right hands; those of our best writers, and our finest speakers.

In some fields and registers we are using English better than it has ever been used: books of history and biography for the general reader; the general level of rhetoric employed by the man off the Clapham omnibus or the wimmin at Greenham Common; school text books; fiction (we may have no mountains as high as Dickens, Jane Austen, or George Eliot; but the general level of novels, particularly genre novels such as crime or historical romances, is higher than it has ever been; and it is coming richly from all over the English-speaking world, from India to Canada); we have no giants at present, but we are still writing true poetry in a greater variety of registers and dialects than ever before; the general level of English among the mass of the people, particularly spoken English, is higher than ever; journalism (I can see that this is a controversial candidate for inclusion among the medal-winners; but those who oppose it should open their eyes by trying to stay awake while reading old newspapers); broadcasting in all its pullulating new forms.

English is not dying. But for several reasons it is going through a phase of rapid change, probably more rapid than any it has gone through before. This book examines the reasons for the change, and the effect that they are having on the many registers and aspects of English that comprise the Queen's English. It makes a cautious attempt to predict how the language will evolve as the century draws to a close, and we approach the third millennium of the Christian Era, and the year 2000, awesome to the superstitious who apprehend a magic in round numbers. It tries to take a robust view, suitable neither for Cassandra nor for Pangloss. Will English break up into dozens of mutually incomprehensible jargons and dialects? Extremely unlikely. Will our grandchildren be able to understand other English-speakers? Of course they will. Will English become the world language? It already has. For scientific and other purposes, the Russians, the Chinese, and even the French have to speak and read English.

I am not an academic linguistician: it is tiresome that we have not yet invented a satisfactory name for the professional students of linguistics. In any case the academics of English faculties have mostly retreated into their private fortress of structuralism. From outside we hear confused and incomprehensible shouts. It is a tragic paradox that, of all academic disciplines, English should have become so impenetrable to those outside the fortress.

I am a philologist or amateur of the language, and a professional journalist, who watches himself at work, as we all do. The worriers and the Cassandras, Disgusted of Tunbridge Wells and Confused of Clapham, want to know what is happening to their language. They cannot wait for the academics to tell them, and they cannot understand the complex and conflicting theories of the professionals, when they do divulge an explanation. This book is an attempt to give them a straightforward answer to a serious question. It is possible to be serious without being either solemn or incomprehensible. The language belongs to all of us, professional and amateur, worrier and feckless, to make of it what we choose. My argument is that the report of the death of English, like the report of Mark Twain's death, is an exaggeration. There is an English Revolution going on, but it is healthy, manageable, and on the whole beneficial.

I thank all the Cassandras and worriers, Panglosses and Dr Johnsons, and other correspondents who got me into this. Many have become not just regular correspondents, but friends. I thank the noble army of logophiles and wordsmiths, in particular: Vanessa Allatson, Denis Baron, Francis Bennion, Henry Button, Robert Burchfield, Sir David Croom-Johnson, Derek Darby, Charles Douglas-Home, Peter Fellgett, Gay Firth, Alfred Friendly, Roy Fuller, Hamish Hamilton, John Harris, James Holladay, David Hunt, Elspeth Huxley, Nicholas Kurti, Bernard Levin, Edwin Newman, John Newman, Frank Peters, Edward Quinn, Anthony Quinton, Randolph Quirk, Isabel Raphael, William Rees-Mogg, Alan Ross, J. M. Ross, William Safire, Christopher Sinclair-Stevenson, Peter Stothard, John Sykes, Philippa Toomey, Laurence Urdang, and Laurie Weston.

# 1/REGISTERS

'He will on different occasions speak (or write) differently according to what may roughly be described as different social situations: he will use a number of distinct *registers*.' T.B.W. Reid in *Archivum Linguisticum VIII, 32*. 1956

'Write with the learned, pronounce with the vulgar.' Benjamin Franklin, *Poor Richard's Almanac*, 1738

Our perception of the English language and how it works has changed radically in the present generation. In the High Victorian world the pristine philologists saw the language in much the same way as they saw Victorian society: as a pyramid. At the top was the Queen's English (not, as it happens, spoken very well by Her Majesty, who retained a faint German accent all her life; she wrote it with naive charm and enthusiasm). The Queen's English was the sort spoken in an Oxford accent by the educated classes in the south-east of England, taught at the great public schools and the old universities, and printed in *The Times* and the books from the main London publishing houses. Lower down the pyramid were lesser kinds of English: some of them perfectly respectable members of the House of Lords of language, such as the dialects and grammars of Scottish and American English; others of them disreputable commoners, unspeakable by the civilized, such as Cockney or Gorbals.

Of course, sensible philologists, such as the great James Murray caught in his web of words at *The Oxford English Dictionary*, recognized that all language is equal, even if some language is more equal than other. But the Queen's English, with correct grammar, and pronounced in received pronunciation, was the standard at the top of the pyramid. As headmaster of the Hawick Subscription Academy James Murray taught the Queen's English. His pupils may have spoken in the soft accents of the Borders, and used one or two regional words in their essays; but they were expected to conform to rules of grammar, syntax, and pronunciation set by the Queen's English, and taught in schools from Penzance to Orkney.

We have come to recognize that such a rigid class system is as silly in language as it is in society. There is not one correct sort of English, and dozens of lesser breeds of English all more or less conforming to the ideal, and having more value the closer they came to the Queen's English, and less value the farther they diverged from it. English is not a pyramid, but a great city with many suburbs and city centres serving many purposes. The same sort of English, whether the Queen's or anybody else's, is not appropriate to all occasions or uses. There is not one standard English, but many overlapping kinds of English with different functions and contexts.

For example we use a quite different kind of English when we are writing a leader in *The Times* from the kind we use when chatting to strangers in the public bar of a pub. If we do not make this distinction, either the editor will receive a great many outraged letters; or we shall be left talking to ourselves in the centre of a circle of uneasy mutters. Students of linguistics have recently named these different varieties of English registers.

*The Times* leader and pub chat are registers that are widely different and easy to distinguish. But there are many registers in the Queen's English, and the distinction between some of them is fine. We use different registers to talk to different people: to the Queen, to our solicitor, to a member of the family, to a child. But we use a different register to talk on the telephone from the register we use to talk to the same person face to face. The great Survey of English Usage being conducted at University College, London, is recording multifold overlapping registers of English in their rich variety. It has a section on the English spoken on the telephone. Because one's English changes if one is aware that a grammarian with a tape-recorder is eavesdropping, the Survey taps the telephones of University College to record the register (not the matter) of telephone English in its natural habitat.

The two major registers, which take in most of the lesser registers, are written and spoken English. Until recently spoken English was the poor relation. The Queen's English at the top of the pyramid was literary standard English, the grammar and spelling of which were taught at schools and universities across the land. English education was largely carried on by writing and reading. Exams, though they might include a French *dictée*, or a viva voce to test whether candidates understood what they had written in their answers, were in writing. When Henry VI founded Eton College in 1440, the tests for the scholars stipulated that they should not only be poor and needy boys of good character, but also that they should have 'a competent knowledge of reading, of the grammar of

Donatus and of plain song.' Serious learning was in written English.
The spoken word was for recreation: 'On the greater festivals, or
when in winter time a fire shall be allowed in Hall, out of reverence
to God and His Mother, or any other Saint, the Scholars and
Fellows shall be allowed to divert themselves for a reasonable time
after dinner or supper with songs and other proper amusements,
and to discuss poems, chronicles of kingdoms and the wonders of
the world.'

The emphasis has recently swung from written to spoken English.
Schools teach by discussion as well as written tests and essays.
Examinations are conducted by multiple-choice questions, in which
candidates tick the answer they deem correct, as well as writing
answers in prose. The telephone, radio, television, and other new
technologies fill the world with the spoken word. Members of
Parliament make their speeches *ex tempore* from a few notes, rather
than writing them out in stately periods, and learning them by heart.
Business of all sorts is conducted by telephone instead of letter.
Among the most popular programmes on the radio are phone-ins,
in which any member of the public can join in public chat with the
presenter. The heroes and sages of the media age are presenters of
chat shows, masters of the spoken word, who may well be vacuous
blabber-mouths, but who are so fluent that they never commit the
unforgivable sin of the new media of the spoken word: drying up.
And tape recorders enable academics to record and study spoken
English more systematically than ever before.

As usual, when a new truth or an old register has been discovered, the pendulum has swung too far away from the written to
the spoken word. Students graduate from universities incompetent
to write a simple sentence in English, though their knowledge of
other matters and their fluency with the spoken word make their
predecessors from previous generations sound inarticulate pedants.
Business by telephone has become slower and less efficient than
correspondence: secretaries perform elaborate exchanges of
stichomythia in order not to lose the battle of telephone technique,
by putting their bosses on the line before the boss at the other end
comes on. History is taught by worksheets, so that children know
assorted information about life on a medieval estate, but not how to
write it down in a continuous narrative. Extreme proponents of
spoken rather than written English argue that all previous dictionaries and similar reference books are flawed, because they have
ignored the submerged nine-tenths of language, the spoken word.
The next edition of *The Oxford English Dictionary*, they say, will be

published on computer, visual display unit, and tape; and will speak the truth about the language that has been silent until now. This last argument is nonsense. All evidence shows that a new word or new meaning is written down and published somewhere almost as soon as it has been uttered into the language. More English is spoken than written. But the written word is still the great standard and stabilizer of language. Even displayed on a VDU it is more tractable than the fleeting breath of the spoken word.

The recognition of spoken English as a separate predominant register, including its oral grammars, vocabularies, and dialects, is the most obvious change that has happened to English in the recent revolution. The promotion of the spoken word at the expense of the written in education and commerce, in politics and the media, is already having profound effects on the language. A spoken language is, inevitably, less formal and rule-bound than a written one. Very few people have the short-term memory and the fluency to construct elaborate periods in speech. The cure for supposing that they can do so is to read the transcript of any spontaneous conversation or broadcast, even between literati, intellectuals, or Professors of Linguistics. It will be full of catachresis and solecism, of errors of number and case, of grammatical sins of omission and commission. The most frequent words will be the two most popular words in the English language, the ones that never get recorded in the dictionaries: *um* and *er*. There will be a plethora of clichés, vogue words, and cotton-wool pleonasms such as 'at this moment in time', telephrases invented to fill time and avoid the mortal sin of broadcasting: silence for thought. Even as you speak, and the words fly away from you into the darkness, you can tell that they are not expressing your meaning exactly. With the written language you can read what you have written, see that it is not quite right, say, 'damn!', rip the paper out of the roller of the typewriter, and start again. Writing English is constructing dovetail joints on the carpenter's bench. Speaking English is fastening two planks together with a nail in a hurry.

The tendency today is towards the quick spoken communication rather than the carefully carpentered job. Accordingly, sentences are becoming shorter, even in writing. The great rolling periods of Gibbon and the other classic masters of literary English seem magnificent, but strange, memorials of a vanished age. The remaining case endings of pronouns, and other grammatical inflexions created for a written language, are melting like snow in the Sahara. Spelling is no longer rated as an almost moral virtue; and punctuation is being simplified and coarsened to a series of dashes, to indicate pauses for breath in the spoken language. We are uninhibited about using in writing slang, dialect, jargon, and taboo words that were recently banned as disreputable from the literary register, when it was considered the top room in the pyramid. English is becoming looser, quicker, and less precise, as we forget to use the millions of fine and distinct tools in the old literary carpenter's box.

If you want to make our flesh creep, as many do, you can predict that this trend will continue, as with Latin after the Fall of Rome, until English becomes a series of loosely connected pidgins, patois, and grunts. There has been a recent vogue in fiction for constructing such decadent and primitive oral versions of English. William Golding did it in *The Inheritors*, that lament for Neanderthal man that is also, as usual, about the darkness in the heart of homo sapiens, and, in this book, about the difficulties of communicating by non-verbal processes. Russell Hoban did it in *Riddley Walker*, that apocalyptic vision of life after the Bomb. Centralized industrial civilization has been destroyed. The lost past is contained in a kind of sacred book called *The Eusa Story*, of which the first chapter is:

'Wen Mr Clevver wuz Big Man uv Inland they had evere thing clevver. They had boats in the ayr & picters on the win & evere thing lyk that. Eusa wuz a noing man vere quik he cud tern his han to enne thing. He wuz werkin for Mr Clevver wen thayr cum enemes aul roun & maykin Warr. Eusa sed tu Mr Clevver, Now wewl nead masheans uv Warr. Wewl nead boats that go on the water & boats that go in the ayr as wel & wewl nead Berstin Fyr.'

Finally they make use of, 'the Littl Shynyn Man the Addom he runs in the wud.'

*Riddley Walker* is fiction. Its oral English displays anomalies and improbabilities in the way that languages develop, even after a great catastrophe. But it exemplifies powerfully and persuasively many of the ways that English is growing, carried to their extremes.

It is possible, and sensible, however, to take a more robust view of the future of English. The centrifugal forces pulling English apart are strong: the dominance of the spoken word; the proliferation of national dialects of English; the new technologies of communication that simplify and distort; the obfuscations of politicians, the euphemisms, clichés, and vogue words of communicators; the ceaseless chatter of English that can be heard coming from miles away as Earth rolls through space. The new registers.

However the centripetal forces making English the world language are stronger: the media of mass communication that spread the word instantaneously around the global village; pop songs; mass tourism, in which the package holiday to foreign parts is a fundamental annual right; above all the printing press, which still flies the standard even if it is no longer at the top of the pyramid.

Within the great register of spoken English, let us examine how the upper register called the Queen's English, or standard English, or received pronunciation, is doing. It may be instructive about the way that pronunciation is going generally.

It is a comparatively recent notion that there is one standard English pronunciation used by the educated classes, and that everything else is a regional or lower class dialect in a different register. In the sixteenth century, that rich period of linguistic energy and standardization, as far as we can judge from their writings, from both spelling, and observations and jokes about accents, the Elizabethans at court in London spoke in a variety of regional pronunciations. Raleigh and Shakespeare would have sounded West Country Mummerset to us. There is evidence that Queen Elizabeth I would have sounded more Boston Brahmin than Sloane Ranger. A letter from her to her successor, then James VI of Scotland, is revealing about her pronunciation as well as her spelling. She spelt as she spoke. James has been whingeing for an 'instrument' or guarantee that she will pay his pension. Elizabeth teases him about his Scottish habits:

> 'Tochinge an *instrument*, as your secretarye terme it, that you desiar to haue me signe, I assure you, thogh I can play of some, and haue bine broght up to know musike, yet this disscord wold be so grose as were not fit for so wel-tuned musike. Must so great dout be made of fre good wyl, and gift be so mistrusted, that our signe Emanuel must assure? No, my deere brother. Teache your new rawe counselars bettar manner than to aduis you such a paringe of ample meninge. Who shuld doute performance of kinges offer? What dishonor may that be demed? Folowe next your owne nature, for this neuer came out of your shoppe.'

James's reply indicates contemporary Lowland Scottish pronunciation, as well as spelling:

> 'And as for the instrument, quhairunto I desyre your seal to be affixit, think not, I pray you, that I desire it for any mistrust, for I protest before God that youre simple promeis uolde be more then

sufficient to me, if it uaire not that I uoulde haue the quhole worlde to understand hou it pleacith you to honoure me aboue my demeritis, quhich favoure and innumerable otheris, if my euill happ will not permitt me by action to acquyte, yett shall I contend by goode meaning to conteruayle the same at her handis, quhome, committing to the Almichties protection, I pray euer to esteeme me.'

The great register of Lallans or Lowland Scots used by James has been dying ever since. But the pronunciation and a few of the words survive. As late as 1983 *The New Testament in Scots* was published, the hobby-horse and life's work of that great Scottish classicist, Professor William Laughton Lorimer of St Andrews. He was a son of the manse, encouraged to learn as many languages as possible, except for Scotch, which was considered a disreputable register. But as a child he started writing down the Scots words and phrases spoken by the aged and impoverished pensioners who inhabited the cottar-houses behind his father's manse. It grew into a learned passion for resurrecting the dead language. His studies persuaded him that Jesus spakna Standard Aramaic – for ordnar, oniegate – but plain, braid Galilee, and that the New Testament isna written in Standard Greek, as the Kirk Faithers alloued. Here is an example of the register:

'Whan some fowk begoud sayin what bonnie the Temple wis, wi its braw stanes an giftit graith an aa, "The day is comin," qo he, "whan thir biggins ye ar glowrin at will be dung doun, an no ae stane o them left abuin anither."' Lorimer calculated that at least twelve different writers had composed the New Testament, ranging from Paul to the author of *Revelation*. He differentiated different registers of Lallans for each of them. The devil was the only character allowed to speak Standard English.

In plays such as *Henry IV, Parts 1 and 2*, *Henry V*, and *Love's Labour's Lost* Shakespeare illustrated the profusion of registers of spoken English. Standard pronunciation started to evolve in the Age of Reason, which sought standards and explanations for everything. As in so many other linguistic matters, Dr Johnson was a pioneer. In the Preface to his *Dictionary* he observed:

'In settling the orthography, I have not wholly neglected the pronunciation, which I have directed, by printing an accent upon the acute or elevated syllable. It will sometimes be found, that the accent is placed by the author quoted, on a different syllable from that marked in the alphabetical series; it is then to be understood, that custom has varied, or that the author has, in my opinion, pronounced wrong.'

Johnson recognized that the pronunciation of English is a slippery register, changing all the time, and that one could get it wrong. He inclined to the classical and the grandiloquent in pronunciation, as in the rest of his English: 'If you were to make little fishes talk, they would talk like whales.' He was a founding father of received pronunciation, though he himself sounded more like John Arlott (the doyen of English cricket commentators, who has a Wessex accent as broad as the Hampshire Avon) than a Hooray Henry (the Southern Counties equivalent of an ageing Preppy, or an upper-class idiot), thank Heavens.

In the nineteenth century received pronunciation became the standard register for the upper and upwardly mobile middle classes. You can see it happening in the nicely differentiated idiom and accent of the characters in the novels of that mistress of the English class system, Jane Austen. But, even at the peak of the Victorian age, received pronunciation was never standard for the upper classes over the whole country. In particular educated northern speech retained echoes of its Northumbrian and ultimately Viking ancestry, for example in the flatter value given to *a* in such words as *past* and *bath*, which in northern standard pronunciation are rhymed with *lass*, not *Marquis de Sade*.

There has always been controversy about the merits of received pronunciation, even at the time when it was rising to the top of the pyramid. Henry Sweet, the founder of modern phonetics, called it Standard English, and described it as, 'A class dialect rather than any local dialect – the language of the educated all over Britain.'

Henry Wyld, the philologist, lexicographer, and Merton Professor of English language and literature at Oxford from 1920 to 1945, defined received pronunciation of the Queen's English as: 'The pronunciation of the great public schools, the universities and the learned professions, without local restriction.' He called it: 'The best kind of English, not only because it is spoken by those often very properly called the best people, but also because it has two great advantages that make it intrinsically superior to every other type of English speech – the extent to which it is current throughout the country and the marked distinctiveness and clarity of its sounds.'

Not everybody agrees with this favourable assessment. A lecturer in English at Cambridge has described it: 'It is not the accent of a class but the accent of the class-conscious . . . the dialect of an effete social clique, half aware of its own etiolation, capitalizing linguistic affectations to convert them to caste-marks. Its taint of bogus superiority, its implicit snobbery make it resented. Its frequent slovenliness and smudge condemn it on purely auditory grounds.'

Back to Professor Wyld for a finer definition: 'It is proposed to use the term *Received Standard* for that form which all would probably agree in considering the best, that form which has the widest currency and is heard with practically no variation among speakers of the better class all over the country. This type might be called Public School English. It is proposed to call the vulgar English of the Towns, and the English of the Villager who has abandoned his native Regional Dialect *Modified Standard*. That is, it is Standard English, modified, altered, differentiated, by various influences, regional and social. Modified Standard differs from class to class, and from locality to locality; it has no uniformity, and no single form of it is heard outside a particular class or a particular area.'

Outsiders as well as natives differ vehemently about the received pronunciation of the Queen's English. As long ago as 1931 Frank Vizetelly, the English-born American lexicographer, philologist, and popular authority in sanctioning American colloquialisms, was moved to describe it as, 'A debased, effete, and inaudible form of speech.'

He wrote, with more class passion than scientific observation: 'The best people of England today talk with the cockney voice that, leaving the purlieus of Limehouse, has reached the purlieus of Mayfair. This is the aftermath of the war, during which the spirit of democracy prevailed, and the pronunciation of the common people left its impress indelibly on the so-called best people, with a few languid drawls, terminal *aws*, clipped *g*'s and feeble *h*'s thrown in for good measure, which later acquired the name of the Oxford voice and steadily debased the coinage of English speech with emasculated voices and exaggerated idiosyncrasies.'

On the other hand, as witness for the virtues of the upper class pronunciation of the Queen's English, Professor Clark of Minnesota: 'Educated Southern British pronunciation certainly has unique prestige throughout the English-speaking world. In America the attitude toward it is in the strict sense ambivalent. It is hardly an exaggeration to say that *all* Americans envy the Southern Englishman his pronunciation. The envy expresses itself in varying degrees and in very various ways, sometimes by the appearance of loathing, but it is envy still.'

I think that this alleged American envy of British received pronunciation has diminished. It was in the fifties and sixties that grand American offices employed receptionists with a classy Sloane Ranger accent. In the eighties Angela Rippon, the television presenter who had fallen out of fashion in Britain, found it hard to break into American television, where she was viewed as the Limey broad with the snooty accent.

In a living language, everything flows and nothing stays still. Even in our life-times upper class English pronunciation has shifted audibly. You can still hear its echoes in old ladies of the debutante class who say *gel* for *girl*, *otel* for *hotel*, and pronounce *garage* as in French, with the accent on the second syllable. You can meet it in bucolic old country gents who talk about *huntin'*, *shootin'*, and *fishin'*. I have been told that the really grand way to pronounce the last two is with *sh* sounded as *s*, *sootin'* and *fissin'*. But I have yet to come across anyone who speaks that way, alas. You can hear it in the BBC Sound Archives, where Florence Nightingale sounds like some Angela Brazil heroine, and Queen Victoria comes over like a mad German professor. You can read the upper class accent sent up in contemporary issues of *Punch* and such publications. To judge from them, the most egregious characteristics of received pronunciation, as spoken by the idle rich, were dropping the terminal *g* from present participles; pronouncing *s* as *th* with a lithp, and *r* as *w*; and interspersing all speech with a scattering of *haws* and *whats*. *Punch* is a satirical magazine, and satire exaggerates. But, to be funny, its guying of upper class English must have approximated to the real thing. Upper standard English seldom sounds its *r*'s except before a vowel: in words such as *dear* and *poor*, the *r* is given the value of the indeterminate vowel sound *er*; so that the words come out as *de-er* and *poo-er*, drawled *de-ah* and *paw-ah*, and exciting derision.

As well as the ceaseless process of change, several factors have combined recently to blunt the angularities of received pronunciation. Some of them may turn out to have affected more than the way we speak, in the revolution in the English language that is going through one of its rapid and violent phases, as after 1066 and in the late fifteenth and early sixteenth centuries.

The Edwardian upper classes wanted to demonstrate their superiority for all to see, in the way they spoke as well as in the clothes they wore. Two world wars, the century of the common man, mass education, television, and a general broadening of horizons have created a revulsion against that most unfashionable of deadly sins: élitism. As at the end of the Middle Ages the feudal structures broke up, and new classes emerged to power, and wealth, and the Queen's English; so we are going through a period when it is considered bad form to flaunt one's class or one's accent. In the holidays public school boys and girls take pains to sound and look no different from their contemporaries in comprehensive schools, by wearing the same hair styles, tight jeans, and unbuttoned accent. Children from middle class homes who go to state schools develop two accents, a posh one for home so as not to upset the parents, and a regional vernacular for school, so as not to upset their schoolfellows and earn the deadly reputation of snootiness.

You can point to many influences that have helped to reduce the wilder excesses of the English, silly-ass class accent, from the Beatles and the sixties generation to great popularizing newspapers such as *The Daily Mirror* and *The Sunday Times*. Of course, snobbery is the Pox Britannica, and there is still a lot of it about, manifesting itself in Non-U vocabulary and idiom, avoided by the fastidious or the careful to make an impression: 'Cheers, squire'; 'Pardon, Reverend'; 'Chummy here', meaning the chap beside me; 'Just the ticket for yours truly'; and thousands of other words and phrases that display aggressive lower-class idiom. But we are all equal these days, or, at any rate, we are all nervously wearing masks. Of course, there are still blinkin' idiots who bray in Bertie Wooster accents that *Punch* of the twenties would know and love. But, in general, the flattening of the English class pyramid has concomitantly flattened received pronunciation.

In parallel to the embarrassment about showing off one's class by one's accent, mass education has created a world of English-speakers who are also English-readers, many of them learning it as a second language from teachers for whom it is also a second language. They create the second great influence on pronunciation, the move towards speaking words as they are spelt. This is easier said than done in a language with such a complex and non-phonetic system of spelling as English, in which such notorious oubliettes for the unwary as *bough*, *cough*, *dough*, *lough*, *chough*, *though*, *through*, *thorough*, *Yarborough*, and *trough*, have the same last four letters, but are pronounced differently.

Nevertheless, because an increasingly higher proportion of English-speakers recognizes words as visible symbols, the speak-as-you-spell movement carries on through the tangled jungle of English orthography. It will continue.

Mass broadcasting has had, is having, and will continue to have immense effect on pronunciation, vocabulary, grammar, and other aspects of English. The influence is not simple, but diffuse. One effect is centripetal, towards standardization, so that a Top of the Pops song can sweep the world overnight with a vogue word or pronunciation, usually mid-Atlantic. It would be tiresome to argue that one kind of English voice is better than another; though I think that a case can be made for saying that some pronunciations, for example, Belfast, in which a lake is a hole in a kettle, and Yoknapatawpha County, are peculiarly impenetrable for outsiders because of idiosyncratic vowel sounds that differ more widely than most from the average or standard pronunciations. The BBC used to have very definite views that one voice was better than another: the BBC, or received, or Oxford, or standard, as carefully enunciated with strangulated vowel sounds by announcers in the days when the man who read the Nine O'clock News had to wear a dinner jacket. The BBC has recently relaxed its standards, so that regional accents are broadcast for the couthie comfort, or bewildered indignation, of British listeners at home. It is noticeable that the BBC standard upper class accent is retained for broadcasts on the overseas services, because these are listened to by learners and others who demand a standard, not rich diversity.

As well as giving the listeners and viewers of the world bugs with which they can eavesdrop on pronunciations and dialects of English from all round the world, mass broadcasting develops its own registers, from GodSpeak, the trendy but solemn elongated vowels of religious broadcasting, to PopSpeak, the matey, classless, chirpy mid-Atlantic of disc jockeys, that was never spoken by anybody outside a broadcasting studio.

Mass package tourism is having an odd little counter-current to the tide of speak-as-you-spell. Until recently the British were John Bulls about foreign languages, and frightened of making fools of themselves by essaying a foreign accent in public. There were always polyglot exceptions, for instance, Queen Elizabeth I, who was ready to have a go with foreign ambassadors. But a more typical example of the British attitude to foreign languages is given in the jokes about speaking Frog in *Henry V*. Now that Brits travel abroad at least once a year, to eat fish and chips and drink beer by the grey-green, greasy Mediterranean, they are bringing home with them the native pronunciations of foreign parts. It is common to hear those arbiters of elocution, the television news-readers, speak of *Firenze*, *Marseille*, and *Barthelona*.

Standardization of the pronunciation of place names all round the world is possibly a worthy objective. There may well be an international committee of UNESCO working on it even now. But it destroys some old English words in the process. *Florence*, the English name for *Firenze*, has been part of the English lexicon since about 1400. Appropriately for two mercantile peoples, it came in originally as the name for gold florins, wools, silks, and wines from Florence. *Florentine* has been an English word for almost as long, as the adjective to describe natives of *Firenze* and their products such as ships, silks, pies, and so on. Note Sir Walter Raleigh in *A Report of the Truth of the Fight about the Isles of the Azores* (1591): 'Their Navy strengthened with Florentines and huge Hulkes of other countries.' Because of the antiquity of trade with the Low Countries and the Rhine, *Cologne* has been an English word and pronunciation for the city and its products since the beginning of the Middle Ages.

The modern craze for mass travel, and a wish to show off that one is much travelled, at present fight with the old English tendency to anglicize tricky foreign names so that one does not have to attempt unEnglish vowel sounds.

The fight is fiercest and messiest over names transliterated from alphabets other than the Roman. *Mahomet* has been part of the English language since John Wycliffe introduced it to us around 1380. 'Mahomet and the mountain' is part of English folk-lore. Recently Arabists and other know-alls have persuaded us that *Mohammed* comes closer to the Arab pronunciation. And now there is a move to change this to *Muhammad*, with a dot under the 'h' if you don't watch out, because this is said to be closer to what the Prophet's own people call him. The battle between robust anglicization and attempts to conform to alien pronunciations is continual, interesting, and unresolved.

British pronunciation of British names is even odder than our pronunciation of foreign names. It is a notorious trap for foreigners, outsiders, and the uninitiated. It is impossible to cause more offence to an Englishman, a Scotsman, a Welshman, or an Irishman than by mis-spelling or mispronouncing his name. Because of the tangled roots of the English language, it is often impossible to deduce the spelling of a British name from its pronunciation, or vice versa. And with names like those old Featherstonehaughs (pronounced by some of them Fanshaw, and others in other dotty ways too tedious to relate), and Redelinghuyes (Redling-hewz), Whewell (Hew-el), Feavearyear (Fev-yer), O'Cathain (O-ka-hoyn), and MacGillesheathheanaich (Mach-gille-he-haneech, with the stress on the *he* and the ch as in loch), living in such rum places as Postwick (Pozzick), Braughing (Braffing), Flawith (Flawith or Floyth), Costessy (Kossi), Saughall (Sawkl), Culzean (Kulayn), Kirkcudbright (Kurkoobri), Troedrhiw-fuwch (on second thoughts, forget it) – and let us avoid at all costs the notorious Welsh fifty-eight-letter tripwire for non-Welsh speakers – British names might have been devised as a shibboleth to sort the native sheep from the alien goats.

Samuel Pepys, the amiable Paul Pry of English letters, pronounced his surname Peeps, according to the strongest evidence. This pronunciation is maintained today by the Pepys Cockerell family, lineal descendants of the diarist's sister Paulina. However, the Earl of Cottenham pronounces his family name, Pepys, as Peppiss. Other branches call themselves Pepys, but pronounce it Pepps or even Pipps.

Adwalton in West Yorkshire is pronounced as the unwary might expect, Adwawlton, except that the locals persist in pronouncing it Atherton, because Heather Town was the old name for the district. There is a place called Okeford Fitzpaine in Dorset, which the locals pronounce Fippeni Ockford; the cynic might suppose merely to confuse strangers. Athelstaneford in Lothian is pronounced both Athelstaynford and Elshanford.

The rich diversity of British place names (and part of its cause: the mongrel language bred from many strains) is perfectly demonstrated in all those names beginning with *Beau*, most of them derived from Norman French. They can be pronounced in as many different ways as the British mouth can manage vowel sounds: Beauchamp (Beetcham); Beauclerk (Boklair); Beaulieu (Bewli); and Beaudesert in Warwickshire (either Bodezert or, just for fun, Belzer).

Many modern tendencies are working to reduce the extravagance of pronunciation of British place and proper names, by docking its prolixities, and smoothing its angularities: the speak-as-you-spell movement; the urge to simplify; mass travel, which means that no man or village, not even islanders, can carry on pretending to be an island; mass broadcasting, which has a tendency to standardize and simplify. Certain tendencies are working to retain the rich eccentricity of pronunciation of British place and proper names: tradition, roots, snobbery, the old British pride in being a peculiar people. Between two such opposing armies, it is no contest. Some of the oddities may be forgotten, in the same way that some local dialects are dying, mainly because of depopulation of the countryside. But roots rule, particularly in such numinous things as names. He would be a rash fool who bet more than twopence that a hundred years from now the Featherstonehaughs or the Pepyses, the inhabitants of Kircaldy and Bobbingworth in Essex, will be pronouncing the names of their families or towns in any way remotely resembling their spellings.

Serious classifiers have pinned down other regular changes in English pronunciation. They note, for example, the English habit of concentrating on one syllable, or in longer words sometimes on two, and letting the others take care of themselves. This habit is in marked contrast to the elegant French equality for syllables. They observe that it is responsible for the most serious charge that has been brought against received pronunciation: that it reduces all vowel sounds to *er*. And they detect such tendencies in it as the recessive accent, or the drift of stress back from the second to the first syllable of three-syllable words. Many words, that originally had the stress on the second syllable, now normally or commonly have stress on the first: for example, *abdomen*, *composite* (except in TUCSpeak, where, exceptionally, it takes the stress on the last syllable in a phrase like 'compósite motion'), *decorous*, *obdurate*, *precedence*, *quandary*, *recondite*, *remonstrate*, *secretive*, *sonorous*, *subsidence*, *vagary*. Other words are affected by this tendency, but have not yet been swept away, so that stress on the first syllable is not yet standard: *Byzantine*, *clandestine*, *contribute*, *distribute*.

Lepidopterists of language have been onto the recessive accent for a long time. As long ago as 1884 Walter William Skeat, the pioneer etymologist and student of dialect, noted in his *Etymological Dictionary of the English Language* that *sonorous* was 'properly' pronounced with the stress on the second syllable, but that it would probably, sooner or later, shift the stress back to the first syllable. It has. To pronounce *sonorous* with its proper stress on the second syllable sounds a solecism today. As late as 1934 George Bernard Shaw was banging on about *sonorous* in a letter to *The Times*: 'An announcer who pronounced *decadent* and *sonorous* as *dekkadent* and *sonnerus* would provoke Providence to strike him dumb.' That is the way that announcers pronounce the words. Providence remains unmoved.

Unfortunately the tendency is not simple. Tides of language are seldom simple. Working against the recessive accent there is a counter-eddy for the stress to drift forwards in four-syllable words, such as *centenary*, *miscellany*, *nomenclature*, *pejorative*, and *peremptory*. Received pronunciation favours stress on the first syllable. But analogy with the antepenult stress of three-syllable words shifts the accent forward in words such as *formidable*, *explicable*, and *commendable*, which used to be 'properly' pronounced with the stress on the first syllable ("'Tis sweet and cómmendable in thy nature, Hamlet'). Nothing excites Outraged of Tunbridge Wells to write to *The Times*, proclaiming that civilization as we know it is coming to an end, more than the tendency of broadcasters to shift their accents forwards or backwards on such words.

These and other influences are affecting our pronunciation, tugging in different directions, like the tides and currents of a peculiarly confused channel of water such as the Pentland Firth, where the landlubber turns green and makes for the rails even in harbour. Pronunciation is changing, as it always has done, and always must in a living language. It is changing faster now than it has at some stages of the long march of English. But there have been other periods of rapid change, such as the years after 1066, the emergence of a national standard from Middle English, and the sixteenth century, with the rise of new classes and new voices. Today's changes are not so radical that they can be fairly described, except for purposes of effect, as a revolution, or, in the cliché and slipshod extension from the jargon of nuclear physics, a quantum jump.

We shall see that these and similar influences are affecting the other registers and parts of English, as well as the ways in which we pronounce it.

One of the most remarkable changes in this generation has been the rapid increase in jargon. The *Supplement to the Oxford English Dictionary* has grown as it is being born, until it promises to be almost a third as big as its parent, the *OED*. When Volume I of the *Supplement*, *A-G*, was published, as recently as 1972, its editor estimated in his Preface that it would be the first of three volumes, and that the *Supplement*, when completed, would contain some 50,000 Main Words. Since then the flood of new words into the vocabulary has increased. The *Supplement* will now just be contained in four volumes, each one fatter than the last, and will record about 60,000 (and rising) Main Words. Most of the increase comes from the jargons or technical vocabularies of new sciences and technologies. Man is in a period of discovery of the world (and of space) as dramatic as the fifteenth and sixteenth centuries, or the first Industrial Revolution. He has to create new words to describe his discoveries. A consequence is that lexicographers of New

English, such as Oxford, Webster, and Barnhart, can produce a thick volume of new words a year, and still not keep up with the spate. Another consequence is that it is no longer possible for a polymath, or a Renaissance Prince, or a crossword-puzzler, or even Dr Johnson himself, to carry in his head a working knowledge of most of the English lexicon that matters.

Another new influence that is causing the sudden rapid growth of the English vocabulary since the Second World War is the emergence of English as the world language. The *OED* is a British English dictionary, but it now has to include New English from the entire English-speaking world, i.e. the entire world, including regions that did not disturb the labours of Sir James Murray and the other founding fathers. Each successive volume of the *Supplement* has to make room for more words from Australia, Canada, Ireland, India, Japan, Russia, Yiddish, and so on. It is particularly strong on the English of New Zealand. Exotic English in *Volume III*, *O-Scz*, published in 1982, included:

Eskimo English: *Piblokto*, a nervous disorder known as Arctic hysteria, and a form of hysterical illness prevalent among Eskimo dogs; *Pingo*, a perennial conical or dome-shaped mound found in the permafrost; and *Qiviut*, the underwool of the arctic musk-ox.

Finnish English: *Penni*, the Finnish monetary unit equal to a hundredth of a *markka*; *Puukko*, a large double-edged, or a small hook-ended, knife (the sources, understandably, differ); *Runo*, a short poem or song on an epic or legendary subject; *Rya*, a knotted pile rug; *Sauna*, we all know sauna, the most naturalized of the words of Finnish English, which in London is developing the secondary and disreputable meaning once taken by bagnio of old Italian English.

Hawaiian English: *Ohia*, technically the *eugenia malaccensis*, the large native hard-wood tree bearing beautiful clusters of scarlet flowers, with long protruding stamens; *Opihi*, the delicious edible limpet of the genus *Helcioniscus*, or its knee-cap or umbrella shell, prized and worn around one's neck as a token of eternal love; *Pahoehoe*, a form of solidified lava that is undulating or billowy in form, and has a shiny appearance; *Pili*, the perennial grass, scientifically named *Heteropgon contortus*, and used as a thatching material in the good old days before Hawaii was covered with concrete tower blocks for the tourists; *Oo*, a black and yellow bird, *Moho braccatus*, belonging to the family Meliphagidae or honeyeaters, and now believed to be extinct; confusingly for us not native in Hawaii and to the lingo born, *Ou*, a green and yellow bird,

*Psittirostra psittacea*, belonging to the sub-family Coerebinae, or honey-creepers.

Hungarian English: *Pengo*, the basic monetary unit of Hungary from 1927 to 1946; *Puli*, a black, grey, or white sheep-dog breed, characterized by a long thick coat that looks as though it has been plaited into cords, the Hungarian shaggy dog; *Puszta*, the great, treeless, Hungarian plain, equivalent, *mutatis mutandis*, to the Siberian steppes or the pampas of Argentina.

One could continue this catalogue of exotic new imports into English from Around the World in Eighty languages. But to do so were nothing but to waste night, day, and time. As English becomes the world language, and as tourism and television make us familiar with other men's back-yards, we are going to continue to find new words to describe foreign currencies, alien foods that have become native from *sukiyaki* and *chop suey* (from the United States, not China), to *poppadom* (which is spelt in as many ways in curry houses as Shakespeare's name was spelt by his contemporaries), objects of foreign nature or manufacture, and green and yellow birds from the other side of the world. The lexicon of English is growing faster than it ever has before, even in such periods of rapid growth as the eleventh and sixteenth centuries.

The emergence of English as the world language is inevitably, and regrettably, simplifying the complexities of English grammar. As Britons themselves, and foreigners from all round the world, are learning English as a second language, the tendency to make it easier to learn is irresistible. The subjunctive mood is dying: even native speakers and writers are uneasy with it. The few surviving case distinctions left over from Old English, like fossils from a vanished world, are going. Even native speakers and writers get into a muddle with their *I*'s and *me*'s. The feminist tendency is turning *their* into a singular, in order to avoid assuming masculine supremacy by saying *his*, or wearing belt and braces by saying *his or her*.

The simplification of grammar, as part of the long progress of English from an inflected to an uninflected language, is regrettable in so far as it reduces the variety of distinctions we can make, and ways in which we can say things. The disappearance of the subjunctive is a serious loss. But a complex grammar is not a virtue *per se*. Some of the Amerindian languages have a grammar of a complexity that makes English look a childish language. Many of the old languages, including English itself, had, in addition to singular and plural, a dual number in order to refer to not one or many, but two objects or people. The dual number died because it served no very useful purpose. English is becoming the world language partly because its grammar is so simple and adaptable. We need not shed too bitter tears even for the disappearance of the subjunctive. If English speakers and writers need to make the distinctions for which the subjunctive was invented, either the subjunctive will not die, or they will devise some new way of making the distinctions.

Immensely increased mobility, holidays, and broadcasting, are eroding the old regional dialects of the United Kingdom slowly, though we are curiously tenacious of such local identifications. When I was a child in Suffolk, I had many friends and neighbours who had never been to London, and for whom the trip of a lifetime was a visit to Ipswich, or a holiday at the seaside in Felixstowe, or, for the genteel, nanny-employing classes, Frinton. Today there is nothing remarkable in a trip to London or the Costa Brava. Many households have a car; and the coach services are good. The Suffolk accent is still enchanting, and you can still hear the dialect *meesen* for the plural of mouse, and *four-a-lete* for a crossroads – but mainly among the old. The rapid drift from the land and mechanization of farming by the grain millionaires is killing the rural dialects. But I observe no such rapid erosion of the urban dialects of Glasgow, or Belfast, or Birmingham. A notable difference is that speakers of urban dialects are aware of registers and dialects of English other than those of their city or suburb. They hear them on television and radio. They experience them in person when they travel to Wembley or Soho. As a consequence, most British speakers have several registers: one for use among mates and neighbours; another posh one for use in the office, or school, or on the phone-in programme.

As the regional dialects of the United Kingdom fade, very gradually (if English lasts another two thousand years, a Glaswegian will never speak like an East Anglian), national 'dialects' of English are proliferating around the world. Almost as soon as the Pilgrim Fathers had landed, it became evident that American English was a different language from British English. We are now learning to recognize the rich dialects of Indian English, Australian English, West Indian English, with their special virtues and idiosyncrasies invented for their particular purposes by those who use them.

Modern technology, from the television set to printing by photocomposition, is having a profound effect on such points of language as punctuation and spelling. If most of our reading in future is going to be done from a screen rather than a page, there will be a strong tendency to simplify and standardize the symbols. In fact, as usual with brave new inventions, reports of the switch from page to screen have been greatly exaggerated. The flickering blue 'books' of the television screen, with instructions to turn to 'page' 2734, remain largely unread except by professionals in the trade. The printed page has immense advantages of convenience, adaptability, portability, and cheapness. You can carry it in your pocket, make marks on it, and read it in the bath. It can also be beautiful, a quality that nobody but a dotty neophiliac has ever attributed to the flickering blue, child-minding, mind-destroying television screen.

Euphemism is supposed to be a peculiarly English vice by the French, and other masters of logical thought and plain speaking. There is certainly a lot of it about. There always has been. If you want to take a gloomy view, you can assert that mass democracy, with Presidents and Prime Ministers winning elections because of their plausibility with euphemisms and empty rhetoric on television, mass advertising, and mass culture have made this an Age of Euphemism. That would be to take too dim (and élitist) a view of the robust common sense of ordinary men and women, who have a tradition in the United Kingdom of standing no guff from their masters. If hypocrisy is a British vice, and hype an American vice, and if both employ euphemism and other tricks of the trade, both languages have a noble tradition of seeing through such pretensions, from Chaucer and Mencken to the modern satirists.

Modern mass communications have encouraged a monstrous growth of cliché. A new pop song, or catch-phrase, or vogue word is heard all round the world as soon as it is first uttered. It becomes a cliché overnight, as fast as the desert blooms after rain. But, like the blooms of the desert, it dies almost as fast. We may produce more clichés today than our fathers did, but they have shorter lives. Victorian politicians could carry on exploring every avenue and leaving no stone unturned, without feeling self-conscious, for half a century. Because there are so many more media for broadcasting clichés today, we get excess of them sooner, that surfeiting, our appetite sickens, and so dies. A crashing cliché such as, 'At this moment in time . . .', or the use of 'situation' as an impressive general qualifier, has a very short shelf-life before it becomes a laughing stock, and is either discarded, or used only ironically, by anybody with any sensitivity for the language.

There is more slang heard and written today than ever before for two principal reasons. The first is the relaxation of the rigid class system of the Queen's English, with the result that ladies and gents let their hair down and use language that would have shocked a Victorian bargee, bargees having been exemplary scapegoats for foul language for some centuries. Remember Dr Johnson's ingenious insult during an exchange of coarse raillery customary among bargees and others travelling upon the Thames: 'Sir, your wife, under pretence of keeping a bawdy-house, is a receiver of stolen goods.' We have relaxed the taboos and thrown away the corsets of language, being more frightened these days of seeming stuffy or not with-it than of seeming low or vulgar.

The second reason for the profusion of slang is the proliferation of different national dialects and registers of English. It is natural that any group speaking and writing its own variety of English should create its own vernaculars and slangs. All these slangs pour into the common pool of English, being broadcast around the world instantly by the mass media. Small boys from Bombay to Melbourne pick up the supposed slangs of Los Angeles or Texas from watching programmes such as *Starsky and Hutch* and travesties such as *Dallas*. Disc jockeys and pop groups spread their native slangs around the world. Human memory being finite, and human wishes to deploy a large vocabulary limited, most people probably do not use more slang than their ancestors did. They simply have a far wider range to choose from, and change it more often, for the same reason that we change our clichés more often: the instant satiety of the Mass Media Age.

In any case, we have come to see slang not as a disgusting excrescence on the face of the Queen's English, but as an ephemeral growth that adds to the hilarity of nations, and enriches the public stock of harmless pleasure. Slang is a sign of healthy growth, not decadence.

In its many registers and parts, English is going through a period of rapid growth and change. It has gone through such periods before, but previous changes have seldom been as rapid or as violent as those taking place towards the end of the twentieth century, as English becomes the world language. If you want to take a gloomy view of what is happening, you can imagine English breaking up into a family of mutually incomprehensible dialects and registers, in the way that the Macedonian world empire broke up after the death of Alexander. That would be a Doomsday view; and a stupid one. There is an English revolution going on. But the analogy is with the prodigious growth of the Industrial Revolution rather than the divisive revolution of the Civil Wars. The forces for cohesion and growth in the world language are stronger than the fissiparous forces. We shall now examine in detail the effects of the English revolution in various aspects of the language.

# 2/SLANG

'Slang is the language of street humour, of fast, high and low life.' *A Dictionary of Modern Slang, Cant, and Vulgar Words*, 1860

'Correct English is the slang of prigs who write history and essays. And the strongest slang of all is the slang of poets.' Marian Evans (George Eliot), *Middlemarch*, XI, 1872

We have a problem of definition about slang. It has been with us for some time, as can be noticed in the nineteenth-century quotations at the head of the chapter. Slang is a district bounded on the north by jargon, on the south by argot, on the east by dialect, and on the west by poetry.

One of its definitions in *The Oxford English Dictionary* is the special vocabulary used by any set of persons of a low or disreputable character; 'language of a low and vulgar type'. We still use slang to mean this, though the revolution of the sixties loosely described as the Permissive Society has brought the rude words into more common use. We might use the French word argot to describe the secret languages of the criminal and disreputable classes.

Another meaning of slang is as the special vocabulary or phraseology of a particular calling or profession, as in medical slang, or golfers' slang. In this sense it is close to one meaning of jargon, but jargon expresses more distaste and imputation of ugliness. This kind of slang can be the cant or jargon of a certain class or period: 'Sloane Rangers' slang', 'Restoration slang'.

Another definition of slang is as language of a highly colloquial type, considered as below the level of standard educated speech, and consisting either of new words invented for fun, or of current words used in some special sense. This kind of slang tends to have a short life and a merry one, passing out of vogue almost as soon as it comes in, as the slang-makers get bored and move on to some new fashion. Nevertheless, a considerable amount of slang establishes itself and becomes accounted fit for literary use, without a whiff of its disreputable past: item, *mob*, a vogue abbreviation of *mobile vulgus*, and a piece of early eighteenth-century slang that vexed the purists. In the *Spectator* issue number 135 Addison complained: 'It is perhaps this Humour of speaking no more than we needs must which has so miserably curtailed some of our Words, as in *mob*, *rep*, *pos*, *incog*, and the like.' *Rep*, *pos*, and *incog* have gone the way of all fashion. But *mob* is still with us, and we use this old bit of slang that has been rehabilitated without any sense of being dirty or vulgar.

This notion of slang as language or idiom that is not appropriate in formal or literary contexts is probably the dominant meaning today. It is likely to be restricted in social status or regional distribution. It tends to be more transitory and metaphorical than standard language. Our trouble is that we are far less certain than we used to be about what is standard language, and what is appropriate to it. Our novelists and other creative writers up in the front line of language use English in a way that is often far from standard. Back at base behind the lines teachers of English, journalists, and other language-makers have less certainty than they did a generation ago about what is slang, and what is acceptable. Some would say that anything goes, and that the class system is as silly in words as it is in life. You can only get away with such classlessness in language if you are a literary genius, and know what you are doing. We may agree that slang is colloquial language of an undignified kind, but at this stage in the proliferation of the language we find it hard to agree on what is colloquial, and we no longer rate dignity highly as a linguistic virtue in many registers and contexts in which we use language.

It can be seen that slang is a shameless Humpty-Dumpty word, used to mean just what the speaker chooses it to mean – neither more nor less. It has become a strong value-word, which contains more judgement about the language and prescription than factual description. One man's slang is another man's colloquialism is another man's vernacular is another man's everyday speech. Before we can judge whether something is slang, we need to know who are speaking or writing, where they come from and what they are trying to do with the language (their register).

The history of such a Protean word can help to untangle its matted connotations. From its earliest appearance slang was a cant word with many overlapping meanings. In addition to those already mentioned, slang was used to mean 'humbug', 'line of business', 'a show', and 'a performance of strolling players'. As a verb it was used to mean 'to defraud'. The common factor was that slang referred to irregular, or shady, or lawless activity variously specialized. From an early date it had a connotation of abusive language, as in 'slanging match'. To slang somebody is an old-fashioned idiom meaning to assault them with words.

The aggressive and abusive undertones of 'slang' find echoes in Scotland and the North of England, where slang tends to mean abusive rather than highly colloquial language. There may be a Viking connection with the Norwegian dialect words *slengeord* (offensive language, and also, interestingly, a new word coined without special reason); *slengjenamn* (a nickname); and the phrase *slengje kjaeften* ('to sling the jaw', i.e. utter rudeness and offensive language).

There are almost as many theories as to why people invent and use slang as there are definitions of its meanings. One popular theory is that slang tends to be the language of the poor, the huddled masses yearning to be free, and the criminal classes, who make up for the drabness of their lives by the colourfulness of their language. Adherents of this theory tend to be romantic middle-class intellectuals. They point to such examples of the working and criminal classes as Cockneys, the early Australian immigrants, and the inhabitants of the seedier suburbs of New York as brilliant inventors of slang. The colourful slang of New York (immortalized by the guys and dolls of Damon Runyon) owes a lot to such national dialects as Yiddish, Italian American, Hispanic American, and Polish American. And this theory takes no account of upper-class societies that are or have been fecund and facund with slang.

Over the centuries Eton College developed a large lexicon of slang for everything from food, 'sock', to an unsatisfactory exercise, 'a rip', because the 'beak' (master) tore a rip in the top of it, to a 'swiping' (birching, with awful solemnity, by the Head Man, on the flogging-block in Lower School, in the presence of two praepostors, one 'tug' or scholar, because he was *togatus* or wore a gown, one 'oppidan' because he was not a scholar and lived in the town outside the College) for those who collected too many rips and were 'sent up' to the Head Man. A generation ago the new boy had a vocabulary of several hundred words of Etonian slang to learn in his first fortnight. If he was a tug and failed his 'Colours Test' he was 'siphoned' over the table in the middle of Long Chamber: i.e. beaten with the piece of rubber pipe with which the poor scholars used to siphon the water for their occasional baths. My impression is that recently the peculiarities of Etonian slang, as well as the agonies of Etonian floggings, have abated.

In the United States the Preppy cult, for the rich children who go to, or claim to have gone to, prestigious private schools, has produced a large lexicon of hermetic slang. It ranges from preferred words and idioms that act as Shibboleths to distinguish Preppies from the common herd to esoteric slang impenetrable by the unPreppy outsider.

A Preppy will refer to his or her father as Daddy, whether talking to him or about him; he is often, but not always, still married to Mummy. Preppies use favoured hurray-words such as 'neat', 'tremendous', 'love' (what a girl feels about ice cream, sailing, add-a-beads, and needlepoint), and 'awesome', as in, 'the saxophone player is awesome.' In parallel there are Preppy boo-words. 'Jacked out' means pissed off; 'rude' means in bad taste, without class, gauche, and bad; 'eat my shorts' means drop dead, go jump in the lake; a 'dork', Preppy slang impenetrable to the outsider, is an unclassy person who does not understand Prep sayings and attitudes; 'dorky' is the adjective, that which is characterized by clumsiness or ignorance of, for instance, how to mix a Bloody (sc. Mary, you dork). Much Preppy talk serves one of the prime functions of slang: to conceal from the authorities or the nosey-parkers activities that are illicit or disapproved of. There is a large lexicon of drink and drug terms. 'Bones' are Marijuana cigarettes or joints or js; 'poo' is champagne, since it is thought to be 'stitch' to refer to champagne as shampoo; 'booted' can mean either to be expelled from school or to have vomited. A large group of idioms refer to sexual intercourse, for hyperbolic boasting in dormitory. The male Preppy boasts that he has hopped on a babe, played hide the salam (short for salami), had a horizontal rumble, done some parallel parking, reeled in the biscuit (lured a girl to bed), or swapped spit (done some French kissing). They are an uncouth lot, or as they would put it, rude, gross, and the worst.

Another characteristic of Preppy slang is to use acronyms and initial letters as a shorthand to mystify outsiders and confirm the Preppy's sense of belonging to an exclusive club. B.M.O.C. (Big Man on Campus) stands for Mr Prep, a prospective husband. N.O.C.D. (Not Our Class, Dear) means, 'He's not for you, believe me.' S.A., of course, is older than Preppy; it is what Montgomery Clift had that Mummy liked. P.D.A. is Public Display of Affection, viz. kissing, necking, sexual relations done outside one's dorm room or frat room.

For outsiders Preppy slang rapidly becomes dorky, the worst, and blown out. Fortunately Preppies never stay in one place for long; indeed, they have a large conjugation of irregular and self-congratulatory exit lines: 'We're out of here'; 'We're history'; 'Let's cruise'; 'Let's get the hell out of Dodge'; 'Let's act like a preacher and get the hell out of here.' Like much slang, these are intended to be both humorous and hermetic.

Slang of the gilded young is not confined to the East Coast of the United States. It occurs all over the English-speaking world, wherever young people wish to form clubs and cliques. At the University of St Andrews the equivalent of Preppies are known as Yaas, because of their English public school vowel sounds. Non-Yaas are called Wee Marys (St Andrews has more students of arts than of sciences, and more women than men). The British equivalent of Preppies are Sloane Rangers, defined, invented, codified, and profited from in 1982. They are said to have their private vocabulary, and their vogue epithets are such hurray-words as 'super', 'extraordinary', and 'good news'. Their boo-words are said to include 'grockly', meaning common, tacky, or non-U. If this is correct, it is a crib from Devonshire dialect, where a 'grockle' is a contemptuous term for a tourist, especially one from the Midlands or the North of England, sitting in traffic jams and a sucker for Devonshire cream teas. Sloanes say such things as, 'How fascinating, absolutely riveting, and rather fun', and go in for hyperbole, understatement of the stiff-upper-lipped, loose-lower-jawed sort, simple-minded British nationalism and snobbery.

Sloane Rangers are not a new idea. Nancy Mitford in a book called *Noblesse Oblige*, derived from the work of Professor Alan Ross, in 1956 coined the notions of U and non-U language and behaviour. Before her comedians of English manners such as Jane Austen, William Shakespeare, and Geoffrey Chaucer noticed the exclusive slangs of the English classes. There is a lot of it around.

In its early sense of low and disreputable argot of the lower classes, slang owes a great deal to Francis Grose or Grosse, the eighteenth-century draughtsman and antiquary. His *Classical Dictionary of the Vulgar Tongue*, published in 1785, and reissued as *Lexicon Balatronicum* (a *balatronix* is a Latin word for a kind of low comic actor) in 1811, was the first man to classify English slang systematically. Lexicography consists partly of copying the work of previous lexicographers. Grose's dictionary has been a primary source of all subsequent collections of slang from Partridge to the *Supplements* of the *OED*, which can afford to open their covers to slang more liberally than the original fascicles.

Grose was an appropriately buckish character for the study with which his name is associated. He was the eldest son of a rich Swiss jeweller who had emigrated to Richmond in Surrey. He got through his family inheritance so quickly that he had to hustle to make a living. Among other occupations he became an illustrator, Richmond Herald, and adjutant and paymaster of the Hampshire Militia. Referring to the last occupation, he said that his only account-books were his right and left hand pockets: into one he put what he received, and from the other he paid out.

On his topographical tour of Scotland he was given an introduction to Robert Burns, who wrote a coarse epigram on Captain Francis Grose, as well as the genial verse 'Hear, Land o' Cakes, and brither Scots', in which occur the revealing lines:

> *A chield's amang you taking notes,*
> *And, faith, he'll prent it.*

Grose was a sort of antiquarian and linguistic Falstaff. He was very fat; full of humour and good nature; and 'an inimitable boon companion.' He was at home in most sections of eighteenth-century society, and had an ear for their slangs and lingos. Lovers of English slang look back to him as the founding father of their study.

His *Classical Dictionary of the Vulgar Tongue* illustrates many of the roots of slang. It shows the progression of slang into standard English. Grose thinks it worth explaining for his readers many words and idioms that no longer have any whiff of vulgarity about them: cat call ('A kind of whistle, chiefly used at theatres, to interrupt the actors and damn a new piece. It derives its name from one of its sounds, which greatly resembles the modulation of an intriguing boar cat'), cat's paw, chicken-hearted, clink (jail), close-fisted, cock-sure, to crow, down in the dumps, dun, to frisk (search), hush money, to kick the bucket, in a pet, to rook, queer (forged, and several other fraudulent and larcenous meanings, but not yet any sexual connotation), shilly-shally, tip-top, snooze, stirrup cup ('A parting cup or glass, drank on horseback by the person taking leave'), white feather, white lie.

One of the more remarkable instances of the longevity of some slang is Grose's definition of 'pig', which the sixties generation thought that it had invented as a rude name for a police officer. Grose has: 'Pig – A police officer. A China street pig; a Bow-street officer. Floor the pig and bolt; knock down the officer and run away.'

Grose illustrates the converse, that most slang is ephemeral. We need his translations for many of the longer idioms and phrases.

How the swell funks his blower and lushes red tape: 'what a smoke the gentleman makes with his pipe, and drinks brandy.' How the cull flashes his queer cogs: 'how the fool shows his rotten teeth.' The cove was lagged for prigging a peter with several stretch of dobbin from a drag: 'the fellow was transported for stealing a trunk, containing several yards of ribband, from a waggon.' The examples of longer phrases are somewhat artificial, as if composed for illustrative purposes by a curious antiquarian rather than uttered for real by a queer cull in a low drinking den.

The last example demonstrates a conspicuous quality of this first serious collection of slang: how much of it has to do with crime and punishment. A deep root of slang is the need for criminals to have a private language. Grose's *Dictionary* is, among other things, a social survey of London crime a century before Mayhew.

Here is a brief selection of the low life and its concomitant slang recorded by Francis Grose.

Carting: The punishment formerly inflicted on bawds, who were placed in a tumbrel or cart, and led through a town, that their persons might be known.

Chalkers: Men of wit, in Ireland, who in the night amuse themselves with cutting inoffensive passengers across the face with a knife.

Ark ruffians: Rogues who, in conjunction with watermen, robbed, and sometimes murdered, on the water, by picking a quarrel with the passengers in a boat, boarding it, plundering, stripping, and throwing them overboard.

Queer plungers: Cheats who throw themselves into the water, in order that they may be taken up by their accomplices, who carry them to one of the houses appointed by the Humane Society for the recovery of drowned persons, where they are rewarded by the society with a guinea each; and the supposed drowned person, pretending that he was driven to that extremity by great necessity, is also frequently sent away with a contribution in his pocket.

The other notable quality of Francis Grose's collection is the great number of sexual and bawdy terms. The 1811 Preface claims that this makes the moral influence of the *Lexicon Balatronicum* more certain and extensive than that of any methodist sermon that has ever been delivered. With its assistance improper topics can be discussed, even before the ladies, without raising a blush on the cheek of modesty.

The writer of the Preface takes a pretty dim view of women when he supposes that it is impossible that a female should understand the meaning of *twiddle diddles* (testicles; Elementary, my dear Watson), or rise from the table at the mention of *Buckinger's boot* ('the monosyllable', as Grose calls it, coyly). According to Grose, Matthew Buckinger was born without hands and legs; notwithstanding which he drew coats of arms very neatly, and could write the Lord's Prayer within the compass of a shilling; he was married to a tall handsome woman, and traversed the country, shewing himself for money. Grose shows the male chauvinism, or at any rate the anti-feminist bias, of much early slang in his entry for 'cunt', which he can bring himself to publish only with two stars in the middle. C**T: a nasty name for a nasty thing.

The *Dictionary* is as rich in sexual slang and sociology as it is in criminal. A Dutchess (sic): A woman enjoyed with her pattens on, or by a man in boots, is said to be made a dutchess.

Muff: The private parts of a woman. 'To the well wearing of your muff, mort: to the happy consummation of your marriage, girl.' Grose's *Dictionary* has dozens of slang terms for the private parts of women; precious few for the private parts of men. This supports the feminist theory that men impose their slang as well as the rest of language on the users of language.

Cauliflower: Also the private parts of a woman (a definition that could be put beside nearly half the entries in the *Dictionary*). The reason for which appellation is given in the following story: 'A woman, who was giving evidence in a cause wherein it was necessary to express those parts, made use of the term cauliflower; for which the judge on the bench, a peevish old fellow, reproved her, saying she might as well call it artichoke. Not so, my lord, replied she; for an artichoke has a bottom, but a c**t and a cauliflower have none.'

'She prays with her knees upward' is said of a woman much given to gallantry and intrigue. Grose also gives a marvellously learned etymology of the condom or French letter. 'Cundum: The dried gut of a sheep, worn by men in the act of coition, to prevent venereal infection; said to have been invented by one Colonel Cundum. These machines were long prepared and sold by a matron of the name of Philips, at the Green Canister, in Half-Moon Street, in the Strand. That good lady having acquired a fortune, retired from business; but learning that the town was not well served by her successors, she, out of a patriotic zeal for the public welfare, returned to her occupation; of which she gave notice by divers handbills, in circulation in the year 1776.' The professional etymologists have found no record of Colonel Cundum or a physician named

Condom or Conton, said to be the inventor of the sheath. It is difficult not to believe in Mistress Philips.

Sex and crime continue to be prolific sources of slang today, two centuries after Francis Grose went around taking notes. 'To hump' is current coarse slang for to have sexual intercourse. But it is not in fact as up-to-date as its users suppose. Grose lists it as: 'Once a fashionable word for copulation.' More truly modern slang and euphemism for the act of love includes, among dozens of variants, 'getting it on', 'doing it', 'going all the way', the coy 'going to bed', and (from Rockspeak) 'slipping a fatty'. One of the most common terms of abuse in modern Britain is 'wanker', derived from the U.K. slang verb 'to wank', i.e. to masturbate. 'Beaver Pie' is modern slang, unknown to Grose, Partridge, and other more recent collectors, for the female genitalia. A 'beef bayonet' is new slang, with the variant 'beef torpedo', for that old totem of slang, the male sexual organ.

Crime continues to augment the river of slang, with new words for old activities or for new laws. 'Sus' came into the language because of a British law enabling the police to arrest suspects for loitering with intent or other suspicious behaviour: it became notorious because of the belief, perhaps justified, that in some parts of cities far more blacks than whites were being sussed by the police. The constabulary sus should not be confused with the Rockspeak 'suss', meaning nous or common sense, whose meaning was exemplified with characteristic philistine vigour by Johnny Rotten (Lydon), the rock singer, in 1977: 'You don't need to be clever to fucking pass an exam, you've just got to have a bit of suss. Either an incredibly good memory or you can suss out the bullshit.' Slang is a particularly complex register of language, because of its vernacular imprecision.

Recent low-life slang for the act of arresting a suspected person is 'to feel a collar' (cf. 'to get or give a tug'). In Grose's time the criminal and shady classes did not wear collars: 'collar day' was slang for an even more portentous occasion than arrest; it meant execution day.

The illicit but trendy drug culture had a potent influence on the slang of low and high life in the 1960s and 1970s. The substances gave us euphemistic nick-names for everything from pot and grass (marijuana) and dust and powder (cocaine: to powder the nose is to ingest cocaine by way of the nasal passages) to Black Bombers, Brown Bombers, and Purple Hearts. The Candy Man is a person who supplies illicit drugs; and Dr Feelgood is a doctor who readily prescribes amphetamines and other narcotics. A Groundman is somebody who remains straight, while others are under the effects of LSD or other Psychedelics, in order to look after their mental and physical welfare. A cap is a capsule containing narcotic substance; Amy is Amyl nitrite, which can be packaged in sealed glass phials known as poppers; cocaine can be called snuff or snow, and, if you are daft and a dickhead, you can snort it. Most of this druggy technical slang remains hermetic for potheads and other druggies. Some of it has achieved a wider popularity outside the drug scene: for example, the adjectives high, straight, heavy, and cool.

Pop and rock music are a prolific new source of slang that has started to flow in the past half century. No doubt the medieval jongleurs had their private jargon and slang. But they did not have the immediate world-wide audience or the influence of their modern successors. There is musical slang in Grose, but it usually reverts to the two principal concerns of his contemporary slang. 'The coves sing out beef': they call out stop thief. 'Silent Flute': See Pego, Sugar Stick, etc.

In the 1960s and 1970s pop music created a new lexicon of Rockspeak. Take the pejorative interjection, noun, and adjective in British slang, 'wally'. In Scottish dialect for centuries 'wally' was a general term of commendation, meaning excellent, fine-looking, or ample. Its etymology is uncertain. Perhaps it came from the Scottish noun 'wale', taken from Old Norse and related to the root 'will', meaning the act of choosing or the pick of the bunch. It developed a specific meaning in Scots slang: made of china or glazed earthenware. Thus it came to mean an ornament or showy trifle. In Scottish 'wallies' are a cheerful name for false teeth, much favoured in that nation of sweet and cake eaters, where young women have been known to ask for a set of dentures as a present on their twenty-first birthdays.

Suddenly in the 1970s at pop festivals spectators started shouting 'wally' in a loud voice, and originally as a cry of approval. When a number of trespassing campers were arrested at a festival on Salisbury Plain, near Stonehenge, they all gave their names as 'Wally', so vexing the courts, exciting the newspapers, and spreading the word.

Inchoate slang is volatile. Because of the apparent mental retardation of the shouters of 'wally', the word reversed its meaning. From being a term of approval, it quickly came to mean an idiot, a simpleton, or a buffoon. As an adjective it means of, or pertaining to, inept bungling, vague or absent-minded, or incapable of thought or action because of drugs. Rockspeak and Drugspeak were connected and influenced each other.

A humper is somebody who is paid to carry gear for a group, the lowest form of roadie; a wally humper is an egregiously incompetent one, who hinders the activities of a crew by mislaying and dropping gear, by asking stupid questions, and, according to an authority on Rockspeak, making cheery, irritating chit-chat such as: 'Heh heh I'm going to sink a few tonight I can tell you mind you it doesn't affect me like that when it comes to pulling talent if you get my meaning heh heh I've got a band meself actually sort of heavy Sabbath sort of thing oops sorry mate does it hurt is it broke never mind plenty more where that came from heh heh.'

Wally as slang for an oversized pickled gherkin sold in fish-and-chip shops has no perspicuous connexion with the hearty-loony wally, unless it be that both are rebarbative.

The slang of Rockspeak is prolific, and, like all slang, seeps into the main stream of the language. It throws up technical terms of the pop racket, such as 'Freddie', the name for a free-style, gormless dance without a partner, characterized by stupid movements of the face and body; the eponym is Freddie Garrity, the funny fellow and focal point of Freddie and the Dreamers. It also covers the water-front of the rest of life that interests the pop world. 'Bammies' are drug-filled cigarettes, usually not very strong. A 'fuck-dog' is a socially unacceptable person, and has been around for longer than is dreamed of in the philosophy of the nomenclators of Rockspeak. To 'cop the bunny' is to interview somebody for the music press; derived, probably, from the old slang of to cop or obtain, and bunny, meaning idle chit-chat, an extension of the British slang to rabbit on about something.

Rockspeak is an efflorescent modern branch of slang; but its roots lie deep in the jargon of jazz, and in the older seedbeds of slang.

The slang of pop music was the most conspicuous and character-istic new language of the teenage revolution of the 1960s. But it was not the only one. Young people have always played with language, as part of learning, and as a shibboleth to distinguish themselves from the adult world. You can observe them doing it in the comedies of Aristophanes and Plautus. The watershed that we have crossed is that for the first time the young are rich and independent enough, and have the means of communication to disseminate their formerly private slangs universally.

They do it not merely with Rockspeak, but with the slangs of fashion and games, of television and drugs, and of the older sources, sex and the shady side of the law. No sooner has some football star said in an interview that he is as 'sick as a parrot' or, alternatively, 'over the moon' about the result of a match, than his words have become a vogue phrase, used until it becomes a laughing-stock, and eventually dies of shame. American and black slang, real or imaginary, are peculiarly influential in parts of the world that look to the United States as the fugleman of fashion and the leader of the teenage language revolution. Therefore young English-speakers from China to Peru call a man a 'cat', a girl a 'chick', and use the verb 'to bug' as a synonym for annoy.

Kenneth Hudson, one of the adult lexicographers of teenage slang, argues in *The Language of the Teenage Revolution* (1983) that since the Second World War a self-conscious and often aggressive teenage culture has developed, which baffles and infuriates the older generation. Its members are anxious to assert at every point the ways in which their life-style differs radically from that of their parents. Mr Hudson maintains that this teenage code is reflected in slang and other linguistic usage, often in subtle detail. In particular he says that the young have invented a code of speaking in inverted commas, a habit concerning which dictionaries will have few clues to offer to posterity. Take, for example, the word 'mum' for mother in England. Because the word is loaded with class connotations, mainly Non-U to use an older categorization, the young protect themselves against the pitfalls of saying 'mum' by placing themselves at a slight distance from the word, either by their tone of voice, or by planning the context carefully. When the young say, 'My mum told me', they are apt to use an accent which is not quite their own, so hunting both with the hare and with the hounds.

I do not believe that this habit of speaking slang in inverted commas or with a funny accent is either as revolutionary or as teenage as Mr Hudson supposes. But it is certainly the case that the world-wide, self-conscious, and fashion-following youth culture of the past twenty years has been the most important new source of slang.

World wars and national military service have been another potent new source of slang in the twentieth century. Warfare, like any other specialized occupation, has always created its own jargon and slang. But the immense citizen armies and the new techniques of instant communication made the two world wars, particularly the first, prolific and fecund breeding-grounds of slang.

We must not commit the hubris of imagining that we have invented all the vivid military slang, as the hippy generation of the

1960s imagined that it had invented an amusing new name for policemen in pig. Drill sergeants, purple with professional indignation, shouting, 'I'll have your guts for garters' at an inept or slovenly recruit, may sound as if they are repeating a recent cliché of military slang. In fact the phrase has been around for four centuries at least. 'I'll make garters of thy guts, thou villain' occurs in Act III, Scene ii of *James the Fourth* by Robert Greene, the witty Bohemian who threw light on the low life of Elizabethan London. An early seventeenth-century parish register has: 'I'll have your guts for garter points.' The combination of guts with garters has less to do with historical male fashion than with slang's propensity for alliteration and assonance.

But it was the world earthquakes of war in the twentieth century, with conscription and all citizens involved in the war effort and war suffering, that enormously increased the stock of slang. It came from the customary sources of slang. Some of it was the crude sexual language of low life, broadcast in the trenches and factories. For example, the First World War brought 'buggery' into common slang idiom in two phrases. 'All to buggery' was used to mean 'completely, destructively, ruinously', as in 'our batteries shelled poor old Jerry to buggery.' And 'like buggery' came in, either as an expletive, 'certainly not!', or as an adverbial phrase meaning 'vigorously, cruelly, vindictively', as in, 'the jankers king (provost sergeant) was making defaulters double on the spot like buggery.' In 1915 Captain Bruce Bairnsfather drew a famous cartoon of two Tommies crouching in a shell-hole, while overhead the barrage raged all to buggery. One of them is saying to the other: 'If you know of a better 'ole, go to it.' This became popular slang and a catch-phrase, and a play of that title in the following year imprinted the phrase in the national lexicon. Inevitably, in the one-track way of slang, 'better 'ole' came to be used by the troops to refer to one's wife's or one's sweetheart's pudend.

Some of the wartime slang expressed the vernacular poetry of the barrack room. As often, slang was used as a sweetener for the bitter facts of death, or the taboo facts of sex. 'Where is old so-and-so?' was a question expecting, and getting, a melancholy answer. The troops of the trenches invented a number of jocular slang catch-phrases to cover up the body. The most famous was: 'Hanging on the old barbed wire (at Loos, or wherever)'. These variant replies referred to a comrade whose whereabouts was unknown or not to be disclosed: 'Died of wounds'; 'On the wire at Mons'; 'Gassed at Mons'. The Retreat from Mons was the first great action of 1914.

There was, of course, no wire used in that desperate movement; and gas had not yet been introduced as a weapon. The phrases were military slang, not history. 'He's up in Annie's room' was another First World War answer to the ominous question, with the implication that the subject of the inquiry was a bit of a lad.

'I don't mind if I do', meaning 'Yes, please', became a ragingly popular Second World War catch-phrase, because Tommy Handley adopted it as a running gag in his radio show ITMA ('It's That Man Again!'). Its variant, 'I don't care if I do', had been in use as jocular slang for two and a half centuries before that. But it was the war, and the wireless, that powerful new broadcaster of language, that turned the phrase into a public nuisance.

From Anzac shandy (a mixture of beer and champagne favoured, or at any rate desired, by Australian and New Zealand troops in the First World War) to Wizard prang, from doughboy and rookie to Fritz and Frog, the wars of the twentieth century have greatly augmented the stock of slang. It is the vernacular of the fox-hole and the NAAFI. It has the traditional qualities of civilian slang, being rude, disrespectful, vivid, and intended to be a private language, unintelligible to the authorities. Much of it is funny, and some of it is clever, with the anarchic beauty of a good joke. Consider the Second World War catch-phrase, 'Illegitimis non carborundum'; literally, 'Let there not be a carborunduming by the illegitimate', i.e., 'Don't let the bastards get you down.' Carborundum, or silicon carbide, is an abrasive material used for polishing and grinding, but its -undum ending makes it look like a Latin gerund. The abrasive phrase originated, probably in army Intelligence circles, in 1939, the happy invention of some frustrated classics scholar, and spread like wildfire through the ranks.

Evelyn Waugh's *Sword of Honour* trilogy and the war volumes of Anthony Powell's *A Dance to the Music of Time* are happy hunting grounds for the slang of 1939–1945 used exactly and evocatively. The best writers do not turn up their noses at slang. They know that it captures the mood of a period better than less highly flavoured language.

War is still a maker of slang as well as widows. Vietnam produced new words from 'Cong' ('Gook' as a contemptuous term for a Vietnamese soldier was a revival of a word previously applied to Koreans, and, in the Second World War, to Japanese) to 'frag', a custom that took 'illegitimis non carborundum' over the top by blowing away one's fellow soldier or gung-ho superior officer by means of a fragmentation grenade. Even the little local difficulty of the Falklands War in 1983 popularized such Royal Marine slang as the verb 'to yomp', which means to carry heavy equipment on foot over difficult terrain. Etymologists are divided over whether the word is onomatopoeic, or is loosely derived from roughly homophonous words in Scandinavian languages meaning to sludge on skis over flat snow. Marines do NATO and other training in Scandinavia.

One way of tolerating the intolerable is by making private jokes, or being rude about it. The wars of the twentieth century are richer in slang, because they now involve entire nations, and because the means of communication can spread the word instantly around the world.

It is impossible to consider English slang without dealing with the Muvver Tongue of Cockney. It is a controversial topic, which has attracted well-meaning and patronizing attention from outsiders, nearly all of them speaking Standard English in an Oxbridge accent. One of the earliest and best of such students was Edwin Pugh in *Harry the Cockney* (1912): 'There is no such being as a typical Cockney. But there are approximations to a type. There are men and women, the sons and daughters of Cockneys, born and bred within sound of Bow bells, and subject to all the common influences of circumstance and training and environment that London brings into play upon their personalities, who may be said to be typical. The average Cockney is not articulate. He is often witty; he is sometimes eloquent; he has a notable gift of phrase-making and nicknaming. Every day he is enriching the English tongue with new forms of speech, new clichés, new slang, new catch-words. The new thing and the new word to describe the new thing are never far apart in London. But the spirit, the soul, of the Londoner is usually dumb.'

That is the traditional, sentimental opinion of Cockney, eloquently expressed. A modern Cockney would reply to it: 'Gerrahvit (Get out of it). It's a lowerol rubbish that Bow Bells stuff. I've lived in Hackney all my life, and I've yet to hear anyone say "I'm going up the apples and pears" or "down the frog and toad", when they mean going upstairs or down the road. That stuff is for tourists. Real Cockney changes all the time; new words and phrases come in; old ones go out.'

Cockney is important to slang, because of the influence it had on the colloquial language of Americans and Colonials, and because it originated two peculiar branches of slang: back slang, and rhyming slang.

Back slang is a puerile type, consisting merely in pronouncing words as though spelt backwards; for example, 'ynnep' for penny, and 'cool' for look. The best opinion is that it was invented by Cockneys. It exemplifies the characteristic wish for a private language, undetectable by outsiders; and it is obsolescent, except among school-children.

Rhyming slang is the idiosyncrasy of Cockney. We can date its origin. In a series of articles for *The Morning Chronicle* in 1849-50 (the basis for his great sociological work *London Labour and the London Poor*) Henry Mayhew called it, 'The new style of cadgers' cant, all done on the rhyming principle.' He suggested that it originated in the language of beggars. Other suggestions are that thieves, who had a motive for baffling the police, and bricklayers, said to have had the most picturesque and private slang in the East End, contributed. A typical example of old-fashioned rhyming slang is: ''Ullo, Fred. Come in awf of de frog an' toad (road) an' 'ave a cuppa Rosie (cup of tea). It's on de Cain an' Abel (table). But wipe yer plates o' meat (feet) 'cos de ol' trouble an' strife (wife) 's just scrubbed de Rory O'More (floor). She's up de apples an' pears (upstairs) 'avin' a bo-peep (sleep). I'm still on de cob an' coal (dole). Get into that lion's lair (chair) and let's chew the fat (have a chat).' Reading that, anybody with any sensitivity for language, or anybody who has been to the East End lately, might reasonably conclude that rhyming slang, like back slang, is obsolescent. He would be wrong. The old instinct to rhyme slang is alive in the 1980s, though it has been diffused through housing estates of London many miles out of earshot of Bow bells.

Take the current use of marbles in British slang, especially in the phrase 'He's lost his marbles.' There is persuasive evidence that marbles are being used in some contexts as rhyming slang for testicles, in the manner of raspberry (tart = fart), butcher's (hook = look); berk (Berkeley Hunt = cunt); scarper (Scapa Flow = go); loaf (of bread = head); and ginger (beer, as in, 'he's a bit ginger'). In this sense the rhyme is with 'marble halls', as in, 'I dreamt I dwelt in marble halls' from Balfe's *The Bohemian Girl*, whose easy-flowing melody, unembarrassed by subtleties of harmony or orchestration, was a great favourite for many years on the smaller English stages.

I doubt whether the marbles that somebody, who is behaving in an erratic manner, is said in British slang to have lost can be classified as testicles in the extreme acceptance of the word without some risk of terminological inexactitude. There is a bold theory from the North of England suggesting that these marbles are an anglicized pronunciation of the French *meubles*. In Lancashire an elderly person who is still with-it can be said to have all his/her chairs at 'ome.

The suggested scenario goes like this. Lancashire woman emigrates to Canada and marries French Canadian. The scene is probably set in Quebec. Lancashire woman comments of a friend that she has all her chairs at home. Friend subsequently behaves in foolish manner. Husband, with imperfect command of Lancashire idiom, says that friend seems to have lost her *meubles*. This explanation has the dotty crossword tidiness of most folk etymology. In support of it we can cite the German slang about somebody who is lacking a penny in the shilling: 'He hasn't got all his cups in the cupboard.' The *meubles* explanation is ingenious, charming, and I don't believe a word of it.

The weight of the evidence suggests that the metaphorical marbles refer to the little grey cells, and the fragile ball bearings up there, that perilous stuff that weighs upon the heart, rather than the testicles. There is a nice quotation from P.G. Wodehouse: 'Do men who have got all their marbles go swimming in lakes with their clothes on?' It comes, as it happens, from *Cocktail Time*; though it could be taken from any number of the Master's oeuvre, since chaps swimming in lakes with clothes on is a stock theme, as common as the formular epithets in Homer. Wodehouse also uses 'few in the pod', another globular image, in the same sense as 'lost his marbles', as in: 'Anyone so few in the pod as to read my Aunt Julia's books.' Not all the marbles that are lost are rhyming slang; but marble halls are still used as slang for balls.

'Bottle' is an example of rhyming slang that is alive, and well, and new. *The Swell's Night Guide*, published in 1846, defined 'no bottle' as meaning no good or useless, with this example: 'She thought it would be no bottle, 'cos her rival would go in a buster.' In the 1970s in London 'bottle' came to be used to mean something like courage, or firmness, or resolve. To have a lot of bottle is to have what used to be described as a lot of spunk. To lose one's bottle was to chicken out. The Milk Marketing Board, poets of the slogan Drinka Pinta Milka Day, picked up the fashionable new slang for an advertising campaign about milk having Gotta Lotta Bottle.

There can be no certainty about the origin of a particular piece of slang, because it is not written down and commentated on until later. But the great weight of evidence supports the opinion that 'bottle' is quite recent rhyming slang for Bottle and Glass (arse). To say that somebody has lost his bottle is to say, in Old Testament terms, that his bowels have turned to water. The metaphor is exemplified by the old story about Nelson. In the middle of a sea battle, Nelson is shot in the shoulder. He refuses to go to the sick-bay, wanting to stay where his men can see him and know that they are led by him. He asks only for his red tunic, so that the men will not see his blood. The look-out calls down from the crow's nest that another fifty French ships have appeared on the horizon. Nelson calls back his midshipman, and asks him, when he brings the red tunic, to bring also his brown trousers.

This metaphor is probably criminal or at any rate low-life in origin. It is new, for it has no connexion with the earlier slang uses of bottle. It is supported by copious scatological variants: for example, 'My bottle was going like a tanner and a half crown' = 'My anal sphincter was contracting and dilating' = 'I was scared out of my wits.'

Because it is vulgar, the slang has been hidden by a second rhyme. Aristotle stands for Bottle, which stands for we know what. It is common in modern Cockney slang to say something like: "E needs a kick up is 'arris', or 'She's got a beautiful little 'arris.' Exceptionally Bottle has been removed from its denotation by a third rhyme. 'That Richard's (Richard the Third = bird; but can also be used for turd) got a smashing plaster.' Plaster = Plaster of Paris = 'Arris = Aristotle = Bottle = Bottle and Glass = Arse. The admen of the Milk Marketing Board, graduates in Eng. Lit. to a man and woman, cannot have imagined what they were asserting.

The population and character of the East End has been greatly changed by the Blitz, the closure of the docks, the movement of people out to new housing estates in the suburbs, and the traditional settlement of the latest waves of immigrants to the east of the City. But it is still a prolific manufactory of new slang. Here are some examples of the way they rabbit down there these days, in addition to saying that somebody has lost his bottle. 'Leave it out' means something like 'Don't be silly.' To bend one's earhole is to talk incessantly. 'Gercha!' means anything from, 'You liar' to 'Go away.' 'Banged it down' means 'wrote' or 'recorded'. 'Give us a bell' means, 'Phone me.' 'Geeing up' is teasing. 'Old man/woman' is father/mother or husband/wife. 'Old geezer' is an old man. 'Done' means 'did', as in, 'The thing what I done.' 'Stroll on!' is an exclamation of surprise. 'Straight up' means 'honestly.' 'Hang about' means 'Hold on.' 'Give it some stick' is to perform strenuously. 'What's the damage?' means 'How much?' 'Turns round and reckons' means 'He says.'

In the same way that some districts, such as the East End of London, are peculiarly rich in slang, so certain trades and occupations seem to be peculiarly prone to inventing and using slang. Thieves were the forefathers. Mayhew considered that bricklayers were particularly facund. The building industry still seems to produce a wide vocabulary of new slang. For example, 'The pay is bad, but the crack (conversation) is good.' That is an Irish word, and illustrates the preponderance of Irish labourers who work on building sites. 'You're not on!' means, 'The answer is definitely no.' 'The bears are growling' means, 'The workers are disgruntled.' 'A rub-a-dub-dub' is rhyming slang for a 'sub', that is, an advance on one's wages. 'Get the pea-pod on the pen-holder' is bricklayers' rhyming slang for, 'Put your hod on your shoulder.'

As with workers on building sites, so with Heralds at the College of Arms, doctors, dustmen, and players of real tennis. People who share an occupation or interest are likely, in the nature of language, to develop private slang for fun. As with Cockneys, so with Californians, Calcuttans, and Kenyans. People who live in a country, or town, or district, will develop their own English slang.

Consequently, there is more slang around today than there has ever been before. There are more special occupational and geographical groups inventing the stuff. And there are more and faster media of communication broadcasting new slang to the four corners of the English-speaking world.

Nothing is here for tears, however; nothing to wail or knock the breast, or write letters to *The Times* complaining that English is going to the dogs. Most slang remains hermetic, the private language of the group that uses it. Even the slang that goes public, and spreads to the rest of us, tends to have a short life, if a merry one. It is the most ephemeral wild flower of language. Much of the Second World War slang cited in this chapter sounds dated, or even incomprehensible, to the postwar generations. In ten years' time the slang of Sloane Rangers and Rockspeak will have become *passé*. It is the most trendy fashion of talk, and accordingly dies the quickest. Those whose slang has frozen in the vogue of their youth, who say things like, 'Old bean', or 'Good show', sound as old-fashioned as linguistic Rip Van Winkles.

We should welcome the new slang, which constantly refreshes and enlivens English from places and preoccupations around the world. It provides substitutes for words that have grown tired in service. The trashy slang that adds nothing to the power or variety of the language is not going to last anyway. Within a year or two it will have become old hat. Then it will become a laughing stock, and die of shame. Occasionally some new slang word or phrase is so apt, or funny, or clever, or so exactly fills a hole in the vocabulary, that it establishes itself and becomes respectable. We should welcome it. The selection process of language is democratic. All of us who use it play a part in deciding what English survives, and what goes out of use. The consensus is right, because we choose the words and idioms that suit our particular needs. The proliferation of slang is a source of strength, not decay.

# 3/JARGON

*'Il n'y a bête ni oiseau
Qu'en son jargon ne chante ou crie . . .'*

*'What's a' your jargon o' your schools,
Your Latin names for horns and stools;
If honest Nature made you fools,
    What sairs your grammars?'*
Robert Burns (1759–1796) First Epistle to John Lapraik

Jargon is a complex descriptive and value word: its meaning depends on the context, and the opinions and judgements of the person using it.

Originally, as illustrated in the first quotation at the head of this chapter, *jargon* was a delightful Old French word, meaning the twittering of birds. By the fifteenth century in French *jargon* had come to mean the *argot des malfaisants*. In most languages thieves and other *malfaisants* develop secret languages that they can twitter in the hearing of outsiders without being understood.

In English jargon has come to mean language that sounds ugly and is hard to understand for various reasons. It has been used to describe a hybrid speech of different languages. This meaning is otiose and obsolescent. We have pidgin for a hybrid language made up of elements of two or more other languages, and used for trading and other contacts between the speakers of other languages. When a pidgin becomes the mother tongue of a speech community, as in parts of the West Indies and West Africa, it is called a creole. We do not need jargon to describe these mixed languages; especially since we have lingua franca in the cupboard as well.

Second, in English jargon is used to describe the sectional vocabulary and register of a science, art, trade, class, sect, or profession, full of technical terms and codes, and consequently difficult, or often incomprehensible, for those who are not in the know. Professionals are usually writing and speaking for other professionals, and can accordingly use their private jargon as a form of shorthand, not needing to take the time, trouble, and space to spell everything out in simple English that the man in the Clapham omnibus or the woman on the New York subway can understand.

When addressing other research chemists, a scientist can say: 'Chlorophyll makes food by photo-synthesis', and they will all understand the platitude he is expressing in simple jargon. When addressing a class of non-scientists, the research chemist could translate his statement into, 'Green leaves build up food with the help of light', without oversimplifying his meaning excessively or begging too many questions. But for a professional audience the jargon is more exact.

A recent and, I dare say, important American research paper concerning the habits of racoons included the passage: 'Although solitary under normal prevailing circumstances, racoons may congregate simultaneously in certain situations of artificially enhanced nutrient resource availability.' I am not a biologist specializing in the Procyonidae, and I do not understand the jargon. But I have an uncharitable suspicion that the sentence means no more than that racoons live alone, but gather at bait. Presumably the simple version was considered not impressive enough for a research paper.

This use of technical jargon to blind outsiders with science has led to the third modern meaning of jargon in English: viz. pompous use of long words, circumlocution, and other linguistic flatulence in order to impress hoi polloi. Various other pejorative names have been invented for the long-winded jargon for which the civil service is, rather unfairly these days, blamed as the principal propagator: gibberish, gobbledygook, barnacular, pudder, gargantuan. It would be tidier if we could select one of these for the pretentious gibberish, and reserve jargon to describe the specialized technical vocabularies of science and the professions, the arts and the services, sports and games, trades and crafts, and all other such groups that develop esoteric languages as a form of shorthand. But, alas and dammit, language is not tidy. And the two kinds of jargon, the specialist vocabulary and the gobbledygook, continually trespass into each other's territory, so that the well-meaning outsider is hard put to it to tell which is which.

Take the following scientific report:

—'This day I shot a condor. It measured from tip to tip of the wings eight and a half feet and from beak to tail four feet. Captain Fitz Roy took the Beagle no further up the river, and at Valparaiso I saw a living condor sold for sixpence. The Chilenos destroy and catch numbers. At night they climb the trees in which the condors roost, and noose them. They are such heavy sleepers, as I have myself witnessed, that this is not a difficult task.'

Charles Darwin wrote that when his science was still pristine, and before its jargon had solidified into complex codes and shorthands. If he wanted to publish that report today in a scientific journal, he would have to rewrite it something like: 'As can be observed from tables 3 and 4, the mean wingspan and length of 132 condors taken at night or purchased (ACME Poultry Inc, Old Market Street, Valparaiso, Chile VP3 7BZ) were 2590.8mm and 1219.2mm respectively.'

I prefer the former version. But I am not a scientist. It is possible that professionals find the tables and the millimetric exactitude and the references more useful than the gripping narrative of Darwin. But I think that we should resist accepting as an axiom that scientific jargon has to be unreadable gobbledygook.

It is often impossible for an outsider to decide whether a piece of jargon is significant technical vocabulary, or gobbledygook. Consider the following short extract from *Tractatus Logico-Philosophus*:

'3.326   In order to recognize the symbol in the sign we must consider the significant use.

3.327   The sign determines a logical form only together with its logical syntactic application.

3.328   If a sign is *not necessary* then it is meaningless. That is the meaning of Occam's razor.
(If everything in the symbolism works as though a sign had meaning, then it has meaning.)'

It is possible to find that piece irritating, and even unintelligible. It was originally written in German, and the system of numbering the sentences is confusing unless you are used to it. It is not fair to take it out of its context: all those sentences stretching back to the one numbered simply 3: 'The logical picture of the facts is the thought.' But the jargon of Wittgenstein is as full of meaning as an egg is full of meat. We may find it difficult to follow the argument; we may not understand the technical terms. However, we should be rash, and indeed wrong, to describe it as jargon in the sense of gobbledygook.

Ludwig is a paragon of lucidity and concise language compared with some modern symbolic philosophers, who argue with algebraic and logical symbols, with which I shall not vex the printer. Of course some modern philosophers write gobbledygook. But most of them use jargon in the sense of highly specialized technical language, intended as shorthand for other philosophers and students of philosophy.

The reason for this is that philosophy has ceased to be the Queen of the Sciences, to be attempted by anybody who wants to understand the world, and has become a private boxing-ring for professionals. There are honourable exceptions, particularly in the field of moral philosophy, such as Freddy Ayer and Richard Hare. But most modern philosophers write dense technical jargon for each other. Under the jargon, what they are saying is significant, important, and often goes back to arguments dealt with in a different way by Plato and Aristotle. It is seldom jargon in the pejorative sense of gobbledygook.

It is a melancholy paradox that linguistics, the science concerned with the study of language, should since the war have developed a jargon that is almost impenetrable to outsiders. Try this passage for density: 'The text of a novel is a system of signs or representamina. The signs stand for something, their objects, in Proust's case certain experiences ascribed to Marcel and others in Combray and other places. The experiences may be regarded as imaginary, to be conceived rather than transcribed. The novel then creates in the reader's mind a system, structure, or tissue of equivalent signs, the interpretants of the first signs. Grammar would study the means and laws by which the signs stand for Combray, etc. Rhetoric would study the means and laws by which one sign gives birth to another. No choice arises which excludes another choice.'

Granted that it is unfair to cite a short passage out of context. You should know that that is the work of Denis Donoghue, Professor of Modern English and American Literature at University College, Dublin, occupant of the Henry James Chair of Letters at New York University, and one of the most luminous of modern academic linguisticians. The outsider raises an eyebrow at the ugly and apparently otiose alternatives of 'representamina' and 'interpretants', but concludes with a sigh that they are probably useful and meaningful terms to other initiates in the mysteries of linguistics, and that the passage illustrates jargon in the sense of technical vocabulary rather than jargon in the sense of gibberish or balderdash.

Linguistics has got itself into deep and opaque water since the war by its concentration on structuralism, the attempt to describe linguistic features in terms of structures and systems. Chomsky inspissated the opacity for benevolent outsiders by changing his mind, and drawing an important distinction between surface structures (the physical features of utterance) and deep structures (the abstract, underlying structures). And linguistics suffers from an inferiority complex common to many of the new, soft, social sciences: it deals with less tangible substance than the hard, well-established sciences, such as biochemistry, and nuclear physics. And its technical jargon has not yet had time to settle down and become established. It longs for the respectability of a true science.

An impatient philistine might conclude that the thing to do with *À la recherche du temps perdu* is read it, and not fuss about its representamina; that English Literature is not a suitable subject for study by sixth-formers and undergraduates; and that most structuralism is jargon in the pejorative sense of pretentious gibberish.

The impatient philistine would be mistaken. Generative linguistics and structuralism are wrestling with important questions in improvised jargon. A hard test would be to ask them to demonstrate that their jargon is of the significant sort by translating their utterances into ordinary English for the plain man. This would be unfair. We do not expect nuclear physicists, or brain surgeons, or microchip pioneers to be able to explain what they are doing in plain English. Modern science has taken giant steps in so many directions that the ideal of a Renaissance man, who can understand everything that is going on, for whom, like Jowett, what he doesn't know isn't knowledge, is no longer viable, to use a suspect term of jargon of the social sciences.

A good journalist ought to be able to translate any jargon into ordinary English. But with many of the modern technical jargons, the result is so plain that it is worthless. Take part of a child's guide to quantum mechanics: 'Probability enters the framework of quantum theory as the intensity of a *wave* whose frequency and wavelength are related to its energy and momentum by Planck's Constant; from a knowledge of the Wave Function, all observable properties of the system may be calculated. Energy Levels, which appear ad hoc in Bohr Theory, arise naturally in quantum mechanics from the interference of waves travelling round orbits.'

That is an oversimplified explanation for the plain man, but it remains hermetic and rebarbative for the unscientific. To translate it into language understandable by the plain man would take an entire book. It is true jargon of the technical kind. There is little room for gibberish-jargon in the experimental sciences, because facts and experiments are chiels that winna ding with jargon, an' downa be disputed.

There is more room for gibberish-jargon in the new, non-experimental and partly experimental social sciences. But it would be philistine to conclude that they are all gobbledygook; and it would also fly in the face of probability. When so many new sciences and pseudo-sciences are making such rapid advances in so many directions, it is not surprising that their technical jargons and gobbledygook-jargon become inextricably entwined. It may take many years for a little child, or, more probably, a middle-aged professor, to proclaim about the Emperor's new jargon: 'But he hasn't anything on.' But sooner or later the jargons of all proper sciences will be disentangled. In the meantime we must not be surprised that jargon is a Janus-word, looking in two directions, with a double meaning. And we may grumble, but we should not be surprised, that philologists of all people have started to discourse in a jargon that we do not understand.

We shall find the same Janus effect of jargon in all the sciences. The experimental and physical ones will tend to have more of the jargon that is descriptive, technical vocabulary; the social sciences that deal with the imponderables and unpredictabilities of human nature will tend to have more of the jargon that is gobbledygook.

We do not need to be as Procrustean as David Hume in his famous test for sorting out analytic and empirical jargon, as the only useful sorts of knowledge: 'If we take in our hand any volume; of divinity or school metaphysics, for instance; let us ask, *Does it contain any abstract reasoning concerning quantity or number?* No. *Does it contain any experimental reasoning, concerning matter of fact and existence?* No. Commit it then to the flames, for it can contain nothing but sophistry and illusion.' This magnificently hard-headed formula would commit to the flames as sophistry and illusion much useful jargon, including Hume's own formula, which is not obviously either abstract or experimental reasoning.

But let us apply Hume's Fork to a volume of modern divinity, viz. a work of the higher Roman Catholic theology, published in 1984: 'Enlightenment, emancipation from self-alienation, utopia, and hope are also terms of crucial importance intended to invoke human existence as a whole and ringing in our ears today. Whether key terms are genuinely of Christian origin or come to Christianity and the Church more or less from outside, critically, perhaps accusing, and in any case challenging, Christians and their theologians are certainly called upon to confront the proclamation of the Christian message with them, to measure the message by them and them by the message and thus bring about a historical kairos which satisfies both Christianity and its unsurpassable message and also the task and longing of the particular historical moment.'

Those outside the Fancy of Roman Catholic apologetics might well be mystified by that short passage, and many others in the twenty thick volumes of theological investigations from which it has been taken at random. Hard-nosed Humeans among them might well mutter, 'Sophistry and illusion', and feel for their matches. But the cautious and the charitable can perfectly well get away with observing that there are a number of terms of theological jargon in the passage, such as enlightenment, emancipation from self-alienation, utopia, historical kairos, possibly even 'hope', which are being used in a specialized way that does not mean a lot to them, but is probably a useful code of shorthand for those who take an interest in such things. No doubt theology, like philosophy, propagates a certain amount of gibberish-jargon. But it also deploys a large vocabulary of descriptive jargon that means something to students of theology.

Theology is different from philosophy because it is a mass sport. In general the rest of us let philosophers get on with their deliberations at a high stratosphere. But everybody from the Pope to the Prime Minister to Ian Paisley thinks that he or she has a right, and more accurately a duty, to tell the rest of us about God. Accordingly theology is exceptional among the sciences for having a whole range of jargons, at different levels and registers. Different audiences understand them differently. One man's descriptive jargon is another man's puzzling utterance is another man's gibberish-jargon.

As a contrast to the high jesuitical jargon just quoted, let us consider some theological utterances from the opposite end of the register:

'My deep personal wish is to have every American free under the direction of God to fight for America; so to fight that America really be free, free from the tyranny of sin, under God's direction, the unseen but ever-present Power. I wish this no less deeply for everyone in every nation.

'I don't want our sons, especially our fighting sons, to go about without an answer. It simply enslaves them. It is not good enough. It will drive them to the same philosophy that rules our opponents. We shall never create an inspired democracy that way. Men must learn to have a faith that will create the right revolution. If we can spread this revolution fast enough we can save America and the world. Unless we have this revolution there will be a revolution of chaos.

'It needs this stronger dose. Sin leaves us with such a dull heavy thud. The blood of Jesus Christ His Son cleanseth us from all sin. That is the discovery everyone is looking for. That is the answer.'

That comes from a revivalist, hot-gospelling evangelist, a forerunner of what is now called the Moral Majority. Such theologians assault the emotions and the check-signing hands rather than the minds of their audience. They use words like sledgehammers rather than precision tools. We could commit their sophistries fastidiously to the flames. But we should notice as we do so that their jargon has a descriptive content of a sort that is intelligible, and even agreeable, to those who go in for that kind of thing. Jargon is that old Janus, particularly in contexts that deal with God and Sin.

Not merely sciences and pseudo-sciences create their jargons of both sorts; but all specialized activities have a tendency to develop private languages for the cognoscenti. One of the widest and most creative of such languages is the jargon of business, unkindly labelled commercialese, and by Sir Alan Herbert called officese. The jargon of business, designed to impress and to sell as well as to convey information, is composed of pomposity, obsequiousness, and circumlocution. It developed an extensive vocabulary of jargon, taught in schools of Business English, as opposed to the other sort. Mockery and mass education have shot down some of its worst old excrescences. But you can still find letters from old fashioned firms which retain the jargon, in which *ult.* means last month, *inst.* means this month, *prox.* means next month, and *even date* for some reason means today. In old commercialese, the writer uses 'advise' to mean inform, says 'we are in receipt of' as a more grandiloquent formula for 'have received', and uses 'beg' as a meaningless prefix before verbs of all kinds, as in 'We beg to bring to the notice of . . .' Old commercialese is rich in 'duly noted', 'esteemed favour', 'friends in the trade . . .' (i.e. competitors), 'enclosed please find', 'as per' (in accordance with), 'and oblige' (please), 'kindly' (please), 'favour' (letter), 'same' (it), 'your esteemed favour duly to hand', 'your good self', and 'assuring you of our best attention at all times.' The classic beginning of a letter in commercialese goes: 'Your esteemed favour of even date to hand and we beg to thank your goodself for same.'

Sir Alan Herbert had a favourite example of officese from a department store to which he owed money:

'Madam,
  We are in receipt of your favour of the 9th inst. with regard to the estimate required for the removal of your furniture and effects from the above address to Burbleton, and will arrange for a Representative to call to make an inspection on Tuesday next, the 14th inst., before 12 noon, which we trust will be convenient, after which our quotation will at once issue.'

Sir Alan, in one of his aphorisms, imagined the businessman who wrote, or more probably dictated, that, justifying the jargon by advising or stating: 'Ah, but in business we have no time to write like a book. You can keep your long words for literature.' Sir Alan pointed out that commercialese comes from the misplaced effort to write like a book, and to be flowery and elegant. By saying simply what he had in mind, without trying to be stylish, the businessman could have reduced his letter from sixty-six to forty-two words:

'Madam,
  We have your letter of May 9th requesting an estimate for the removal of your furniture and effects to Burbleton, and a man will call to see them next Tuesday forenoon if convenient, after which we will send the estimate without delay.'

He could have saved even more time and typing, and reduced his letter to thirty-five words, by recasting its form slightly:

'Thank you for your letter of May 9th. A man will call next Tuesday, forenoon, to see your furniture and effects, after which, without delay, we will send our estimate for their removal to Burbleton.'

Forenoon is a useful old word that has gone out of fashion. But the demonstration still stands that business jargon is extremely unbusinesslike.

Some of the old commercialese may sound archaic. But the urge to make the business of making and selling things sound not just respectable, but noble and heroic, continually makes a hundred new flowers of commercial jargon bloom. 'Due to retirement, a vacancy exists in the top management team for a Sales Director whose main task will be the continuation of profitable market expansion that has emanated from aggressive marketing and developing policies. A comprehensive remuneration package will be offered and relocation assistance will be given should this be necessary.' To take Sir Alan's hoe to this jungle of commercial jargon might make it unfashionably barren: 'We have a vacancy for a Sales Director to carry on our recent rapid expansion. He will be paid the rate for the job, with all perks and benefits, and helped to move house if necessary.'

Nevertheless, the suspicion persists that much modern sales and marketing jargon is gobbledygook intended to impress rather than inform. There is a lot of euphemism and hyperbole in commercialese, so that salesmen become Sales Professionals or Sales Executives, and shop assistants become shop ladies, and then Sales Executives. Translate the jargon: 'We are looking for young men and women who are seeking an opportunity of joining a young professional and dynamic brand leader.' All these gung-ho pro-adjectives seem to mean no more than that the firm has not been established for very long, that its products are well-known, and that its staff are on the young side, and very keen on their jobs.

Commercialese, the jargon of trade and business, sales and marketing, has more gibberish than descriptive content. But it also speaks in a formal code, which is understood by those who use it, and who might be shocked by plain speaking that called a spade a spade, or a comprehensive remuneration package, pay.

Journalism is another pseudo-science that creates its own jargons. Journalese is popularly supposed to be one of them: the kind of English found in the tabloids and pops, featured by use of colloquialisms, superficiality of thought or reasoning, clever or sensational presentation of material, sentimentality and chauvinism, considered characteristic of newspaper writing.

In fact a good journalist uses the traditional plain style of English prose, without tricks or artificialities. It should be simple and clear, for it will be read by people in a hurry. 'Always remember that you are competing for the attention of a little old lady in Hastings with two cats,' said the head of *The Times* Washington bureau to Claud Cockburn, cub reporter. He went on, tearing Cockburn's 5,000-word article in half and dropping it into the waste paper basket, 'On this occasion, Mr Cockburn, the cats win.'

Short sentences are easier to understand. The longer the sentence, the more danger there is of confusion or ambiguity, and the more likely it is that the reader's attention will be lost. Newspaper English should not sound affected, and should be neither archaic nor exaggeratedly contemporary in tone. Newspaper jargon should be clear, to the point, impartial, and sensible: the professional tone that should be one of the essential virtues of the prose style of a good newspaper.

What sort of should is that, pray? It is an auxiliary verb of obligation that is more found in the breach than the observance in Fleet Street and other centres of the inky trade. The need to grab the attention of the inattentive reader, and hold it while he hangs from a strap in the Underground or Subway, encourages the use of screaming type-faces and sensational words in journalese. As Rupert Murdoch said, justifying pin-ups in his papers in 1969: 'We have to compete with newspapers which have double-page spreads on pubic hairs.'

Journalese employs ostentatious syntax. And ever at my back I hear *Time Magazine*'s contorted jargon hurrying near: backward ran sentences until reeled the mind. The New Journalese of the 1970s consisted of bombarding the reader with barrages of irrelevant detail: at 7.13 the Prime Minister had her second cup of coffee; hot milk, no sugar. By now she had read all the morning papers, and was ready to dictate the first draft of her speech.

The laws of libel and defamation force journalese to use certain codes that are jargon. For example, in accounts of court cases 'company director' and 'second-hand car salesman' are polite codes for crook; 'model' means prostitute; and 'top gynaecologist's daughter', as a description of the latest girl-friend of one of the royal princes, indicates that the girl is a good sport.

Confidentiality and protection of sources impose other codes of jargon on journalese. The Lobby or political journalists working at Westminster are given off-the-record briefings by government and opposition, on Lobby rules, i.e. on condition that they never reveal whom they have been talking to. Accordingly, they have developed a jargon, who runs may read, which political truth imparts. When a Lobby correspondent writes about 'a characteristically robust dismissal from sources in Whitehall', it is quite clear that Mrs Thatcher has denied the rumour personally, and probably hit him with her handbag as she did so.

Headlines impose the constraint of brevity on journalese. Headline jargon prefers PROBE to INVESTIGATION, not simply because it sounds more sensational, but because it has five letters instead of thirteen. For similar reasons it favours SHOCK rather than REVELATION, HORROR rather than ACCIDENT, ROW rather than DISAGREEMENT. The necessity to compose a significant headline in thirteen characters across a single column turns the mildest sub-editor into a Procrustes with language.

A headline is not an act of journalism; it is an act of marketing. But it still needs to make sense. There used to be a competition at *The Times* to compose the most boring headline of the year. Claud Cockburn won it with:

SMALL EARTHQUAKE IN CHILE

NOT MANY KILLED

But more often than not the compression of headline jargon leads to obscurity and misunderstanding. In *Ars Poetica*, that early and sensible manual for hacks, Horace made the point:

*brevis esse laboro,*

*Obscurus fio* . . . .

One of the classic double entendre headlines of journalese jargon occurred during the last war:

ALLIES PUSH BOTTLES UP GERMANS

More recently, when Harold Wilson had a Cabinet reshuffle, or, as we say in the trade, preferring a four-letter word when available, 'axed' some colleagues, a sub delighted London with the headline:

WILSON TAKES OUT HIS CHOPPER

Journalese of headlines favours puns. The following was put above an unfavourable review of a production of *Antony and Cleopatra*:

THE GREATEST ASP DISASTER IN THE WORLD

Newspaper headlines tend to exaggerate rather than understate. But there have been classic meiotic headlines, for example:

J.J. ASTOR DROWNED IN LINER MISHAP

That was above the report of the sinking of the *Titanic* in one of Astor's papers.

More often the artificial brevity of headline jargon produces double entendre, obscurity, and confusion, and adds to the gaiety of nations. As in:

SQUAD HELPS DOG

BITE VICTIM


FEW HAVE ENTERED

MISS CARMICHAEL

(the name of a pageant in Carmichael, California)

DEAD EXPECTED TO RISE


MAN EATING PIRANHA MISTAKENLY SOLD AS PET FISH


COLUMNIST GETS UROLOGIST

IN TROUBLE WITH HIS PEERS

The separate genres of journalism each creates its own jargon, as any specialized subject or activity always does. The third word in the previous sentence, *genre*, comes from the jargon of Lit. Crit., and is a term heavily disputed by the *cognoscenti* (there goes another one). If you are engaged in the jargon, you can trace the origin of *genre* as a critical term back to Aristotle's *Poetics*:

> 'Our subject being poetry, I propose to speak not only of the art in general, but also of its species and their respective capacities; of the structure of plot required for a good poem; of the number and nature of the constituent parts of a poem; and in the same way of any other matters on the same line of inquiry.'

Since Aristotle much shot and ink has been expended on the way to divide the genres, and thumping big books written drawing the distinction between the outer form of a genre, for example dipodic verse and Pindaric ode, and inner form, as it might be pastoral and satire. Dictionaries of modern critical terms are published describing in tedious detail such terms of jargon as 'dissociation of sensibility', Existentialism, ambiguity, and organic form in literature. Those concerned professionally in specialized and higher Lit. Crit. must be allowed to develop their own technical jargon; allow them or not, they are going to anyway. Readers of book reviews in the newspapers for the general public have a right to expect English without too much specialized lingo. And they will suspect, uncharitably, that a critic who parades Lit. Crit. jargon is more concerned to demonstrate his credentials as a very superior intellectual, than to review the book.

Janus jargon shows its two faces in all the genres of journalese. Criticism of the visual arts is a notorious jungle of jargon, which may be technical shorthand for professionals, or gibberish and gobbledygook for cynical outsiders. Here is a sentence taken at random, I promise, by the *Sortes Virgilianae* method of opening the book and stabbing with a finger, from one of the best received books of art criticism in 1982. It won the *Prix de la Confédération des Négociants en Oeuvres d'Art*, the jargon equivalent of a gold medal, that year:

> 'The effect of the real in the image insists on setting up *a scale of distance from the patent site of meaning* which is read as *a scale of distance towards the real*.'

Let us agree that quoting a single sentence out of context is unfair (you should see some of the other sentences). Let us admit that for professionals it may be useful technical jargon. But let us say, frostily, that any writing that has to use extensive italicization to make its point is clumsy writing that could be improved by recasting. And let us note, with an apprehensive shiver of distaste, the use of such gallicisms as 'the real', and images 'insisting', and 'patent'. Such jargon makes us suspect that the writer is more interested in establishing his status than in conveying meaning as clearly as the language allows.

Writing about painting, like writing about music, is notoriously difficult. The best thing to do with paintings is to paint them or look at them. The best thing with music is to play it, or listen to it. Writing and reading about them are secondary activities, two stages from 'the real', as we say in the trade. The higher critical journalese is like the soft social sciences: it deals with complex intangibles, less tractable than the hard stuff of the physical sciences, or the factual journalism of it happened yesterday. And it is correspondingly anxious to demonstrate its bona fides as a significant contribution to human knowledge.

In a series of admirable art lectures about the Venice Exhibition at the Royal Academy in 1984, a lecturer, talking about the exquisite small sculptures that were the biggest surprise of the show, deployed, with a certain amount of other art jargon, the word 'isocephalic'. She was making the point that all the heads in the sculptures came to the same level in a straight line, in contrast to other sculptures and paintings she had been considering. That 'isocephalic' is a good example of a useful term of technical jargon as a form of shorthand among experts. It uses one word to say what it would take a dozen to say less exactly in simpler language. It is not a word that many of us are going to use often in our daily business.

If you let them, balletomanes will explain the difference between an Enchaînement and an Entrechat. Crime reporters will go on about GBH and 'Sus'. Sports writers will entertain us with jargon about track records, and cherries, and gut feelings in their heart of hearts, and the image, bizarre to outsiders, of a runner 'kicking' around the last bend. Music critics will puzzle outsiders by reference to the rich brown timbre of the cello, mean-tone tuning, and rhythm as an element of melody. General reporters call carbon paper 'a black', single-paragraph 'fillers' NIBS (News in Brief), and an item that must on no account be 'spiked' an 'Editor's Must'.

It is natural and desirable that specialized interests should develop their technical jargons, in order to speed and shorten communications between those who share the interest. When they could, if asked, translate the jargon into sentences intelligible by the intelligent outsider, even if, in the case of complex disciplines such as biochemistry or musicology, it were to take several books of plain man's translation, then they are using the hard jargon of a technical vocabulary. When their jargon is untranslatable into simpler language, however long and laborious the translation, then they are using jargon as a smokescreen, like the Sibyl at Cumae crying *Procul, o procul este, profani* to outsiders, warning them to keep away from mysteries that they are too dim to understand.

As you would expect in human affairs, the distinction between the two faces of jargon is seldom as clear-cut as has just been stated. Most jargons contain elements of gibberish and showing off as well as hard technical codes and shorthands for the initiated. Very few jargons consist of nothing but hot air. The sillier the speciality, the woollier the jargon. But, of course, the judgement of what specialities are silly is a value judgement and a matter of opinion. (Up to a point, Lady Copper.) We should not be surprised, therefore, that the jargons of cults and sects are peculiarly flatulent, and that their propagators find it almost impossible to translate their mumbo-jumbo into everyday language. The purpose of such jargons is to convey hysteria and mysteria, not meaning.

The romantic novels of Mills and Boon and Barbara Cartland are not high literature; but they are bought and enjoyed by millions. They have their own, low-level jargon, that bears the same relation as the grunts of Neanderthal man to the full range of modern English. The jargon has to convey a rose-tinted atmosphere of love, without becoming specific. Passionate kisses are admitted at intervals, and, these days, a certain amount of indistinct bodice-ripping; but definitely nothing below the belt. The Romance Language of romantic fiction has to imply its meaning, through a stock of formular epithets and situations as conventional as anything in Homer. It is designed to hint and tease without offending any taboos.

Take a typical passage, if you will pardon the expression:

> 'Her words made Conrad draw in his breath.
> 'Then he was kissing her again, kissing her passionately, but at the same time, with a reverence he had never given another woman.
> 'Delora had filled the shrine in his heart that had always been empty.

'Now he knew she would be there always and for ever, and he would worship her because she had brought him the true, pure love for which all men seek as they voyage over the difficult, unpredictable and often tempestuous sea of life.

'"I worship you," he said against her lips.

'There was no further need for words.'

There was no further need for words, because the lexicon of Romance jargon has just been fully deployed. In it chaps are called names like Conrad, and girls names like Delora, quite unlike the names of those who are reading it on the way to work. Rhetorical repetition, tautology ('always and for ever'), banal metaphor, and short paragraphs are part of the jargon. There are code words, often connected with religion (reverence, shrine, worship), that adumbrate passion delicately. It is a candy floss jargon. But do not mock it. It may contain a high proportion of gibberish-jargon; but it is one of the most widely diffused and popularized of private lingos.

At the other end of the scale of jargons, the sciences have a higher proportion of significant technical words in their languages. Nevertheless, of all the proliferating jargons, it is the jargon of sociology, or Sociologese, that has the worst reputation for gobbledygook with the general public.

The social sciences are comparatively new; and it usually takes a century or two for the jargon of a new science to settle down. Most sciences deal with matters beyond the ken of the rest of us. Sociology deals with the everyday affairs of everyday people. Accordingly, we have the unworthy suspicion that they prefer an abstruse jargon to make their everyday subject sound more scientific. Sociologese has certainly been partly responsible for the proliferation of such pretentious vogue abstractions as constructions with 'situation', which have become a laughing-stock, and are dying of shame.

Nevertheless, if you are looking for a rich example of gobbledygook-jargon, you could do worse than look in the professional journals of sociologists, where you will find such jargon as, 'a relatively unstructured conversational interaction', which is a pompous description of what the ordinary man would call an informal chat.

Here's a piece:

'The examples given suggest that the multiformity of environmental apprehension and the exclusivity of abstract semantic conceptions constitute a crucial distinction. Semantic responses to qualities, environmental or other, tend to abstract each individual quality as though it were to be experienced in isolation, with nothing else impinging. But in actual environmental experience, our judgements of attributes are constantly affected by the entire milieu, and the connectivities such observations suggest reveal this multiform complexity. Semantic response is generally a consequence of reductive categorization, environmental response or synthesizing holism.'

We can detect bits of meaning, as if by flashes of lightning, in that monstrous cloud of jargon. 'The multiformity of environmental apprehension' must mean that we are aware of our surroundings in a number of different ways; 'semantic responses' are the words we use to describe what we see; and 'environmental experience' is our observation of our surroundings. But I should not care to give a plain translation of that paragraph, nor try the patience of the printer by attempting one.

Faced with such gobbledygook-jargon, it is tempting to dismiss all sociology as a pseudo-science, the principal purpose of which is laboriously to redefine everyday platitudes in pompous jargon. That would be an understandable, impatient reaction, but it would be a mistake. Over the past century sociology has discovered important new truths about us and our world. As in any other discipline, there are brilliant and lucid scholars working in it, and brilliant scholars who are not lucid (Talcott Parsons), and pseuds and charlatans who give the trade a bad name. But the proper sociologist can present truth without gobbledygook. Here is a typical passage from Émile Durkheim, a founding father of sociology, translated from French:

'Instead of stopping at the exclusive consideration of events that lies at the surface of social life, there has arisen the need for studying the less obvious points at the base of it – internal causes and impersonal, hidden forces that move individuals and collectivities. A tendency to this sort of study has already been manifested by some historians; but it is up to sociology to increase consciousness of it, to illuminate and develop it.'

Durkheim, Weber, and their best successors demonstrated that it is possible to explain the ways in which society works without sending up clouds of impenetrable jargon.

Psychology is another new science that has the same sort of

trouble with its jargons as sociology. It has not had time to establish its vocabulary. In any case the Freudians, Jungians, Adlerians, and other later disputing sects of the science, that is part medical, part social, part metaphysical, and part gobbledygook, cannot agree on what the simplest terms are to mean. Its jargon has been widely plagiarized and picked up by the general public, which lives in a scientific age, and is anxious to sound scientific. And very often the general public gets hold of the wrong end of the stick, even if the psychologists can agree among themselves as to what is the right end of the stick. As a consequence the jargon of psychology has been widely abused in Freudian English. In it somebody who is a nervous traveller, worried about missing the train, is described as neurotic or even paranoid. Somebody who cannot make up her or his mind is called schizophrenic. Somebody else refuses fish, for example, on the exaggerated grounds that he is allergic to it. The jargon adds to the gaiety of nations. But it confuses the serious work of psychology and psychiatry; and occasionally it wounds the feelings of those, or the friends of those, who are really suffering from the conditions so lightly bandied about.

In parts of the world much given to analysis and psychiatry, such as California, Freudian English has developed into a secondary jargon, described as Psychobabble. In Psychobabble, analysts' terms are mixed with the latest slang, misunderstandings of the other social sciences, and the jargons of the cults and other charlatanries that infect that fair State. 'Upfront' means honest; 'heavy' means serious or grave; people say things like: 'She and Harry hadn't finalized the parameters of their own interface.' And California is where it's at, you know, in the jargon situation.

But the latest and fastest growing of the technical jargons, as we move into the age of the silicon chip, is Computerese. It has already given us such popularized technicalities as 'interface' and 'input'. Like many new jargons, deficient of vocabulary, it converts nouns into verbs, as 'to access' and 'to format'. It then converts the verb back into a gerund noun again by adding -ing. For example, 'window' is a vogue word and metaphor of Computerese. It refers to the latest technology that allows a computerist to keep a dozen or more items on his screen at the same time, as on a crowded desk. This has created the verb 'to window', and then the gerund 'windowing', or keeping a cluttered VDU screen. The bright new word has already been picked up by the bower-birds of marketing, who have, characteristically, got the jargon slightly wrong. 'Our window for this product is very small' is used to mean that the product will be obsolete very quickly.

Other terms of Computerese from Silicon Valley in California are:

'A Gating Event' means a crux or turning-point: the gate on a silicon microprocessor chip is a key element in controlling its logic.

'Bandwith' means the amount of information exchanged in a conversation. It is derived from the jargon for the breadth of information in certain computer devices. You would not want to have a protracted conversation with somebody whose bandwith was small.

'He's pushing things on the stack' means he is getting overwhelmed: one stacks trays of circuit boards in a computer.

'To core dump' means to get everything off one's chest: it comes from the jargon for emptying out a computer's central memory.

'He's a read-only memory' is unkind. It means that, as a courtier said of Louis XVIII, *il n'a rien oublié et n'a rien appris*. It comes from read-only memory, or ROM, a computer part that cannot be altered by the user. A more sophisticated version is PROM, or programmable read-only memory. You can even get EPROMS, E standing for erasable.

'I'm interrupt driven' means that my life is frantic and disorganized. Computers are designed to avoid such human failings.

*InfoWorld Magazine*, which deals with computer science and Computerese, has devised a language mingled from the two latest Californian jargons, Psychobabble and Computerese.

Babbler 1: 'I'm starting to relate to what you're saying. At first I was as down as my computer is when power spikes and bad vibes surge through the lines and don't go with the data flow, but now I think I'm beginning to feel a sense of wellness about this thing.'

Babbler 2: 'Yeah, and you know, if you think of bad vibes on a power line as an analogue to bad vibes in the central nervous system, you've really accessed something important. People are really computers. They feel good; they feel bad – just like you and me. They relate to each other and interface with each other; people interface with each other; people interface with computers. Really cosmic parameters.'

Babbler 1: 'Wow! I'm accessing it!'

Computerese is an instructive example of how fast jargon is changing in the present English revolution. Computers are a field where technology is moving extremely fast: too fast, in fact, for language to keep up with it. You frequently hear computer people talking about 'Core Store'. They are referring to the memory of the computer, that is, the part of the computer that holds data that *is* being processed. (Note, in passing, how Computerese has turned *data* into a singular. Computers deal with such prodigious numbers of data that computer people cannot think of their raw material as one datum, plus another datum, plus another datum . . ., but rather as numerous as the sands of the desert or the stars in the sky. So they treat *data* as an aggregate noun, like sugar, in which the essential point of the noun is choosing to ignore the individual grains or components, and considering the collection as though it were a packaged unit. In Computerese small numbers of *data* are as embarrassing to enumerate as wild oats. *Data* is. Purists need not repine. A similar process of translating an original Latin plural into an eventual English singular has happened before, to words such as *agenda* and *stamina*. It is happening to *media*.) Computerese still widely uses the term Core Store for the memory of a computer, even though it has become an anachronism in ten years. Since the early seventies the ferrite cores that were the basis of memory have become obsolete, and are no longer used. They have been replaced by silicon chips.

In the same way, one still regularly hears the users of Computerese refer to the Processor as the CPU (Central Processor Unit). This is another instant anachronism. CPU is an obsolete echo from the far-off days, all of ten years ago, when all computers were large computers, and the processing unit or CPU stood in the middle of a large computer room, surrounded by the peripheral units, i.e. the devices that supplied input data, and printed output *data* as it poured like sugar out of the CPU. In those days central and peripheral were precise descriptions of the lay-out of a computer room. *Nous avons changé tout cela*: or rather the advent of the silicon chip and the microcomputer (in which both processor and input/output can be housed in one small device) has destroyed the descriptive validity of the terms. However, they are still widely used.

Computerese is a classic example of how the vast and hurried strides of modern science and technology are changing the English language. The strides are so fast that even that swift runner, language, cannot keep up.

Some jargons are unjustly attacked for obscurity because of a misunderstanding of their purpose. Such are the jargons of parliamentary draftsmen, solicitors, the Inland Revenue, and local authority notices. This is not to assert that all parliamentary draftsmen, lawyers, inspectors of taxes, and clerks of local authorities write jargon that is free from gobbledygook. That would clearly be an absurd assertion. But on occasions, when they are writing, they are writing not for the general public to understand, but in order to construct formulae that will be shipshape and watertight against every leak and storm of case law and precedent. Such jargon is not meant to be read with ease. It is meant to be interpreted and applied by lawyers, in much the same way as a mathematical formula.

For example, here is a typical note from Hackney Council on the subject of the refund of overpayments of rates:

'(1) Without prejudice to ss 7 (4) (b) and 18 (4) of this Act, but subject to subs (2) of this section, where it is shown to the satisfaction of a rating authority that any amount paid in respect of rates, and not recoverable apart from this section, could properly be refunded on the ground that –

(a) the amount of any entry in the valuation list was excessive; or
(b) a rate was levied otherwise than in accordance with the valuation list; or
(c) any exception or relief to which a person was entitled was not allowed; or
(d) the hereditament was unoccupied during any period; or
(e) the person who made a payment in respect of rates was not liable to make that payment,

the rating authority may refund that amount or a part thereof.'

It goes on for paragraphs, measureless to man, as interminable and impenetrable as an invocation to Baal by Chaldaean priests. Presented with it, the rate-payer hoping for a refund of an overpayment of his rates, might well tear her hair, and scream about the obfuscations of the jargon of local authorities.

She would be justified, but mistaken. That document is not meant for her, unless she is a lawyer in rating law, or a masochist (note the Freudian jargon) interested in such matters. Hackney's leaflet is spelling out in laborious but watertight detail the exact circumstances in which a refund on the rates is allowed, so that only those entitled to a refund get one, and, less urgently, so that nobody who is entitled to a refund fails to obtain one. If the rate-payer wants to know how the law applies to her particular case, and whether she is personally entitled to a refund, she would do better to consult a lawyer or a Citizens' Advice Bureau. These places serve a useful purpose, like vultures, in a world in which the law, like most other things, has become too complicated for the amateur to understand.

To expostulate the jargons of all the sciences, arts, trades, sports, professions, and other specialized interests, why day is day, night night, and time is time, were nothing but to waste night, day, and time. The same general principles apply to all jargons. Every jargon, in greater or lesser proportion, is a mixture of hard technical terms that are useful codes for the cognoscenti and gobbledygook that is used to sound grand, and blind the eyes of the ignorant with long words. The harder, and older, and more professional sciences will have less of the gobbledygook-jargon. Some of them, perhaps symbolic logic or old-fashioned algebra, will have none at all. The newer, softer, empirical sciences, which have not yet had time to establish their jargons, and which treat the imponderables of human nature and the cussed behaviour of human beings, will tend to have a higher proportion of gobbledygook. Some totally unscientific pseudo-sciences or disciplines, like a completely corrupt and irrational cult, which exists only to brainwash and exploit its victims, may develop jargons that consist entirely of gobbledygook, with no descriptive content at all.

The prolific ramification of knowledge in the modern world means that there is more jargon about than ever before. The ideal of Renaissance Man was that he should know something about everything; and some of them, like Erasmus and Leonardo, gave an impression of coming near to achieving it.

> 'First come I; my name is Jowett.
> There's no knowledge but I know it.
> I am Master of this college:
> What I don't know isn't knowledge.'

When the first edition of the *Encyclopaedia Britannica* was issued in three fat volumes by a 'Society of Gentlemen in Scotland' between 1768 and 1771 (it included, among much other interesting matter, the news that California was an island), there were plenty of people around who knew everything in it, and some who knew a great deal more.

Since then the old sciences have split up into thousands of more specialized branches, so that an organic chemist, for example, speaks a language as different from that of a theoretical chemist as Hittite from Babylonian. Hundreds of new disciplines, particularly in the social sciences, have been invented and rapidly advanced to the frontiers of knowledge. Man has reached for the stars, chattering jargon as he goes. All the new modes and categories of knowledge necessarily and immediately create their own jargons. So do the hundreds of nationalities and groups and special interests that are speaking English as a world language. In the eternal silence of infinite space, earth can be heard from far away as the planet that talks, and much of what it talks is jargon.

There are more professional physicists making a living today from physics than have existed before from the time of Archimedes until now. (If invited to prove this popular assertion of folk lore, the prudent man clears his throat, and moves on to talk about something else.) It must also be true, though equally tiresome to have to prove, that there is more jargon in the English language today than has been there since the immigrant Angles, Saxons, and Jutes started to develop their jargon of *Englisc*. It is the world language. As Jakob Grimm (1785–1863), the German philologist, recognized: 'In wealth, wisdom and strict economy, none of the other living languages can vie with it.' It has to express all the knowledge and opinion of all the learning and pseudo-learning in the world.

English today is a language encrusted with layers of new jargon. This is a result of the explosion of knowledge rather than a fundamental change in the language. It means that there are many lexicons of technical terms that the ordinary English-speaker cannot understand, and need not trouble to learn. It means that more popularized technicalities are adopted, plagiarized, and misunderstood by the ordinary speaker than ever before. In particular, English towards the end of the twentieth century has a propensity to abstract and impressive-sounding blanket-words from the social sciences.

But jargon is a source of strength in the language. It enables those with a particular interest to talk to each other in a sort of code or sub-language, without bothering the rest of us in the crowded and noisy world. If their knowledge is true and important, and their jargon sound, we shall certainly pick up the best bits of it, like magpies, to decorate our discourse. We may get it a bit wrong. In which case the specialists may need to invent a new jargon. Neurosis is a term that has been so widely popularized that psychiatrists are having to invent new words.

Along with the hard, shiny new technical jargon, inevitably comes the tinsel language of gobbledygook-jargon. For every quark and quasar you will have any number of situations and parameters of interaction. But the fastidious and the purist need not throw their hands in the air in despair at the decay of the language because of the proliferation of gargantuan pudder-jargon. Language purifies itself in the same sort of way that the ocean does. Popularized technicality goes in impatient vogues. It has a brief life. As a dead body or other decaying matter does not last long in the sea, so meaningless jargon does not last long in the language. Anybody with any sensitivity for language already finds some other way of speaking about what would have been called, ten years ago, the environment situation. There is a lot of jargon around, and it increases every day. But you do not have to learn it unless you want to. That is the point of jargon.

# 4/DIALECT

'The whole earth was of one language, and of one speech.' *Genesis*, XI, 1

'Language changes every eighteen or twenty miles.' Hindu proverb

English is the world language. Let us now praise famous men and women, from Shakespeare and Milton to Jane Austen and Dorothy Parker, from Chaucer to James Joyce, and from *Moby Dick* to the wit of James Thurber. Many languages have great writers; but no other language has produced such a variety of great writers in so many genres and styles of literature. This is enough to explain why people want to learn English; but not why it has become a world language. It is a necessary, but not a sufficient, reason for English being the world language from China to Peru.

Other, less elevated, reasons contributed to what has happened. For English to have become a world language, it needed large populations of native speakers of English. This was a necessary, but not a sufficient, reason; cf. Chinese and Hindi, which are spoken by large populations.

There must be a wide geographical spread of native speakers. This is a necessary, but not a sufficient, reason; cf. Spanish.

You need native speakers of inventive genius, and of industrial and commercial enterprise. This is a necessary, but not a sufficient, reason; cf. Japanese and German.

You need a sustained period of political and economic leadership to spread the word. This is a necessary, but not a sufficient, reason; cf. Russian, which shows no sign of spreading in the Soviet empire.

All these factors played a part in making English the world language. But in fact what has emerged is not a single language, but a bunch of overlapping dialects. The English they speak in Bombay is a quite different and distinct dialect from the English they speak in Birmingham or in Brisbane. The Doomsday view of the English language is that it is breaking up into a cluster of overlapping and mutually unintelligible dialects; and that by the end of the century English-speakers from different parts of the world will no longer be able to understand each other.

To an extent this is already true. An English-speaker with a heavy Glasgow or Ulster accent may have difficulty in making himself understood, for example, to an English-speaker from Watts County, Los Angeles. I think that the Doomsday view is unduly pessimistic and alarmist. The centrifugal forces of geography and racial and cultural difference may be pulling English apart. But the centripetal forces of mass foreign travel, television and radio, pop songs, and, still above all, the printed word, are far stronger. A thousand national and regional varieties may bloom, but English will survive as the world language.

Even if Doomsday were to come, and English were to split up, it would not be the end of the world. It happened to Latin, which was a beautiful and expressive and economical language. But the fragments that grew away from the death of Latin were not bad languages: Italian, French, Spanish, Portuguese, Rumanian, and the rest of the Romance languages are worthy successors. Virgil and Tacitus are great. But so are Dante, and Racine, and Borges, and Camoens, and generations of writers who have enriched the world.

A dialect used to be considered the local variety of a language that occurred in a rural district. In parts of England we call a donkey a moke; in other parts we call it a cuddy, a nirrup, a pronkus, and other charming names. You can draw linguistic maps with isoglosses showing the distribution of these dialectical differences. Local dialect is fading away, as society becomes more centralized, and people move around more, and hear people speaking on the television and the radio from places outside their village. National dialects grow stronger, as English-speaking countries develop their peculiar vocabularies and idioms. A century ago English had a common core of literary and colloquial English spoken by all English-speakers: around the outside were the outposts of language, known by some but not all English-speakers. These were such kinds of language as technical jargon, scientific and foreign words, archaic, vulgar, slang, and dialectal English.

Today the pattern has changed. English has become a Commonwealth of languages. Around the central core, and overlapping it and each other, are Strine, Bombayspeak, Black English, South African English, Boston Brahmin, the quare delights of Belfast English, and all the rest of the family. These national dialects enrich each other and the central core by borrowing and lending. We wear each other's clothes, eat the food of other regions and nations, borrow the fashions and styles of countries on the far side of the world; and use their English to describe them. Wearing a kimono, she eats a poppadom and raps beaucoup about the current hassle over Black English.

The dominant voices in changing English are American, partly because so many millions are using the language over there, and partly because they lead the way for the rest of us in so many sciences, arts, and fashions. From across the Atlantic new vocabularies, idioms, and grammar flow into the central sea of English from tongues as exotic as Eskimo and Algonkian and as familiar as Hispanic English and the English of the seventeenth century that came over with the Pilgrim Fathers.

Yiddish is one of the strongest and liveliest sources of new English, or Yinglish, partly because of the excellence of American Jewish novelists from Malamud and Roth to Grace Paley. From gonef to kibitzer, Yinglish is continually enriching the language. Where would critics and other journalists be without chutzpa (though some of us are glad to write it rather than have to pronounce it) to describe the quality of rascally brazenness and shameless gall that shocks and amuses? You want an example of chutzpa? How about Hymie the Gonef? He broke the Eighth Commandment – by stealing the Bible.

It is not just Yinglish vocabulary that we are adopting, but Yiddish grammatical structures, idioms, and deadpan Jewish humour. For example, consider the characteristic Yiddish usage of taking a predicate adjective or noun and sticking it right in front of the sentence for emphasis: smart, he isn't; beautiful, she's not; a genius, Harry isn't; quick, the new technology ain't.

Solemn students of linguistics call this idiom topicalization. Leo Rosten, the witty student of Yinglish, calls it 'fronting'. I know Dickens used it occasionally. It is common practice in German: *Schön ist sie nicht*; and in other Germanic languages, Danish, for example: *Skon er hun ikke*. But it is a conspicuously Jewish idiom, and it adds to the varieties of emphasis and innuendo available in English.

'From that (this) he makes a living?' is a particular instance of fronting. A Jew asks his son: 'Exactly what did Einstein do that was so smart?' 'Einstein revolutionized physics. He proved that matter is energy. That when light goes past the sun, it *bends*. That . . .' 'Awright, awright,' said the old man. 'But tell me: from that he makes a living?'

Here is a nice example of fronting an adjective for emphasis. It comes, natch, from the great S.J. Perelman. Thirty-five hundred feet below the plane, two turkey vultures clung to a snowy crag, and picked idly at some bones. 'This sure was a delicious scenario writer,' ruminates the elder, stifling a belch. 'You'd have to go all the way to Beverly Hills for one like him.' 'Listen,' said his companion, 'that bad I don't need *anything.*'

Call Jack Benny for example of repetition for emphasis and irony. The robber, confronting Jack, who, as you know, used miserliness as one of his funniest comic props: 'Your money or your life.' One of those long Benny pauses. Robber (more menacingly): 'I said – your money or your life.' Jack, vehemently: 'I'm thinking. I'm *thinking.*' Jack's real name was Benny Kubelski.

And here is an example of the flexibility of Yinglish to reverse a meaning through nothing more substantial than emphasis. One day Stalin appeared in Red Square, waving a sheet of paper in the air. 'Comrades,' he cried, 'this is a wonderful day for Russia and for Communism. I have just received this letter from Comrade Trotsky. Let me read it to you: "Joseph Vissarionovich; you were right, I was wrong. You are the true guardian of Socialism. I should apologize to you."'

An old Jew at the front of the crowd held out a hand: 'If I might see the letter, Comrade Stalin.' 'Certainly,' said Stalin, and handed it over. The man looked at it. 'As I thought, Comrade; you haven't read it properly: "*You* were right, *I* was wrong? *You* are the true guardian of Socialism? *I* should apologize to *you*?"'

Consider the work that Yinglish gets out of the simple little word 'again'. Leo Rosten has categorized nine different ways of using 'again' as an expletive or particle, what the Germans call a *Flick-wort*, to give emphasis or colour.

They range from '*Again* he's here?' (But he was here only yesterday) to '*Again* I should apologize to that *Schmuck*?' (You must be daft even to suggest it).

Another idiom of Yinglish that exemplifies the deadpan Jewish deployment of sarcasm, and has been adopted by English-speakers generally, is the trick of accusing somebody of idiocy by denying the obvious. Question: 'How would you like an all-expenses-paid trip to Bermuda?' Answer: 'I prefer to spend the winter in a foxhole in the Gray's Inn Road.'

You can accuse somebody of asininity by echoing a question. Question: 'Don't you want to meet a wonderful boy and get married and have a fine family?' Answer: 'No, I don't want to meet a wonderful boy and get married and have a fine family.' (Meaning: 'How daft can you be to ask such an idiotic question?')

You can affirm indignation by repeating the question in the form in which it was asked, with varying intonational emphasis. Question: 'Did you send your mother flowers on her birthday?' Answer: 'Did I send my mother flowers on her birthday?' Rosten distinguishes eight separate meanings for that answer, depending on where you put the stress. For example, if you put the accent on *flowers*, you imply: 'Flowers were just the *beginning* of what I gave my mother on her birthday.'

Another Yinglish idiom that has passed into common currency is repetition, to escape the obvious, and maximize persuasiveness: 'I'm going, I'm going.' The difference between 'You'll like it' and 'You'll like it. You'll *like* it' is as monumental as the difference between plain and bloodless 'I don't know' and 'I don't know, I don't *know*', which is a defiant confession of ignorance. Hamlet also used repetition: I know, *I know*. But this kind of repetition for emphasis is characteristically Jewish, and its popularity is enriching Yinglish, and increasing the varieties of expression available to all of us.

If it is true that for many purposes English is the most flexible and expressive of the 2,769 languages that are still being spoken around the world (and I think it is) Yinglish is its liveliest dialect.

Every dialect that has sprung out of English develops its own idiosyncrasies of vocabulary and grammar, idiom and nuance. From the moment that the Pilgrim Fathers crossed the Atlantic, the language that they spoke started to diverge from the language of their countrymen that they left behind. The pleasant use of 'fall' to mean autumn, when the leaves fall from the trees, which we think of today as peculiarly American, was standard English of the seventeenth century. Look at Raleigh's *Reply to Marlowe*:

> *A honey tongue, a heart of gall*
> *Is fancies spring, but sorrows fall.*

The usage survived in the New World. In the Old World 'autumn', which had been around since Chaucer, obliterated 'fall'.

As far as we can judge, from rhymes and other clues, the American accent and stress of English is more 'correct', i.e. older, than the British accent. Shakespeare and Queen Elizabeth I spoke English that sounded more like a modern American's than a modern Englishman's.

In Yinglish we particularly notice the Yiddish grammar and word order that has been imposed on English to give it new meanings. In Australian English or Oz English, we particularly notice the slang.

All dialects of English develop their own slang. It is notable that Strine and Cockney are two of the richest slangs. One explanation that has been suggested is that slang is the peculiar gift of the poor, who use it to bring colour and richness into their lives. Ergo, or not, as the case may be, Cockney, which was spoken in the poorest parts of London, and Australian, which was first spoken by transported convicts and poor emigrants, are peculiarly rich in slang.

Your average Oz bastard may be a drongo, and even Blind Freddy could see the point we are making. If it was raining palaces, I'd get hit on the head by the dunny door. He's made a real blue and caused me a lot of strife; and I don't want to bag but he's a real bull artist; and this sort of sheer bastardry and sticking his bib in just gets me off my bike, and I feel like going in boots and all. On the other hand, let's not have a barney or go for the big spit or have the dingbats. She'll be apples.

Let us consider Oz dialect as a paradigm for the way in which all dialects of English develop their own slangs and colloquialisms. Oz slang has been popularized in England recently by the prevalence of brilliant young Australians over here in such trades as journalism. Australians make good journalists because they are as game as Ned Kelly, inventive with language, and not hampered by the English class inhibitions and sensitivities.

The Ozzification of London was exemplified in the sixties by the renaming of the bed-sitterland of the Earl's Court Road as Kangaroo Valley, and by a popular strip cartoon entitled 'Barry McKenzie' in the satirical magazine *Private Eye*. The creator of the latter, Barry Humphries, said that his invention, the dreadful Barry, spoke a kind of pastiche in which 'words like *cobber* and *bonzer* still intrude as a sop to Pommy readers, though such words are seldom, if ever, used in present-day Australia.'

The first way in which a dialect develops out of English is to name the animals, birds, trees, plants, and other creatures in the new world. *Kangaroo* is an example of a peculiarly Australian addition to English. Much Australian dialect for natural history was taken over from the original Australians, the Aborigines: boomerang, billabong, corroboree, bingey, humpy, gibber, mulga, and warrigal.

Of course, it was not as simple as that. Language never is. Bandicoot is an Indian word, emu is Portuguese, and Piccaninny is West Indian. Dialects affect each other as well as the muvver tongue, which is what Cockneys call English.

Other Australian dialect words come from attempts to communicate between the original natives and the incomers; the pidgin that has produced words such as *mary* meaning a woman, and *walk-about*, which has been adopted by the Queen and ambitious politicians.

The dialect develops to record social as well as natural conditions. On the one hand there are all the Outback words – the backblocks, the back of beyond, the black stump, Woop Woop – and a large range of words connected with the bush. There is the bush-baptist, the bush-carpenter, and the bush-lawyer; there is the real bushman with his bushcraft; there is the bushfire, of course, and the bush telegraph; you can get bush-sick, or just go bush.

On the other hand Oz early developed *a pure merino* as slang for somebody who was insistent on his or her social status. To go *on the wallaby track* was to tramp the outback in search of work (as though following the track made by the wallabies). The *government stroke*, the indolent working style of a government employee, originally on road work, had been recorded by the middle of the nineteenth century.

There is a notably large group of dialect words showing how important sheep are and have been in the country's economy – all the special wood-shed senses of words like blades, blow, board, bin, class, clip, dagger; the bare-bellies, kelpies, sheep-dog trials, jack-aroos, and rouseabouts (the odd-job men on a sheep station).

This is the world of the squatter, the runholder, the grazier; the stockrider and the stock and station agent are characters in the story that goes back to *Clancy of the Overflow*.

Dialect developed from persons or place-names, or from figures in Australian folk-lore. A *Jacky Howe* is Australian slang for a sleeveless flannel shirt, named for its eponym, a shearer who lived from 1855 to 1922. '*Sing 'em muck*' as a self-depreciating comment on Australian culture is a catchphrase from the supposed advice of Dame Nellie Melba to Clara Butt on undertaking a tour of Australia. '*Doing a Melba*' is to make a habit of returning from retirement in a number of 'farewell' performances. *Blind Freddie*, representing the highest degree of disability or incompetence, is probably folklore, but has been derived from a blind hawker in Sydney in the 1920s. Barcoo is a river and district in Queensland. Hence comes such dialect as the *Barcoo salute*. 'I see you've learnt the *Barcoo salute*,' said a Buln Buln Shire councillor to the Duke of Edinburgh. 'What's that?' said the Duke, waving his hand again to brush the flies off his face. 'That's it,' said the man from the bush.

Not just language, but life, and even sport is changed by a change of geography. So Australian dialect evolves the language of Australian Rules football, wood-chopping, and surfing; the vocabulary of the life-saver and the shark patrol. New words are brought into the language to describe such Australian preoccupations as the Art Union (a big lottery), the Cup, the Ashes, the trots, bikies, bludgers, and beer-ups. Nothing is more Australian than boiling the billy and having your tucker.

Many of the words in this sporting and social class are not indigenous but transmogrified. They did not begin life in Australia, but they found new life there. *Dinkum* meaning honest or genuine, *bowyangs* meaning a string tied round the trouser-leg below the knee, worn by labourers, and *damper*, the sort of bushman's bread of flour and water we used to bake in the hot ashes of bonfires, were originally dialect words in England. They were taken to Australia by the early immigrants, and have survived there, while they have died back home. Words, like people, have a new life when they leave home. As *fall* survived in amber in America, so *skerrick*, meaning a scrap or morsel, *larrikin*, a hooligan, a *ringer*, the fastest shearer in the shed (from Northern English dialect meaning anything superlatively good), and *shanghai* meaning a catapult, survive in Australian dialect, though they have passed out of currency in the parts of Britain where they originated.

Another rich source of Strine slang is class and professional rather than regional dialect. Many of the early settlers were from the poor and criminal classes, whose principal crime consisted in being poor. Australian accent and slang most closely resemble Cockney, with the Cockney diphthong and the tendency to run syllables together, so that 'Australian' comes out as Strine, and 'Emma chisit?' is Strine for 'How much is it?' 'Heather hip ride' is what Strine pronunciation of 'head of the hit parade' sounds like to an outsider. Here are some examples of English working-class and thieves' argot that have crossed the world to Australia and flourished there, while they have died away Back Home. Nineteenth-century Cockney tailors and costermongers in the East End used to chiike or chy-ack each other around Petticoat Lane and points east. Australians of all classes still chiack or tease each other. 'Bloody' is the universal Australian as well as Cockney adjective. To 'plant' or hide stolen goods, a 'school' for a collection of gamblers, and a 'skinner' for a betting coup which skins the bookies or some other mugs, are all Victorian thieves' slang from the Muvver Tongue of Cockney, which have flourished Down Under.

In all dialects of English, some words and phrases are minted for the new world; others are words imported from overseas which have either survived while they have become obsolete elsewhere, or diverged semantically from their original meanings in their new language. A third category of slang is widespread around English dialects, so that it is impossible to give credit for its creation to any one dialect. 'That'll be the day', as an ironical rejoinder meaning, 'Wanna bet? That'll never happen', is widespread, drawled out of the side of the mouth, in Hollywood films. Some credit its introduction to New Zealand servicemen, however. There is no certitude in such matters. 'Bum to mum', as an injunction to abstain from sexual intercourse, is said to have been invented for the monastic practices of Australian Rules football. The coach tells his team on Fridays, 'Well, it's bum to mum tonight, boys', because they might wear themselves out in sexual activity. Nobody knows, but it sounds Australian.

This brings us finally to a peculiarity of Australian dialect, its dislike of class distinction, its macho and jock qualities, its wish to sound like one of the boys, and its foul-mouthedness. A high percentage of all slang is rude. Strine slang is ruder and better than most. A 'knock' meaning either an act of copulation or a promiscuous woman (Strine is notably male chauvinist) is Australian. To 'knock' in its sense of meaning of 'disparage' may be originally Australian or originally American. 'Knockers' meaning the female breasts are British, I regret to say.

Strine, like other dialects of English, has in the past twenty years become notably less bashful about its sexual slang. Today it is more sensitive about terms of racial insult like 'abo' and 'boong', and terms of social disparagement such as 'poofter'. 'Pom' as the universal description of a Brit is still considered conventional rather than racially offensive, thank God. Nobody knows exactly its derivation. Maybe it is children's rhyming slang: 'Immigrant, Jimmygrant, Pommygrant.' Maybe it is derived from the bright red pomegranate colour that newly arrived Brits turned under the Australian sun. The expression in full should be 'Whingeing Pommy bastard'.

Strine, like the other great dialects of English, has developed its idiosyncrasies of grammar, pronunciation, semantics, and syntax. Its slang is its peculiar glory.

In India there are fifteen official languages and a thousand or so others. English is the only common linguistic ground from Bombay to Calcutta, and from Delhi to Madras. Only about 2 or 3 per cent of the population speak it; but this educated élite provides the men and women who run the country.

Like Yinglish, Indian English or BombaySpeak has its idiosyncratic syntax: note the Indian habit of tagging the question, 'isn't it?', on to the end of sentences, regardless of the number and gender of the subject. The Singapore Chinese are also inclined to tag 'is it?' on to the end of the sentence, even though it has no agreement with what has gone before. 'The women went shopping, isn't it?' Like Strine, BombaySpeak has its own characteristic slang and dialect to describe its natural phenomena. Among the many words that have come into the central core of English from India are 'curry', natch, from the Tamil word for a relish with rice, *kari*; 'jungle' from the Hindi *jangal*; and 'khaki' from the Urdu word *khaki*, meaning dusty. Like all the dialects of English, Indian has its characteristic pronunciations and body-language, including the charming and useful waggle of the head from side to side to indicate diffidence.

English is the putty language. Like its other users, Indians squeeze it and mould it to suit their peculiar needs, and add some native ingredients. As the conspicuous peculiarity of Indian English, consider its formality and old-fashioned correctitude. Most Indians learn English not by the spoken word in their homes, but at school from books. As a consequence, Indian English tends to be characteristically formal, even pedantic. Expressions and words in common use tend to have a period flavour for speakers of other dialects of English.

The bereaved are always condoled, and the Prime Minister is always felicitated on her birthday. Boxing fans are described as followers of the roped square. Criminals, unless specifically identified, are dacoits, and bandits are described as miscreants. Louts are called antisocial elements. They are never caught by the police, always nabbed; just as political parties always bag seats at elections. For a British or American English-speaker Indian English has the effect of a time-machine, taking him back to the idiom and vocabulary of his childhood. This is because it is learnt from text-books, which are, by definition, going out of date as soon as they are published.

Criminals do not flee. They abscond. Reports of bus crashes in the Indian press frequently conclude: 'The driver is absconding.' This, incidentally, is often prudent of him. A driver of a bus that crashes in rural India runs the risk of being beaten by survivors to within an inch of his death.

Miscreants may abscond on fleetfoots: what Brits call plimsolls, and Americans call sneakers. If caught they eventually become undertrials, viz. people awaiting trial: in India that can be a very long wait. Dacoits are often killed in gun battles, which are always described as encounters. Eve-teasers, or young men who annoy girls, are sometimes found on a lorry, the colloquial name for a bus; and the girls cannot retaliate because their hands are full of copies: exercise books. COPS NAB EVE-TEASERS shout the headlines (to the relief of the girls: there being too much bottom-pinching and leering these days); but it transpires that some Eve-teasers are absconding also, perhaps thanks to fleetfoots.

In finding your way around Indian cities and buildings, it is important to know frontside from backside, partly because the taxi drivers so often seem to be strangers to the areas they work in, and one directs them by saying: 'Turn rightside; now leftside; here's backside.'

Office English has its own codes: 'Is Mr Banerji on his seat?' 'No, he is out of station. He is on tour. He has left for some place. Please leave your good name. Come back after some time.'

In Indian English 'some time' is a phrase that makes *mañana* sound urgent.

Mr Banerji may be a youngman (the two words are always welded together) engaged in rural uplift (helping the poor), or what in India are always called 'the weaker sections'. He calls his rupees 'bucks' or 'chips'; and chooses his clothes from rolls of suitings and shirtings. As winter draws on he gets into warmer 'wearunders'. If a politician, he does much felicitating to keep in with his superiors, and tries to please the common man (the general public) as featured in newspaper headlines such as 'Bad News For Common Man'.

The Government in Delhi is often called the Centre, and the authority in the ruling Congress Party, in essence Mrs Gandhi, is called the High Command. Politicians sometimes talk darkly of 'the foreign hand', by which they usually mean Pakistan or the United States. Lovers meanwhile are enjoined to tell their sweethearts: 'I am longing to have a rap in your sweet bosom.'

You could write a whole book about the Indianization of English, the particular and delightful dialects of English spoken in India. Professors have. They note the grammatical and syntactical idiosyncrasies of Indian English, such as leaving out the reflexive pronoun in reflexive verbs (*enjoy*, *exert*), or the peculiar syntax of verbs by which 'I am doing it since six months' is used for 'I have been doing it . . .'

In lexis they note that Indian words have been insinuating themselves into English ever since the reign of Elizabeth I, when such terms as *calico*, *chintz*, and *gingham* had already found their way into London docks and English shops, and were lying in wait to enter English literature.

In style and tone they catalogue such Indian idiosyncrasies as:

1. Latinity, by which an Indian might prefer *demise* to *death*, or *pain in one's bosom* to *pain in one's chest*.
2. A propensity to polite forms. The main reason for this is that originally the registers of English introduced into India were administration and the law, both polite and formal registers.
3. A tendency to phrase-mongering, such as *Himalayan blunder*; *nation-building*; *change of heart*; and *dumb millions*.
4. Initialism, the passion for official initials that exceeds even the official registers of American English. 'HE'S PA has written DO to the ASP about the question of TAS. The DC himself will visit the SDOPWD today at 10 AMST.' That means, expanded for slow British-English speakers: 'His Excellency's Personal Assistant has written a demi-official letter to the Assistant Superintendent of Police about the question of Travelling Allowances. The Deputy Commissioner himself will visit the Sub-Divisional Officer of the Public Works Department today at 10 am Standard Time.'
5. Moralistic tone: Indians cannot keep God out of it.
6. Clichés: Indian English has a tendency to elaborate clichés, such as 'better imagined than described' (easily imagined); 'do the needful'; 'each and every' (pleonastic for 'each'); 'leave severely alone' (for 'leave alone').
7. Deletion of pronouns, and other contractions, by which, for example, 'an address of welcome' in British English becomes 'welcome address' in Indian English; 'a bunch of keys' becomes 'key bunch'; and 'love of God' becomes 'God-love'. Some pundits think that this tendency follows Sanskrit compounds.
8. Yes-no confusion: 'You have no objection?' 'Yes, I have no objection.'
9. Reduplication and repetition, as in, 'Who and who came to the party?' This feature is common to all South Asian languages, and has been adopted into Indian English.

10.  Bookishness: Most Indians are taught their English formally
from books, using authors such as Shakespeare and Milton.
It is not surprising that their dialect is somewhat bookish,
and often more correct and beautiful than British English.
Indian English does not sound conversational, because
English has seldom been taught as a spoken language in
India.

Take the dialect of Newfoundland English as an example of the
way that language evolves to fit historical and geographical circumstances. Newfoundland has been a somewhat isolated and
independent English-speaking enclave for nearly four centuries,
and its inhabitants have been adapting the language to suit their
purposes for far longer than other dialects and jargons of English.
    The earliest fishermen to settle on the east coast of Newfound-
land came mainly from the ports and villages of the English West
Country, from Bristol round to Hampshire. The second important
linguistic strain was brought in during the seventeenth century by
the helpers or servants annually carried from south-eastern Ireland,
mainly through the port of Waterford. The modern dialect of
Newfoundland English retains traces of both these sources in its
vocabulary and its pronunciation.
    Because of the geography and industry of Newfoundland, some
words such as cod and haul have developed a distinctly higher or
more general degree of use than in other dialects of English. Other
words have been given a new form or meaning in Newfoundland:
for example, cat means, among many other things, a newborn seal
pup, a pine marten, and a game like hurley played on ice. Dog
means, among many other things, a male seal, and also, confusingly, the gunner's assistant who carries his ammunition on a seal
hunt.
    Other words that have become obsolete in native British English
have survived, preserved as it were on ice, in Newfoundland. For
example, 'to fadge' meaning to manage on one's own; 'dwy'
meaning a short, sharp shower of rain, hail, or snow; and 'still'
meaning a stretch of smooth water in a river.
    Other words acquired important local nuances because they
stand at the centre of semantic fields of great regional importance.
As you would expect, they tend to have a lot to do with the sea and
that old cod-fish: barren, bay, coast, harbour, ice, and so on. Other
terms such as bank, ledge, and shoal reflect a complex system of
classification of water bodies according to the types of ocean floor

significant for a coastal fishing people. 'Bloody country', as Winston Churchill said to his doctor, Lord Moran, while they were flying over a desolate expanse of rocks and great pools that is Newfoundland.

The way that English has developed in Newfoundland argues against the view that the dialects and other proliferating sublanguages of English are flying away from the centre so fast that they will soon be incomprehensible to each other. Newfoundland English has gone its own rugged and centrifugal way for four centuries. But the rest of us can still understand what the old codwallopers are saying.

It is the English dialects of countries where English is a second or tenth language that tend to be incomprehensible to English-speakers from the main stream. Yet English still permeates into such countries with strong native languages of their own, to the impotent rage of purists, and the amusement of innocent bystanders who understand that language always has worked by permeation and osmosis. Japanese is a good example of a strong independent language that is nevertheless being affected by the worldwide spread of English. Japanese words from samurai to sukiyaki come into the central core of English, maybe being subtly changed in the process by alien film directors or alien cooks. English words infiltrate Japanese, producing the exotic dialect of Japanese English or Janglish.

You often find the first signs of this new dialect in restaurant menus, where tourists who speak no Japanese are expected to eat. Janglish has produced such cheerful old chestnuts on menus as 'sand witches' and 'Miss Gorilla' (mixed grill). In 1983 the Asahi Evening News Publishing Company produced *Wasei Eigo o Tadasu*, which listed some of the idiosyncrasies of the Japanese dialect of English. They included 'orchestra box' for orchestra pit; 'cuffs button'; 'art flower' for artificial flower; 'one man car' for a bus without a conductor.

In Janglish you can have a chat with a 'Carrier Woman' (Japan's version of the shopping-bag lady) wearing 'Arm Free Grand Slam Munsingwear', while sipping a Georgia American Type Coffee named 'Come With The Wind', or 'have a sun-fill time' (Hi-C orange drink), before going on to the Matsuda Advice Ski School for a lesson in schussing, or rushing back to the *danchi* to try a 'Home Paamu-Oh, Wonderful Feeling!' or Shiseido French shampoo that creates *des cheveux merveilleusement bouclés*, while blowing a few balloons of Bubup Bubblegum. You can sample

Glico Chocolate Aphro's 'Extra-fine half bitter chocolate for true lovers' or 'Petite Vague du Marib Lotte Micre Grind Method Romantic Chocolate with your Beautiful Time. Lotte is your favourite brand.' A poetic Janglish lexicographer reports that his favourite specimen was embroidered in gold on the back of a scarlet satin windcheater worn by a post-Elvis Japanese youth: 'Here comes Colorific Show with Groovy Jump into the dreamy paradise on taking it make you groovy over satisfaction! Yes!'

Japan has been opened to the linguistic effects of mass tourism and the rest of the outside world only in the past thirty years. As time goes on, the peculiarities and impenetrabilities of Janglish will be reduced. But the facts of geography and culture will ensure that the dialect of English spoken in Japan will always be different from all the other dialects.

On the other side of the world a language almost as hermetic as Japanese is worried about the infiltration of English. In 1983 the jubilee research fund of the National Bank of Sweden gave Professor Magnus Ljung of Stockholm University a grant to investigate Swinglish, the corruption of the Swedish language (as in *det Svenska språket*) by the universal bindweed of English.

Professor Ljung himself is of an age that he would not be caught dead in *tajt jeans*. Nor would he refer to them in such Swinglish terms. He would call them *trånga*, the idiomatic or old-fashioned Swedish epithet, which literally means 'crowded'. But crowded jeans are out (*ute*) in the trendy talk of Swinglish, in the same way that the teenagers who wear them tend to *fajt* rather than *slåss*, the correct Swedish word for 'fight'.

Swinglish has produced such dialect titles as a disco in Söder, the southern suburb of Stockholm, which calls itself 'The Place No 1 in South'. At its best it has produced the phrase *Ha en trevlig dag* (Have a good day), which previously did not exist in Swedish, presumably because most Swedes did not expect or know how to have one.

Swinglish has given birth to such hybrid sentences as *Var är mina boots?* (Where are my boots?), when the original Swedish word for boots is *stövlar*. *Våt färg* (wet paint) is a construction lifted directly from English, replacing the Swedish idiom *ny målat* (newly painted).

Professor Ljung has been interrogating two thousand Swedes about their linguistic attitudes. Sixty per cent claimed that their Swedish was being corrupted to Swinglish by watching English programmes on television; twenty-six per cent blamed English books, newspapers, and magazines; the remaining fourteen per cent recognized that their use of Swedish was changing, but could attribute the change to nothing in particular. More than half confesssed to using the English plural-ending in 's' instead of the Swedish *or*, *ar*, *er*, or sometimes nothing at all.

Professor Ljung blamed the young and poorly educated mainly for Swinglish. But he admitted that many educated Swedes deplored the corruption of their *språk*, but none the less used fashionable English phrases and words. The main centre for resistance to Swinglish is the remote north of Sweden. But down in Stockholm a trendy man these days signs off with a *baj baj*, puts on his *tajt jeans*, and heads for the Place No 1 in South, where, in immaculate Swinglish, he chats up the local *krumpet*.

But the best example of a dialect of English in a foreign tongue comes from our old friends and enemies across the Channel, the French. It is generally agreed that they manage their language better in France. They did, after all, set up their Académie Française in 1635 to do just that. Statute XXIV: 'The principle function of the Academy shall be to labour with all care and diligence to give certain rules to our language, and to render it pure, eloquent, and capable of treating the arts and sciences.'

Of course, not everyone shares the high opinion of the French language held by the French. Mozart, writing to his father: 'If only this damned French language were not so badly fitted to music.' Horace Walpole: 'The most meagre and inharmonious of all languages.' However, ignoring such trouble-makers, sensible men of Francophile goodwill are generally agreed that the Frogs have managed to keep their language more pure and eloquent than lesser tongues.

Whoa, there. Hold on. In spite of the worthy labours of the Academy, about a twentieth of French is now made up of *anglicismes*, as far as one can calculate these imponderable matters. *Le Monde* contains an English word in every 166. The language of Racine and Voltaire is polluted with nasty *Pouding* words like pub, and nasty *Yankee* words like Women's Lib.

This is clearly deplorable. But it is only a recent phenomenon that vile words such as 'merchandizing' and 'juke-box' have started to come into French. Or is it? *Ouest* for west, which wears its Anglo-Saxon origins like a bowler hat, is recorded in French from the twelfth century. It is one of the earliest *anglicisme* loan-words in the French dialect of English. *Rosbif* has been around for three and a half centuries. Voltaire recorded as an agreeable example of

Franglais that maîtres d'hôtel in his time were starting to talk about *un roast-beef de mouton*. *Comité* for committee was given the thumbs-up by the Academy in 1762.

Some anglicisms hide their Englishness under an old-fashioned French beret. *Insanité*, *finaliser*, and *inoffensif* look authentic French. But they are loan words, created from English words with Greek or Romance roots. Another large and enjoyable group has been created in the French dialect of English from English elements to make words that have no meaning in English. *Auto-stop* is not a policeman stopping you to make sure that you are wearing a seat-belt, but the practice of hitch-hiking. *Un record-man* is not a disc-jockey, but an athlete who holds a record.

The English dialect of French has an equivalent group of Frenchi-fied words that are not commonly used in French. The rudest example is *cul-de-sac* which was bowdlerized into *impasse* in France to avoid mentioning *cul*. There are some Gallicisms in English French for which there is no exact English equivalent: for example, mews, chic, naïf. There are others that have been adopted as the standard English name of the thing in question: debris, coupon, ballet. There are others that express an idea that could not be expressed in Anglo-Saxon words without intolerable circumlocu-tion: *bête noire* and *enfant terrible*. To use French words in English in other instances, where there are exact English equivalents, seems pretentious, ostentatious, and rude. But we do it; and that is how dialects grow.

The common market in languages with loan-words and dialects is as natural and healthy as travel to other countries. It has always happened since the Tower of Babel; and it always will. In his book *The French* (1983) Theodore Zeldin remarks sharply: 'The real cause of dissatisfaction with foreigners in France comes not from the French feeling humiliated by borrowing from America or from other countries, but from an annoyance that foreigners are not borrowing much in return.'

An interesting group of English dialects is Pidgin English, which was once spoken in different forms around the world from West Africa to the South Pacific, and from the Straits of Malacca to the West Indies, wherever the sun never set on the British Empire. A pidgin is an artificial language composed of elements of two or more other languages, and used, usually for trading contacts, between speakers of other languages. It is said to be derived from 'Business-English', the name given by the Chinese to the Anglo-Chinese lingua franca. They pronounced business as 'pidgin'. And we have confused the meaningless pidgin with the significant pigeon; a confusion that accounts for the expression, 'that's my pigeon'.

Pidgin English is still current today in West Africa, in the wilder parts of Australia, and in Papua New Guinea. It has contributed many words to the central stock of English, in addition to 'pidgin' itself: *piccaninny* is a West Indian formation on the Spanish or Portuguese word *pequeño* meaning 'little'; perhaps directly on the Portuguese diminutive *pequenino*. '*Savvy*', originally a verb ('You savvy what I'm saying?'), now usually a noun meaning 'know-how' ('She's got plenty of savvy'), is another Portuguese word translated into English by the dialect of a pidgin.

When a pidgin becomes the mother tongue of a community it is called a creole. This has happened in the West Indies and the United States South, and in Hawaii, where the creolized English dialect is known as 'da Hawaii kine talk'. It has happened in Sierra Leone, where Krio is the mother tongue, an enchanting dialect of English, with infusions from Spanish, Arabic, Yoruba, and other local languages. Krio may seem alien to speakers of other dialects of English, but the roots are there underneath. *Baksay* meaning the bottom is taken from 'back-side'. *Bak sit drayva* is merely the genteel local pronunciation of 'back-seat driver'. *Bad briz* is a bad breeze or wind in the stomach. To *pul bad breeze* is to fart. *Krach am fo mi* ('Scratch her for me'), often said or sung to a bridegroom who is taking the bride away on honeymoon, is an injunction to have sexual intercourse with her regularly and frequently. It might take one longer to work out why a *bakanti* means an over-head scissors-kick in the Krio dialect of English. It has nothing to do with wild, drunk women. The scissors-kick was first demonstrated in Freetown by sailors from HMS *Bacchante*.

The English dialect of South Africa is the lingua franca of a multilingual society, for only some of whom English is the mother tongue. Many black South Africans, for example, speak two languages of European origin and two or more Bantu languages. Like the other dialects of English it has its peculiar pronunciation, vocabulary, idioms, and grammar. Some South African English has been part of the central core of the language since the Boer War: words such as 'Boer' itself, 'kaffir', 'kraal', and 'veld'. Other words and usages have become internationally known through reports of the different and yet deeper conflict that now smoulders in South Africa: 'homeland'; 'passbook', which Africans themselves call the 'domboek' or 'stupid book'; 'normalize', a weasel word used only of sport, meaning to make non-racial; 'international', when applied to hotels and restaurants, means that they are permitted to serve black patrons and guests; 'repatriate' means to send urban blacks to the 'homelands' of their particular nations, which can result in a town-born black being repatriated into a country he has never seen; 'white-by-night' describes an urban area that does not permit living-in domestic servants; the 'yellow route' is what South Africans call the exodus of Rhodesian whites from the country that has become Zimbabwe.

Other aspects of South African English have become known to the outside world through the work of such talented writers as Roy Campbell, Stuart Cloete, Athol Fugard, Dan Jacobson, Alan Paton, Olive Schreiner, and Laurens Van Der Post.

Because of the political troubles in South Africa, political language is the most conspicuous part of the dialect that impinges on the consciousness of the outside world: words and ideas like grand and petty apartheid, Bantustans, separate development, resettlement, and nie-blankes. But like all dialects of English it has evolved a language to deal with its geography and history. 'Jointed cactus' was identified as a noxious weed in 1903, and is now one of the most serious agricultural problems in the country; 'Veld fever', a nostalgia for the veld and open spaces, is a common theme in much South African poetry, both Afrikaans and English. 'Ostrich' has come into the language from South Africa, where the silly bird, so useful in metaphors and cartoons, is classed as farming stock, the meat being used as pets' food, and the eggs for cakes and omelettes. From biltong to sjambok South African geography and history have written themselves into English.

Like all dialects of English, South African has developed its own grammar and colloquialisms. It is idiomatic in South African English to say that one is 'bad friends' with somebody else, meaning that one is in a state of usually temporary enmity with him or her, as in, 'I'm bad friends with her this term.' In South African the word 'sleep' means 'to lie down', not necessarily 'to be asleep', as in, 'I was sleeping on the ground in the middle of the scrum and someone stood on me.'

Like other dialects, South African English has a lively slang, which deserves wider currency. A 'blood budgie' is a mosquito; a 'flat dog' is a crocodile; a 'fence creeper' is an animal (often a bull) that knocks down and walks over fences; 'fuse' is slang for cigarette; to 'come (or slip) on your guava' means to make a fool of yourself; a 'staffrider' is someone who travels illegally on the outside of suburban trains without paying the fare; a 'long drop' is a pit privy; and a 'ruggerbugger' is a recognizable, aggressively masculine type, fanatical about sport, and usually partial to all-male gatherings.

The Boer War brought the African veld into the parlours of Brixton and the pubs of Highgate. The history and politics of our century diffuse the language of South Africa into the school-rooms of Delhi and the apartments of Los Angeles.

In the apartment blocks in Watts County, Los Angeles, they speak Black English, a dialect said to be peculiar to American blacks, and peculiarly impenetrable by outsiders. Ain nothin in a long time lit up the English language profession like the current hassle over Black English. Like what we bees needin is cognizance that sho-nuff brothers and sisters rappin am not necessarily linguistically deficient, but don disprove that in living vibrant colour, in which 'bad' is a term of approbation, and there are other codes intended as shibboleths and mystification for foreigners.

The self-consciousness of Black Power is a newish factor affecting Black English. But there is no reason to suppose that it will not evolve in the same way as other dialects of English, developing its own grammar and vocabulary, which will enrich and be enriched by the other dialects. Apart from pidgins and creoles, there are no examples yet of an English dialect breaking away from the common core to become a separate language. And, in spite of the forebodings of linguistic doom-watchers, there is little prospect of it happening. The age of instant mass communication makes such a breakaway unlikely.

# 5/CLICHÉ

At this point in time every man Jack, every mother's son, every principle of decency and humanity, and the whole of Grub Street, grub and grubbage, are agreed again and again on unimpeachable authority that your common or garden cliché is a flat, stale, and unprofitable blemish of speech, to be avoided once and for all by all good men and true in the ongoing prose composition situation. There are at least a dozen clichés in that sentence. I set out with the intention of writing the whole of this chapter at one fell swoop in clichés. But the boredom of that first sentence sent me headlong into the arms of Morpheus (there's another one, dammit). And to continue in this vein (there's another) would be harsh and unnatural punishment (and another) for you, dear readers (another), who would fold your books, like the Arabs, and as silently steal away (a quotation cliché, and why bring the Arabs into this?). Not every man Jack, mother's son, etcetera ad nauseam (there's another) is agreed about what constitutes a cliché; so let us start there. Are you sitting comfortably? That's a British radio catch phrase in the process of becoming a cliché. Good; then I will begin.

A cliché is a stereotyped expression or a hackneyed phrase that has been used so many billions of times that it comes out of the mouth or the typewriter without causing a ripple in the mind of the speaker, or the typist, or the listener, or the reader. It is a trite tag more honoured in the breach than the observance: note, dear reader, that that Prince of Denmark cliché is used there correctly for once. An editor's job is to go through his author's copy checking all facts and spellings, cutting the first and last sentences, and removing all clichés and all attempts at jokes. If you do your duty to this chapter, Christopher dear, it is going to end up unconscionably short, and you will have to pad it out with large drawings and cross-headings in big type.

A cliché was originally a word of the technical jargon of the French printing trade in the nineteenth century. It was a stereotype block, the past participle used as a noun of the verb *clicher*, to stereotype. A cliché was a cast obtained by dropping a matrix face downwards upon a surface of molten metal on the point of cooling. Printers in early Victorian English type foundries called the process 'dabbing'. I have it on unimpeachable authority (cliché, cliché) that the word is onomatopoeic. That is, it imitates the plopping sound that the matrix made as it fell into its hot bath. My unimpeachable authority (vide supra), the sage etymological lexicographer Dr C.T. Onions, hazards the suggestion (there's another of the little blighters; they are everywhere) that the immediate source of the word is the German *klitsch*, meaning slap, crackle, or plop.

Ernie Bevin, the great Labour Foreign Secretary, when asked for his opinion of Anthony Eden's speeches, replied: 'Clitch, clitch, clitch'; so restoring the first fine careless rapture (wise thrush clitch) of the plopping sound of the original use of the word. Winston Churchill, that magpie plagiarist of other men's clichés, as all prolific politicians have to be, when asked the same question about the unfortunate Eden's speeches, replied: 'They consist entirely of clichés – clichés old and new – everything from "God is Love" to "Please adjust your dress before leaving".'

By the middle of the nineteenth century French literati, shortly followed, as usual, by British literati, had transferred the word from printing jargon for use as a metaphor for stereotyped language. *Discours cliché* was the original French cliché. Wordfowlers with a passion for classification can divide the cliché up into its various species.

You can start with idioms that have been so indiscriminately overused that their points have been blunted and they have become clichés. You can pick and choose far and wide by leaps and bounds and by hook or by crook to find such idiom clichés, which are often doublets. The English have a strong affinity for alliteration and rhyme, neither of which was much liked by the classical Greek and Roman poets. But the Anglo-Saxon bards depended upon alliteration as an ornament and a mnemonic. Rhyme from France gradually replaced alliteration as the tool of poets.

Alliterative clichés are such agreeable jingle-jangles as rack and ruin, wishy-washy, to chop and change, with might and main, bag and baggage, safe and sound, slow but sure. Rhyming clichés are high and dry, harum-scarum, hocus-pocus, fair and square, wear and tear, higgledy-piggledy.

Etymological digression: there is an ingenious Presbyterian derivation of hocus-pocus. It is said to come from *hoc est corpus*, 'this is the body', in the Roman mass when it was allowed to be said in Latin. In the same anti-Papist way, patter, meaning rapid, glib, and insincere spiel, is derived from rattling off the paternoster like a meaningless formula. Alas and dammit, the suggested etymology of hocus-pocus is phonus-bolonus. It is in fact derived from *hax pax max Deus adimax*, a meaningless magical formula coined in the sixteenth century by rapscallion and vagrant student activists. Such rhyming and alliterative doublets may be redundancies of language, but they are blood and bone of English. It would be a duller, more jejune language without them.

There are masses of doublet clichés that are grown out of neither alliteration nor rhyme, but out of our national tendency to jibber-jabber, never to use one word or phrase where we can think of two. Such plain doublets are blood and bone, dust and ashes, sackcloth and ashes, null and void, heart and soul, for good and all, six of one and half a dozen of the other, ways and means, tooth and nail, etc. ad lib. et naus.

We could then invent a category of battered similes and hack-neyed proverbs that have become clichés, falling off the lips with a dull clitch that makes no echoes. Such are as cool as a cucumber, as fit as a fiddle, as large as life, as rich as Croesus, as old as the hills, as thick as thieves, as steady as a rock. Many of these are venerable pensioners of the language, for whom one should have a sneaking respect, if only because of their longevity. The first instance of the coolness of cucumbers being used as a simile that I can find in Eng. Lit. comes in Beaumont and Fletcher's *Cupid's Revenge*, first played in 1615: charmingly, 'Young Maids were as cold as Cowcumbers.' That Rabelaisian religious controversialist Thomas Nashe wrote 'As right as a fiddle' in 1596. 'I see the puppets, the wheelbarrows everything as large as life!', 1799. The humorous suffix '. . . and twice as natural' was first added in 1836.

Croesus was a simile for riches as early as 1577; the hills were said to be old in 1500; thieves were said to be thick in 1833, but the writer added 'as the proverb goes', indicating that they had been thick before that comparatively late date; the undoubted steadiness, or originally firmness, of a rock was favourably commented upon in 1541: 'The word and promise of an occupier must be as firm and fast as the rock of stone.' Quite right too. These ancient similes and proverbs may not convey as much meaning as when they were first coined, but they are lovely old incantations.

Our Linnaeus of clichés might next notice a large category drawn from the jargons of trades and professions, sports and games, politics and the weather, and other national preoccupations. Sticking to one's last, keeping a straight bat and a stiff upper lip, setting one's hand to the plough, asking a leading question, and darkening somebody's door are examples of occupational clichés. Linnaeus can organize them in their various subspecies. Let us merely notice the proliferation and exuberance of nautical clichés, as is fitting for an island race. By and large seafaring clichés, often misunderstood and misapplied, stretch from Scilly to Ushant, and from knowing the ropes to sticking to one's guns, and from leaving the sinking ship to being between the Devil and the deep blue sea.

That seaman's Devil is the source of much agreeable confusion in clichés among landlubbers. The Devil was the name that caulkers gave to the seam in the upper deck planking next to a ship's waterways. They called it that because there was very little space to get at this seam with a caulking iron, making it a stinker of a job, like cutting one's right thumbnail or fitting studs in a dress shirt with oneself inside it, assuming that one can find the studs in the first place. There is your origin of the nautical cliché 'Between the Devil and the deep blue sea', since there is only the thickness of the ship's hull planking between this seam and the sea.

Ancient mariners claim that the cliché 'the Devil to pay' is theirs also, from that same old garboard seam known as the Devil. It was difficult for the caulkers to pay in the oakum and hammer it home. Devil to pay and no pitch hot is the sailor's term for a sticky situation with no obvious solution. That sounds all shipshape and Bristol fashion, and I do not want to argue with the nautical cliché profession. But the earliest citation of this cliché that I can find is in Grose's *Dictionary of the Vulgar Tongue*, published in 1788, where he has an entry under 'To pay' for smearing the bottom of a ship or boat over with pitch: 'The devil to pay, and no pitch hot or ready.' I have to point out that there are examples of the cliché about paying the Devil nearly four centuries earlier than this, which evidently refer not to caulking, but to alleged bargains with Satan, and the inevitable payment to be made to him in the end. When Swift wrote in his *Journal to Stella*, 'The Earl of Strafford is to go soon to Holland, and let them know what we have been doing; and then there will be the devil and all to pay', it does not seem to me that the garboard seam was in his mind, but 'I'll burn my books! – Oh, Mephistophilis.'

Our next broad category of clichés might be non-idiomatic

phrases, which shone brightly when they were first coined, but have become tarnished by constant use. These are expressions so hackneyed that they are knock-kneed, spavined, and fit for the knacker's. When the first sub-editor writing a headline or football manager being asked how he felt about the defeat of his team said that he was as sick as a parrot, a reference to the sensational cases of Psittacosis from West Africa in the early 1970s, it was a sharp, amusing phrase, depending upon how ghoulish your sense of humour was. It has been so overused since then that it has become a cottonwool phrase, a cliché that has lost its shine. To explore every avenue and to leave no stone unturned are two political clichés of this class. No politician with any sensitivity for language could use either of those phrases seriously. Yet you hear them at it still, all the time. There are a lot of politicians in business who use language as a blunt instrument to bludgeon their audience rather than a tool to convey exactly what they mean. Exactitude is a dangerous commodity in the muddy business of politics.

In this orgy of classification that we have fallen into, we could subdivide these non-idiomatic clichés into general all-purpose ones; political, economic, and sociological ones of the managing classes; journalistic ones of the hacking class; and literary clichés of the literati.

As a matter of fact at this moment in time it is my considered opinion that all the world and his wife are in blissful ignorance of the cohorts of clichés that can be paraded alive and kicking and the picture of health in a single sentence. There is nothing new in the vexation of non-idiomatic clichés. There is evidence in *Twelfth Night* that Shakespeare recognized that his contemporary equivalents of our low-profile scenarios and ongoing situations were tiresome:

'Who you are and what you would are out of my welkin;
  I might say *element*, but the word is overworn.'

Halcyon days, castles in Spain, the staff of life, Good Queen Bess, and Hobson's choice are all in their various ways specimens of non-idiomatic general clichés.

In politics, economy, and sociology the basic clichés and questions do not change. It is the answers that change from time to time. It is going too far to say that economists live by taking in each other's washing; but it is certainly true that they spend a vast amount of time mangling each other's clichés. In this politicoeconomico-sociological sub-division we can include such old favourites as exploring every stone and leaving no avenue unturned, bloated plutocrats, blue blood, the economic factor, and a far-reaching policy; and such new vogues as U-turns, bull points, coming to the crunch, the soft centre, the hard left, and Social Democracy.

Journalism could be defined as the art of recycling old clichés. Oliver Wendell Holmes said, unkindly, that profanity was vitriol, slang was vinegar, but reporter's cliché-padded English was rancid butter. We hacks are that way because we have superficial knowledge of everything, but an ability to express it well in familiar phrases. Hear what comfortable words are popular with journalists: in this day and age, climate of opinion, in the ultimate analysis, the scenario, to orchestrate and sometimes to harmonize, within the framework, to probe, bombshell, bonanza, brainchild, SHOCK HORROR (in headlines), the Cinderella of something or other, minuscule (meaning very small instead of its technical meaning of an early script), the Fourth Estate, the Dark Continent, a modern classic, of that ilk (when used incorrectly to mean 'of that kind'; it always is used incorrectly); dear old Scylla and Charybdis, grass roots, blueprint, backlash, confrontation, dichotomy, and O my paws and whiskers so many more that to carry on would be tedious. Let us draw a veil (cliché) over journalistic clichés, pausing only to remark that they overlap the other categories, and that the hardest worked cliché is better than the phrase that fails. It has been well said: 'Journalese results from the efforts of the non-literary mind to discover alternatives for the obvious where none are necessary, and it is best avoided by the frank acceptance of even a hard-worn phrase when it expresses what you want to say.'

The next category of cliché that one could define would be the literary cliché. The boundary between literature and journalism is a broad, blurred Everyman's Land, from which journalism gains as much as literature loses. But the literary cliché can be distinguished from the journalistic as being found in an ivory tower rather than a suburban semi; as wearing blue stockings rather than braces and spotted bow tie (did you know that the eponym who gave the name to the literary-journalistic cliché 'bluestocking' was not a woman but a man, viz. Benjamin Stillingfleet, who indulged in blue worsted instead of black silk stockings and intellectual conversation instead of cards at Elizabeth Montagu's salon?); as appearing in the Books Pages and the small reviews rather than the news pages and the popular press.

The sort of cliché I have in mind is Rabelaisian humour; seminal apotheosis; Pandora's box; a sop to Cerberus; Catch 22; the *literati* and *illuminati*; the Fleshly School of Poetry; *panem et circenses*. I am uneasily aware that I use some of those, and that when I do I am caught *in flagrante delicto* (Latin and legal cliché translated by A.P. Herbert as 'in flagrant delight') showing off what I suppose to be my superior education and culture. These literary clichés are the jargon of Lit. Crit. English Literature is a lake in which elephants can swim and lambs can paddle (literary and theological cliché). It is almost impossible to write about it without allusion, reference to other writers, quotation, and, I dare say, élitism and pretentiousness. But we should try, we should try.

Cliché is the shorthand of the *cognoscenti*. It is not surprising that the jargon of the wordsmiths of Eng. Lit. should suffer from logorrhoea more than that of other specialized trades. The material we work with is words, allusion, reference, books that we have read, or can pretend that we have read. The best criticism by someone like Lionel Trilling is easily accessible for anybody who can read what is snobbishly described as the 'higher' journalism. But it is no good pretending that the Lit Crit of somebody like Leavis, or, on the other hand, Roland Barthes, is immediately perspicuous (there's a Lit Crit cliché for you). It would be just as silly to pretend that they are writing nonsense. Perspicuity is a virtue, and opacity a vice in Lit Crit as in all branches of English. It would be Neanderthal to insist that a big review of an important specialist book in let us say *The Times Literary Supplement* or the *Book Review* of *The New York Times* should be written in the vernacular of *The Sun* or *The New York Post*. It would be as silly as insisting that everything in *The Melody Maker* should make sense to an academic who does not know Genesis from Adam and the Ants.

Had we but world enough, and time (quotation cliché), and patience; and had the publishers but money enough; we could run through all the other categories and sub-divisions of non-idiomatic clichés in the various jargons and specialities of human knowledge. We should discuss legal clichés from ten years before the Flood until the conversion of the Jews, devoting pain to such phrases as 'in my humble opinion', 'as Your Lordship pleases', 'the burden of proof', 'it appears to be without foundation', 'we must assume as proved'. I am particularly sorry to give up the section on sporting clichés, from 'sick as a parrot' and 'over the moon' to 'Eclipse first and the rest nowhere' (Obs.). But you get the idea. Let us move on to our third main group of clichés.

These are quotations and phrases from foreign languages. This group has been diminished since classical quotation has ceased to be the parole of literary men all over the world. It is no longer obligatory to put at least one Latin quotation in every *Times* leader. The new technology of photocomposition will get it wrong anyway; and I broke two of our expensive VDUS (visual display units to you) by trying to keyboard some moving lines of Theocritus in Greek into them. If you try quoting Latin in a Parliamentary speech you will be shouted down as an élitist.

Nevertheless, English, that most hospitable of hosts to foreigners (at any rate to foreign languages) still houses a vast stock of foreign clichés. We can divide them into tags apprehended without reference to the author, and direct quotations, used as the parole of a literary man, or, to look at it another way, to show off that we are cultivated fellows whose bedside reading is Horace or Racine. Although it is no longer a compulsory subject for our brightest and best children, Latin still provides by far the largest stock of tags and quotations in English.

OK, let us be systematic about this. That sort of systematic efficiency is not necessarily an odious opiate, though it usually is, especially in tables and 'graphics' in newspapers intended to make life easy for those who find more than three sentences of continuous prose too much for them. Here follow examples of tags in foreign languages that have become clichés in English.

Latin: Ab origine; arbiter elegantium; de mortuis (followed by pregnant pause); genius loci; de gustibus non disputandum; terra firma; omnia vincit amor; sic (meaning 'I know that this is wrong, but see what a superior person I am to have spotted the error'); tempus fugit; status quo; sub rosa; and hundreds more, if we can allow ourselves a piece of Latin that has not yet been clichéfied, dein mille altera, dein secunda centum.

Frog: Affaire de coeur; après nous le déluge; bon mot; bête noire; carte blanche; c'est la guerre; c'est magnifique mais ce n'est pas la guerre; cri de coeur; embarras de richesses; éminence grise; je ne sais quoi; homme moyen sensuel; mot juste; pour encourager les autres; tout comprendre c'est tout pardonner; cherchez la femme; and, O brouhaha and tohu-bohu, thousands more if this goddamned systematic catalogue hadn't sent me to sleep.

German: Angst; Drang nach Osten; ersatz; Gesundheit; kaputt; Kitsch; Bildungsroman (also a literary cliché); Realpolitik, Weltgeist; etc.

Italian: basso profundo (and dozens of other musical terms; Wop is the parole of the language of music); la dolce vita; inamorata, or, oddly, less commonly, inamorato; lingua franca; magnifico; prima donna; uomo universale; etc.

Spanish: Aficionado; caudillo; hasta la vista; junta; machismo; peccadillo; supremo; vamoose; vigilante; vaquero, in Westerns, where they ride thundering into the white silence of those empty midday streets; etc.

Portuguese: Auto da fé; Russian: babushka; Afrikaans: apartheid; Persian: baksheesh; Sanskrit: avatar; Turkish: effendi; and so on, and so on. I am not going to try Greek, in order to spare the compositors Sturm und Drang. This system is all very well, but let us abandon it before it drives us up the wall and round the twist. English is stuffed as full of foreign words and phrases that have become clichés as a London Underground train in January is stuffed with flu germs. Some of them are useful. Some of them express a meaning that is not so neatly available in native English. But I guess that, before using one of these foreign tags, one should ask oneself whether one is doing it because it expresses a meaning not otherwise so succinctly available, or in order to show off one's familiarity with foreign lingo. The former is the better reason.

It would be puritanical and pedantic to ban all these foreign tags from good English (whatever question that shifty 'good' begs) merely because they are foreign. Some of them say things that could not be otherwise expressed without intolerable circumlocution. Just try saying 'mutatis mutandis' in only two other words. What the phrase means literally is: 'having made those changes that had to be made.' I suppose that 'allowing for the appropriate and consequential changes' is as close as we are going to get in English. I think that the Latin is neater. The same merits of neatness and exactitude justify hundreds of other foreign tags that have been Anglicized, from 'faute de mieux' to the Tongan 'taboo' and the Arabic 'algebra', which is taken from 'ilm aljebr wa'lmuqabalah', the science of redintegration and equation. It is an accident of etymology that we say algebra instead of 'almucabala', which was popular as the name for the tiresome business in the thirteenth century.

Quotations from foreign languages become clichés when they come to the mind or the typewriter automatically, as an incantation, without a distant echo of when they were first said, by whom, or in what context. You know the sort of thing. 'Arcades ambo'; 'et in Arcadia', of which there were at least two quite separate translations even in antiquity; 'facilis descensus Averni' (a misquotation,

'Averno' is correct); 'nil desperandum'; 'Persicos odi, puer, apparatus'; 'pulvis et umbra'; 'quis custodiet ipsos custodes'; 'sic transit gloria mundi'; 'timeo Danaos et dona ferentes'; 'post equitem sedet atra Cura'; the gramophone needle seems to have stuck in a Latin groove. So what about 'Vous l'avez voulu, Georges Dandin, vous l'avez voulu'; 'plus ça change, plus ça reste la même chose'; 'nous avons changé tout cela'; 'lasciate ogni speranza voi ch'entrate'; 'El Caballero de la Triste Figura'; 'Es un entreverada loco, lleno de lucidos intervalos.' Let us omit Greek, Russian, and other languages in other than Roman scripts.

Whether a foreign quotation is a cliché depends upon the speaker, the audience, and the context. But most of those that I have just listed are so well known that there is no glory in demonstrating one's familiarity with them, and no pleasure in recognizing the dear old things. Quotation is a high pleasure and a password among reading people. But, as with material food, one's taste becomes more discriminating as one grows older. As a child one guzzles sweets and quotes all the famous old lines, which are famous because they are *good*. As one grows older one's taste turns to subtler flavours and less well-known quotations. As a general principle I hold these truths to be self-evident (watch it, a cliché, query, clitch) that it is bad manners and showing off to use a pretentious foreign phrase when there is a perfectly good English equivalent, and to make a foreign quotation that is so hackneyed that it is spavined and knock-kneed. As in all matters of taste, the judgment of what is hackneyed or pretentious will vary from person to person. Is 'bugbear' quite the same as 'bête noire'? If yes, is it preferable to it? I don't know. Is 'virtually' better than 'to all intents and purposes'. I think so. It is undeniably shorter.

The fourth main class of clichés consists of overused and hackneyed quotations from English Literature. I get pissed off (vulgarism, and just about a colloquial cliché in louche circles) with lights that are always dim religious, Government changes that are invariably sea-changes, things of beauty that are joys for ever. These venerable fossils of the language come, as you would expect, in quantities from the Bible, Shakespeare, and other masterworks of English writing.

The Authorized Version of the Bible is so fundamental to the English language that it is a mine of golden clichés from 'In the beginning' to 'And behold a pale horse'. They include such old favourites as gall and wormwood, in jeopardy of their lives, the flesh-pots of Egypt, balm in Gilead, fishers of men, the law of the

Medes and the Persians, the Mammon of unrighteousness, a fire-brand plucked out of the burning, a howling wilderness, to spoil the Egyptians, the voice of the turtle is heard in our land, their name is Legion (usually misapprehended), and 'Come out, come out, thou bloody man, thou son of Belial' (a cliché of Trinity College, Oxford, for shouting over the wall at Balliol next door). We may not even be sure of the exact meanings of some of these lovely, archaic incantations; but they rise irresistibly to the lips or the keys of the typewriter like conditioned reflexes when the right stimulus is given.

In the same way we could, if we had a mind to, compile a thumping big concordance of Shakespearean clichés that rise to the lips without causing a ripple in the little grey cells (Agatha Christie cliché). They would include those old slings and arrows of outrageous fortune, to be or not to be, when shall we three meet again, Double, Double, toil and trouble, tomorrow, and tomorrow, and tomorrow, Friends, Romans, countrymen, lend me your lugs, and dozens more. And we have not even started on Keats's thing of beauty, Milton's dim religious light, and Dickens's Barkis still willin'.

An engaging sub-section of quotation clichés are those that are regularly misquoted. I am escaped BY the skin of my teeth (really WITH). A POOR thing, sir, but mine own (ILL-FAVOURED). Cribbed, cabined and confined (CABIN'D, CRIBB'D, CONFIN'D). Water, water everywhere AND NOT A drop to drink (NOR ANY). A little KNOWLEDGE is a dangerous thing (LEARNING). Screw your courage to the sticking-POINT (PLACE). THE last infirmity of noble MINDS (THAT . . . MIND). Make assurance DOUBLY sure (DOUBLE). Tomorrow to fresh FIELDS and pastures new (WOODS). When GREEK MEETS GREEK, then COMES the tug of war (GREEKS JOINED GREEKS . . . WAS). The devil can QUOTE Scripture for his purpose (CITE). Chewing the CUD of sweet and bitter fancy (FOOD).

You will get no thanks for pointing out the correct versions of these cliché-quotes, if you are rude enough to take the trouble. We are a race of hardened and shameless misquoters (itself a faint misquotation).

No doubt we could elaborate the classes of clichés into further subdivisions ad infinitum, ad libitum, until the cows come home. But there is no need to. Every man Jack and woman Jill of us agrees that clichés are lice on the locks of language, and are to be avoided by careful writers and speakers at all times, are we not? Well, aren't we? Well, actually, since you ask, Dear Reader, no, not I. Life is so full of clichés, and the language is so full of clichés, that silence will reign supreme (clitch and exaggeration), if you deny us the use of cliché. So many millions of people have spoken and written so ceaselessly since the Tower of Babel that it is almost impossible to find ideas and phrases that have not been used many times before.

Poets and philosophers mint brand new language. The rest of us have to make do with the common currency that passes ceaselessly from hand to eye and mouth to ear. The most overworked cliché is better than an extravagant phrase that does not come off. Clichés become popular often because they are the best way of saying something. 'Journalese results from the efforts of the non-literary mind to discover alternatives for the obvious where none are necessary, and it is best avoided by the frank acceptance of even a hard-worn phrase when it expresses what you want to say.'

Hobson's choice, and castles in Spain, and riding one's hobby horse, and having a finger in every pie are all aged clichés. So is a white elephant. So is a sop for Cerberus. So is *Sunt lacrimae rerum*. So is *cherchez la femme*. But they all vividly express ideas that cannot be expressed otherwise without intolerable circumlocution and periphrasis, to indulge in a spot of the old c. and p. Just you try expressing the meaning of *sunt lacrimae rerum* in English without using at least twice as many words and an apostil explaining that Aeneas is looking at paintings in Dido's national gallery. The three words are loaded with references and connotations. You would be cutting off your nose to spite your face if you denied yourself in every circumstance the use of the brightest and most economical and most beautiful phrases invented by man, simply because they were clichés.

OK, OK: some battered ornaments are so battered that they are unusable. I cannot see myself having need of Jupiter Pluvius, or the Dark Continent, or Good Queen Bess, except in parody or sarcasm. I do not expect to explore every avenue or leave no stone unturned. But I am not going to renounce them absolutely, on principle. The day may come when I need them.

Quotation to flaunt (not flout, in Ted Heath's popular misapprehension) one's superior reading and look down one's nose at one's reader is affected and despicable. So is the use of a foreign language to display one's polyglotism, when there is a perfectly good English alternative. But quotation is a pleasure, the parole of the educated, the password of the amusing. One should verify one's references to make sure that one quotes accurately. One should lay off intolerably hackneyed quotations that have become trite. We all develop favourite quotations with which we irritate our friends and editors, who are often the same people. One of mine is: 'No arts; no letters; no society; and which is worst of all, continual fear and danger of violent death; and the life of man, solitary, poor, nasty, brutish, and short.' I resolve not to use it again in this book. But promises and pie-crust are made to be broken: there's another of the pests.

I should avoid suffering a sea-change even into something rich and strange, Philip, unless the sea comes into it somewhere. I should lay off being cribbed, cabined and confined. But, if you must, get it right as cabined, cribbed, confined, bound in. But you go ahead and write *bête noire*, if you cannot think of an exact equivalent in English. In short, dear reader (clitch), I am determined to have my cake and eat it (incorrect clitch, when you think about it, for to eat my cake and still have it), to have my finger in every pie, and to reserve my right to pull a cliché out of the vast cupboard of the English language, if it is the best way of saying what I want to say.

# 6/EUPHEMISM

'Any euphemism ceases to be euphemistic after a time and the true meaning begins to show through. It's a losing game, but we keep on trying.'

'Any fool can tell the truth, but it requires a man of some sense to know how to lie well.' Samuel 'Erewhon' Butler.

Euphemism is the British linguistic vice (Lancastrians are the exception); just as hyperbole is the American; coarse slang the Australian; blarney the Irish; pedantry the Indian; and a whining pronunciation the South African. The concept, however, is Greek. It comes from the Greek word and prefix meaning to speak well of, to use words of good omen. During sacred rites the Greeks were expected *euphemein*, to avoid unlucky and improper words; just as in our churches, except the extremely ostentatious, one is expected to avoid bad or loud language. Before the performance of a Greek tragedy, which was a religious as well as a dramatic festival, heralds called on the audience *euphemein*. There are classic examples in Greek of euphemism in the sense of not giving things a bad name in case they turned round and bit you. The Erinyes, those terrible avenging Furies with snakes for hair and stones for hearts, were commonly called the Eumenides, the kindly ones, in the vain hope of appeasing them. The Black Sea, notoriously inhospitable and dangerous, was known as the Euxine, the sea that was kind to sailors.

The word and the rhetorical figure of calling a spade an entrenching implement passed from Greek into other European languages. Note Horace in one of his patriotic triumphal Odes (Carminum Liber III, 14) calling on the boys and girls at the thanksgiving festival for Augustus' victory in Spain to practise euphemism:

*Vos, o pueri et puellae*
*iam virum expertae, male ominatis*
*parcite verbis.*

'And you, boys and girls who have no experience of men so far, keep quiet at the back there and avoid words of ill omen.'

Euphemism means the substitution of a mild or vague or periphrastic expression for a blunt or harsh or indecent one. We do it for various reasons ranging from religious reverence and common decency to prudery and genteelism. We all do it, not just the hypocritical Brits. In the Fiji Islands when the natives practised cannibalism, they used to call human flesh 'long pig' to distinguish it from the other staple of their diet, 'short pig' or pork. In Italy, when poisoning was a common form of getting one's way, and a snobbish Roman might say, 'I am dining with the Borgias tonight', but no Roman was ever able to say, 'I dined with the Borgias last night,' it was considered bad form to speak bluntly of *veleno*. What you said was that a certain death had been assisted, *aiutata*. In France the lethal but inconspicuous medicine used by impatient heirs to remove those who stood between them and the inheritance they coveted was called *poudre de succession*, inheritance powder.

The matter of euphemism changes from age to age and from society to society, depending on what topics are found so dangerous that they demand the substitution of a favourable for a more accurate but offensive expression. According to Bronislaw Malinowski, the pioneer structuralist anthropologist, the Trobriand Islanders of the early twentieth century were unashamed in word and deed about sex, but bashful and euphemistic about the dangerous act of eating, which they preferred to do in private and refer to obliquely by innuendo. But, generalizing wildly, we can assert that most societies, especially primitive ones, are euphemistic about God and religious affairs; that as they become more civilized they become euphemistic about purgatorial matters of defecation and micturation; that many of them, particularly Victorians, have linguistic taboos about sex and all that.

The opinion that we are becoming less euphemistic as we become more civilized will not survive a moment's consideration. We may be franker about God, and religion, and excretion, and copulation. Our modern taboos are class, and race, and colour, and money, and death. We are the society that calls a second-hand car salesman 'a used vehicle merchandizing co-ordinator', and a filing-clerk an 'information retrieval administrator'. We describe poor and backward countries as underdeveloped, then developing, then Third World, moving in mealy-mouthed sensitivity on to a new euphemism as soon as the latest one picks up offensive connotations. We have followed the same cycle from black, to darky, to coloured, to negro, to Afro-American, to non-white, and back to black again, which has become beautiful.

Our poor are disadvantaged. Our stupid are less able. Our dunces at school are less academic. Our rich and cultivated are less deprived. Things stolen or looted are liberated. And death is our last taboo. *The Book of Common Prayer* evolved during the sixteenth century spoke with solemn simplicity: 'When they come to the Grave, while the Corpse is made ready to be laid into the earth . . .'; 'We therefore commit his Body to the ground; earth to earth, ashes to ashes, dust to dust; in sure and certain hope of the Resurrection to eternal life.' We are less sure and certain, and our language has accordingly become more vague, from undertakers to Evelyn Waugh's *The Loved One*, where most cemeteries provide a dog's toilet and a cat's motel. I suspect that in our Age of Explicitness our last insults will be mortuary and decompository metaphors. A car will crash into the back of another one at the lights. The driver of the one in front will jump out, red-faced and shaking his fists, and shout at the one behind the unmentionable words: 'You putrefying old corpse . . .'

[GOD]

In the reign of Charles II, a certain worthy divine at Whitehall thus addressed himself to the auditory at the conclusion of his sermon: 'In short, if you don't live up to the precepts of the gospel, but abandon yourselves to your irregular appetites, you must expect to receive your reward in a certain place which 'tis not good manners to mention here.'

Thomas Brown, *Laconics*, 1707

We are mighty bold about using four-letter words in these liberated days. I wrote the first 'cunt' to appear in *The Times* of London in 1972. The reason was scholarly not sensational or lewd. Volume I, A-G, of the majestic *Supplement to the Oxford English Dictionary* was published, known familiarly as the four-letter volume because it treated for the first time the most popular previously unmentionable sexual words. Oxford printed it, with the note: 'for centuries, and still by the great majority, regarded as a taboo-word; until recent times not often recorded in print but frequent in coarse speech.' Its earliest citation in English was the street name in the City of London circa 1230 'Gropecuntlane'. I dare say that the same implication lingers euphemistically in the eight Love Lanes that still survive in London. It seemed worth recording the interesting fact for readers of *The Times*.

But the oldest four-letter word, far older than such Johnny-come-lately words for private parts and acts, is called in Greek The Four-

Letter Word, Tetragrammaton. It is the Hebrew word for God, YHVH, still never spoken or written by a pious Jew, but vowelled by the rest of us as Jehovah or Yahweh. The English, a notoriously godly, and profane, and God-bothering people, have tended to euphemism in religious matters. The French, who never let their religion affect the rest of their life, have no embarrassment about saying *Mon Dieu*! Puritanism and euphemism are strong in the English, so we have devised hundreds of ways of mentioning the awful word without saying it.

There is evidence that this nervousness about naming the deity came in at the Reformation. The Shipman in Chaucer's *Canterbury Tales*, admittedly not a man of nice conscience, made no bones about exclaiming: 'For God's bones tell us a tale.' In *Henry IV Part 1*, first performed in 1596–7, the Second Carrier, whom from other internal evidence we can judge to be a ribald and raunchy rogue, at two in the morning at any rate, shouts: 'God's body! the turkeys in my pannier are quite starved.' Such bluntness was becoming blasphemous, and, what is more, dangerous. And at the same time towards the end of the sixteenth century we find a proliferation of euphemistic abbreviations for invoking bits of the deity: 'Zounds' for God's wounds; 'Zooks' or 'Gadzooks' (what God's hooks were remains obscure); 'Od's bodykins' or 'pittikins' (body or pity); 'Gadsbudlikins'; 'Gadsnigs' and 'Gadsniggers'; and dozens more.

By the same process and at the same time God spawned a litter of euphemistic substitutes: Cocke, gough, gog, gosse, and gom. The two last have given us By Gosh! and By Gum!, those charmingly old-fashioned exclamations. Gee may come from G . . ; and Jee whiz! certainly comes from Jesus. Lord was euphemized to Law, Losh, Lawks (a portmanteau for Lord and Alack) as in *Pickwick*: 'Lawk, Mr Weller, how you do frighten me.' Sblood, slid, snails, and struth (still current, just, among old-fashioned ejaculators) are euphemisms for God's blood, lid (lid?), nails, and truth. 'Drat it' is a euphemism for saying: 'God rot it!'

Other euphemisms for getting round naming Him Who Shall be Nameless included such attributive sobriquets as the Almighty, the Creator, the Eternal, or the Deity. Jesus came to be identified euphemistically as the Redeemer, the Saviour, the Anointed, the Paschal Lamb, and so on. The diffidence about naming the unnamable is not confined to the Jewish and Christian religions. Muslims also feel it. It is a cardinal point of Islam that Mahomet was the last, the 'Seal', of the Prophets, and that the Koran, which was revealed to him, is the final and unalterable message of God to mankind. There was a fascinating instance of pictorial euphemism in 1981 when a western film of the life of Mahomet had to be substantially remade, after protests, to avoid depicting the Prophet or his book, except obliquely.

Reverence or superstition taboos the names of kings as well as God. You do not have to read far into *The Golden Bough* before meeting euphemisms from Paraguay to Zululand for the names of kings and other sacred persons, of relations, of the dead, of gods. In ancient Greece, those cities ignorantly supposed to be models of rational civilization, the priests of the Eleusinian mysteries might not be named. It was a legal offence to pronounce their names. The pedant in Lucian describes how he met one of these nameless personages dragging to the criminal court a rude fellow who had dared to name the priests, even though he knew perfectly well that from the moment of their initiation it was unlawful to do so, because they had become anonymous, having lost their old names and acquired new, sacred, and euphemistic titles. We are still just as euphemistic. We address the Pope not by his name but as Your Holiness, and the Archbishop of Canterbury as Your Grace. We address the Queen as Your Majesty and then Ma'rm, and refer to her as Her Majesty, or, familiarly, H.M. Not even her intimates address her by her name, though irreverent younger members of her Household are said to refer to her as Brenda behind her back.

Similar euphemism cloaks the names of all important office-holders in Britain. It is polite to address senior politicians by their titles, as 'Prime Minister' or 'Minister', rather than by their names. On formal occasions the correct verbal address of an Archbishop is 'Your Grace'; on social occasions 'Archbishop' is the form. His most reverend surname and Christian name are reserved for intimates on the most informal occasions, as the actress said to the Archbishop. When a Bishop of the Church of England is con- secrated, he loses his surname for official purposes. In future, for such solemn occasions as writing letters to *The Times*, he will sign himself by his christian name followed by the Latin abbreviation of his See and a cross, for example 'Fred Roffen　' (a tarnished silver Latin abbreviation for *Durobrivae*, which was the original name of Rochester), or 'Tim Londin　' for our hypothetical Bishop of London (*Londinium*).

On formal occasions, or if you are his employee, you should address a Duke as 'Your Grace. On social occasions 'Duke' will do.

The correct verbal address for the former wife of a peer other than a Duke on formal occasions is 'Madam'; on social occasions 'Lady Surbiton', or whatever the title of her dead or divorced husband happened to be; employees are advised to address her as 'My Lady' or 'Your Ladyship'. In the last example the difference is purely grammatical, e.g. 'Yes, my Lady'; but, 'Will your Ladyship come this way?' There is no need to labour the examples. Substantial volumes devoted to the correct form of euphemistic address of title-holders and other officials are published by Debrett's and other specialists in such linguistic niceties.

It is easy to mock this euphemism about nomenclature, which I suspect that the English carry to farther extremes of pedantry than other societies; though I note that Americans tend to address their first citizen as 'Mr President', and I bet that not many Russians address the Chairman of the Presidium of the Supreme Soviet by his surname, fewer still by his first name. Dread of naming the powerful is an ingrained, atavistic instinct in most races. It may be silly, but it is also useful. For many years I was embarrassed about how to address the Chairman of *The Times* when we passed each other in the corridors engaged upon our several duties. For a while I had an editor who was a great believer in christian names as catalysts for democracy and teamwork. But that seemed impertinent in the case of the Chairman; far more impertinent such matey vocatives as 'cobber' or 'digger'. Mr followed by his surname felt unduly pompous and plonking. We eventually settled for bobs and grunts and grins that would have provided a chapter for an anthropologist. The embarrassment was solved by a subsequent editor who addressed the chairman splendidly and effectively as 'Chairman'. He said that he was a great believer in addressing office-holders by their official titles, though, oddly enough, he was not greatly amused by my experiment thereafter of addressing him at every opportunity as 'Dear Ed'.

The converse of this English euphemism about calling people by their proper names is the old-fashioned custom of English men of addressing close friends by their surnames *tout court*. I suspect that this goes back to their prep and public schools where that was how they got to know each other. For an Englishman of a certain age and class 'Dear Howard' is the most intimate form of address in his vocabulary. Christian names are reserved for his wife and family, though you only have to read Jane Austen to observe that this was not always so. This admirably straightforward convention of calling a spade a spade outrages the gentle euphemistic instincts of women and public relations officers, who did not have the advantage of being sent away to a boarding school, and who address one as 'Dear Philip Howard' for fear of being thought unfriendly or stand-offish.

The superstition about naming the deity is extended to his opponent, for whom there are numerous euphemistic and ponderous sobriquets from the Prince of Darkness to Old Nick, and to his opponent's habitation, which may be referred to as the other place, the bottomless pit, and a dozen other allusions to avoid calling it hell. There is an agreeable popular etymology that derives Deuce, the euphemism for His Satanic Majesty that came into English in the seventeenth century, from the Latin 'deus' or God. We could take this as an interesting survival of the Albigensian and Manichaean heresies of two deities, one of good, one of evil. Unfortunately, like most popular etymologies, it is untrue. There was no chronological contact between the Middle English 'deus' and the emergence of Deuce centuries later. The best authorities think that Deuce can probably be identified with the exclamation made by a dicer on making the lowest possible throw, viz. a two.

Names are the peculiar properties of the persons named. You only have to get somebody's name wrong or mis-spell it to notice how sensitive we still are about our names. It is always those with illegible signatures who are the angriest. Euphemism about naming names survives from the beginning of speech, when to know something's name was to have magical power over it. We are still superstitious about naming God and the Devil, the Queen and Madam Chairperson.

### SEX

'Nothing is so much to be shunned as sex relations.' St Augustine, *Soliloquies*

We are wrong if we suppose that sexual euphemism was an invention of the Victorians, although it is true that they carried it to new heights. All ages and most societies have been cautious about the naming of parts. The Greeks used their word for a rose-bush as a euphemism for what we had better describe, in the decent and still euphemistic obscurity of a learned tongue, as *pudenda muliebria*. In 1982 J.N. Adams published a long and scholarly book devoted entirely to *The Latin Sexual Vocabulary*, including *telum*, a weapon or tool, a metaphor that is used in most languages. Greek baby boys called it their kokko, their laloo, or their lizard. In Latin it was your sparrow (or ostrich?), your *titus* (dove), or your turtle-dove. Adult Romans called it instrument, branch, dagger, stake, sword, tail, throat, or worm. Note that Romans were more aggressive and more insinuating. In twelfth-century Latin one called it one's hammer, and that was that. Roman nannies taught little girls to call their place their piggy. This agreeable euphemism produced, through the diminutive *porcellana*, the French word for what in English is called Venus' shell, the *porcelaine*, which in turn gives us porcelain from its shining smoothness. In Latin euphemism, your pubic hair is your fern, your balls are your allies, or your witnesses, or your twins. Those who called their laloo their sickle, or tiller, or ploughshare, were using hyperbole, not euphemism, making poetry not prudery.

We might suppose that Restoration letters were outspoken about sex; and so they were, naming the formerly unnameable. But they were also rich in outrageous metaphor and other sexual euphemism. Their exemplar, Rochester, was a witty master of the suggestive power of allusion. In 'A Song of a Young Lady to her Ancient Lover' he has her say:

> 'Thy nobler part, which but to name
> In our sex would be counted shame . . .'

and carry on, being explicit without naming anything. There is a natural human tendency to euphemism about naming sex and its bits and pieces. It is evident in every language, even, perhaps especially, in writing intended to be erotic. *Par exemple*, from the seventeenth-century French classic of venery, *L'Ecole des filles*, which could not be described as prudish, and is kept clandestinely shut away in the Private Case of the British Library, Susanne, the experienced older woman, explains the facts of life to a young virgin:

'I call it the cunny. Sometimes it's called the sheath or the thingummy, the little hole, the mossy hole, and so on. And when a boy does what I've described to a girl, it's known as putting his yard in her cunny, or rather one says that he mounts her or rides her . . .' And so on, through labyrinths of metaphor that is as euphemistic as it is erotic.

The patron saint of euphemism was Thomas Bowdler (1754–1825), who personified the refined reaction to eighteenth-century bawdy, and became the eponym of the verb 'to bowdlerize'. The expurgatory instinct was strong in his family. His mother, Elizabeth Stuart Bowdler, published a critical commentary on *The Song of*

*Solomon* in which her numerous purifying emendations included the substitution of 'bridal chariot' for the inflammatory 'bed'. In 1818 Thomas published in ten volumes his *Family Shakespeare*: 'in which nothing is added to the original text; but those words and expressions are omitted which cannot with propriety be read aloud in a family.' In his preface Thomas wrote of Shakespeare's language, 'Many words and expressions occur which are of so indecent a nature as to render it highly desirable that they should be erased.' He also complains of the unnecessary and frivolous allusions to Scripture, 'which call imperiously for their erasement'. Much of the blue-pencil and scissor work was in fact done by his sister Henrietta Maria, known as Harriet, though this was a well-kept literary secret. She cut out lines on aesthetic as well as euphemistic grounds. Apart from deleting what upset them, they tended to rewrite: 'Heaven bless us' for 'Jesu bless us!'; 'vile Glendower' for 'damned Glendower'; 'Well Susan's dead' for 'Well, Susan is with God.' When criticized by intellectuals, Bowdler replied patiently: 'If any word or expression is of such a nature that the first impression it excites is an impression of obscenity, that word ought not to be spoken nor written or printed; and, if printed, it ought to be erased.'

Having euphemized Shakespeare, Bowdler turned his attention to Gibbon, producing an edition of *Decline and Fall* 'reprinted from the original text with the careful omissions of all passages of an irreligious or immoral tendency'. It came out a good deal shorter than the original, the famous fifteenth and sixteenth chapters about the rise of Christianity, masterpieces of irony and polemics, being particularly truncated. Bowdler had enough self-confidence to assert in his introduction that Gibbon would have approved of his plan, and that his version would be adopted by all future publishers of the book. In fact it was not so much of a success as Shakespeare, Gibbon being caviare to the general. But it enabled Bowdler's nephew to claim in a footnote that it was the peculiar happiness of his uncle so to have purified Shakespeare and Gibbon that they could no longer 'raise a blush on the cheek of modest innocence, nor plant a pang in the heart of the devout Christian'.

Bowdler's counterpart across the Atlantic was Noah Webster, the lexicographer, who tried to make the Bible fit for family reading. He turned 'fornication' into 'lewdness' and 'teat' into 'breast', not realizing the melancholy truth for bowdlerizers that euphemism is actually more suggestive than plain-speaking. Wombs are out in Webster's Bible. A stink is reduced to an ill savour or an odious scent. Onan does no more than frustrate his purpose, and the scarlet whore of Babylon becomes the scarlet harlot, which sounds like the beginning of a rugby song.

It was the age of Mrs Grundy. Mrs Grundy herself, symbol of British prudery and euphemism, was born in 1798 in *Speed the Plough*, a play by Tom Morton. She never appears in the play, but Dame Ashfield, the farmer's wife, constantly worries about her, until Farmer Ashfield exclaims: 'Be quiet, wool ye? Always ding dinging Dame Grundy into my ears – What will Mrs Grundy zay? What will Mrs Grundy think?' Mencken gave as an example of American Grundyism the fact that by 1821 'rooster' had been substituted in every possible context for the ambiguous 'cock', the latter having acquired an indelicate anatomical significance. Accordingly, in a novel by T.C. Haliburton called *Sam Slick*, a young man tells a girl that her brother has become a 'rooster-swain' in the Navy. But on balance my favourite piece of nineteenth-century Grundyism is Leigh Hunt's revision of the insult directed at the Cook by Chaucer's Manciple, 'Thy breath full sour stinketh.' He emended this to, 'Thy breath resembleth not sweet marjoram.'

The euphemizing instinct raged through the nineteenth-century lexicon. It tried to cover anything to do with sex. The sexual organs became the 'private parts', 'parts of shame', or mere 'parts', or were disguised with more elaborate euphemisms, such as, 'She shielded her modesty', 'She blushed at his manliness', or 'The assault was conducted on Love's Throne.' Within a marriage sexual activity was described as 'conjugal relations' or 'connubial rites'. Outside marriage it was a 'romance'.

Pregnancy came to be 'expecting' or 'in the family way' or 'to be bow-windowed' or the French *enceinte*. Giving birth to the baby became *accouchement* or 'lying-in' or 'confinement'. The arrival of the new baby was euphemized into 'the little stranger' or 'the patter of tiny feet'. It should not be supposed from this eruption of euphcmism that the Victorians were uninterested in sex. The evidence that we have, from, for example, the memoirs and the numbers of prostitutes, indicates the opposite. There was a proliferation of euphemisms for the prostitutes that thronged the towns, as you can read in the pages of Mayhew. They ranged from 'erring sister' to 'a woman of easy virtue'. Harlot took over from whore, itself a euphemism, being ultimately derived from the Latin *carus*. Feminist writers have listed more than a hundred Victorian terms for a prostitute, and noted with more truth than poetry that they were almost all dysphemisms, or aggressive put-downs like 'nymph of darkness' or 'perfect lady'. It was in this period that 'gay' began to slide to mean sexually promiscuous and now homosexual. Feminist writers note, more in anger than in sorrow, fewer than twenty terms for a sexually promiscuous male, all of them highly euphemistic and commendatory in a nudging and winking smoking-room style, such as 'Gay Lothario' and 'lady killer'. Menstruation was not referred to. The Victorian woman would say that she was feeling poorly or had domestic afflictions. If she came from the gay and shady classes, she might say 'The captain is at home', or 'My little friend has come for a few days'.

Euphemism spread to other parts of the body than the sexual bits. Breasts were unmentionable, and became the chest, or bust, or contours, or charms, or 'the upper part of the body'. Buttocks became the seat, the posterior, the fundament, (for women) the *derrière*, the promontories, the fleshy part of the thigh, and a dozen other circumlocutions that it would be tedious to list. The belly became the abdomen or stomach or, in a significantly nursery usage, the tummy. Anthony Trollope's publisher changed 'fat stomach' in *Barchester Towers* to 'deep chest'. Even legs were suspect, since they led to other things, and were euphemized to 'understandings', 'nether limbs', or just 'limbs', in the same way that extreme Grundys are said to have covered the nether limbs of their chairs and pianos to avoid shocking the susceptibilities of their women, whom they preferred to refer to as ladies or females depending on their class. Whether it was cause or effect or a bit of both, extreme sexual euphemism was a symptom of extreme Victorian interest in sex, as well as adding to the gaiety of nations. The truth of the matter is that human beings have always been interested in sex, and attempts to disguise the fact merely exaggerate it.

The same sexual euphemism attached itself to clothes, with the same ludicrously disappointing results for the euphemizers. Whatever genteelism you invent for the clothes that men wear around their legs and forks rapidly becomes suggestive to the suggestible. Breeches became trousers became small clothes became irrepressibles and a string of similar humorous circumlocutions. John Wolcot summed up the difficulty in a poem called 'A Rowland for an Oliver' of around 1800:

> 'I've heard that breeches, petticoats and smock
> Give to the modest maid a grievous shock
> And that my brain (so lucky its device)
> Christ'neth them inexpressibles, so nice.'

Knickerbockers became knickers became inexpressibles. Mrs Amelia Jenks Bloomer, the New York feminist reformer and founder of the women's rights magazine, *The Lily*, urged her readers to wear knickerbockers for bicycling and other outdoor sports. Controversy, and also convenience, eventually relegated bloomers, of which she is the eponym, to euphemism beneath the skirt. Stockings became hose. A book of etiquette of 1859 pronounced: '*Stockings* is considered extremely indelicate, although *long socks* is pardonable.' Smock became shift became chemise. All that shift means is a change of garment. But it acquired such improper and inflammatory connotations that as recently as 1907 its use sparked off a riot at the first production, at the new Abbey Theatre in Dublin, of J.M. Synge's *The Playbody of the Western World*.

### EXCRETION

As Luther observed, it is a melancholy, or possibly an entertaining, part of the human condition that the organs of generation are closely connected with the organs of urination and defecation. The subject is taboo in most societies, and fenced around with euphemism. Readers of the Authorized Version of the Old Testament will find it easier to understand if they are told that when somebody is said to cover his feet, it is a euphemism for relieving himself. A lavatory is, etymologically, a vessel or apartment for washing one's hands; cf. the modern genteelism, 'I'm just going to wash my hands.' One of the early English euphemisms for the lavatory was the jakes, for Jacques's or Jack's house. Sir John Harington, godson of Queen Elizabeth I, published a Rabelaisian treatise called *A New Discourse of a Stale Subject Called the Metamorphosis of Ajax* in 1596. Stale is a euphemism for urine; Ajax = A jakes. In it a prudish gentlewoman, having to announce to her lady the arrival of a Mr Jacques Wingfield, blushes and stammers, 'Mr Privy Wingfield.' He was banished from court for his rude jape, but not for long. Royals enjoy lavatory humour.

The most popular modern upper-class U excretory epithet for the jakes is the loo. It is a convenient little word, though twee, but its derivation is a scholarly crux. Here are the principal etymologies suggested:

1. It is a corruption of the French *l'eau*, as in 'gardyloo' shouted from the high flats in Edinburgh before emptying one's chamber pot into the street. Dr Johnson was not the only visitor to find the practice repulsive.
2. It is a beheaded pun on Waterloo, which has the same begin-

ning as water closet. James Joyce, master of puns, specifically made the full pun in *Ulysses* (1922): 'O yes, *mon loup*. How much cost? Waterloo. Watercloset.'

3.  The French used to put the numbers 00 or 100 on the lavatory door in hotels, as a variant of the letters w.c. for water closet. British soldiers returning from France during or after the First World War misinterpreted 100 as loo.

4.  Professor Alan Ross has an appropriately U etymology. It concerns a practical joke that was played at Vice-Regal Lodge, Dublin, when the first Duke of Abercorn was Lord Lieutenant in the decade after 1866. Each bedroom door had a card on it giving the name of the occupant. Some joker changed all the cards, and the name of a young woman called Lou for short ended on the lavatory door. She seems to have been Lady Louise Hamilton, who died in 1940.

We shall not be surprised to find that the acts and places of defecation and micturation are cloaked in euphemism in most societies and cultures. It is seemly that they should be. Maybe in the barrack-room and the Trobriand Islands, if Malinowski is a reliable witness, they refer to such matters in plain language. Life would be crude if we all did. The difficulty is to find a euphemism that is not twee or pregnant with class overtones. Toilet, which comes from the French word for the cloth that covers a dressing table, is irredeemably suburban genteel in British English at present. Even more genteel are the variations on such pairs as Mermaids and Divers that are used on lavatory doors in pubs. There is a lot to be said for the manly antique euphemism, jakes.

### MONEY AND POLITICS

Euphemisms about God and sex have a whimsical ring even for the most prudish in our age, which does not take sex and God as seriously as most preceding ages. But our euphemisms about politics and money are deadly serious, because we take the subjects seriously. What used to be known crudely as Labour Exchanges and Distressed Areas are called Jobcentres and Development Districts. When somebody on the BBC said, 'The Chinese use manipulative methods,' I thought for a moment he was referring to Chinese skill at osteopathy and massage, until I realized he was talking about bribery. When totalitarian countries speak of liquidation, they mean assassination. When almost any country attacks another, it calls it liberation. There is quite as much euphemism about in the world, particularly in the jargon and thought processes of international organizations, as there was in the heyday of Euphemia Grundy. But it is applied to different objects. Euphemism arises from deeply ingrained human instincts, not all of which are bad. They range from religious reverence, to common decency, to the powerful wish to be liked, to prudery and genteelism, to a terror of life. Not all euphemism is bad; but much of it is silly.

The language of politics in an age of mass democracy, and mass dictatorship, for that matter, for dictators still have to keep the troops happy, is necessarily full of euphemisms, obfuscations, hypocrisies, doublethink – in short, not to be euphemistic about it, lies. From Plato to the present forgettable rulers of the Soviet Republics, political thinkers have believed in the efficacy of useful lies for the good of the state. The *locus classicus* of political euphemism is in Newspeak, the official language of Oceania, devised by George Orwell in *Nineteen Eighty-Four* to meet the ideological needs of Ingsoc, or English Socialism.

You remember how *The Times* in his novel referred to one of the orators of the Party as a *doubleplusgood duckspeaker*; it implied high praise, in that he had quacked out orthodox opinions like a duck. *Oldthinkers unbellyfeel Ingsoc*, or, as we still say in our blunt, uneuphemistic way: 'Those whose ideas were formed before the Revolution cannot have a full emotional understanding of the principles of English Socialism.'

Oldthinkers unbellyfeel Ingsoc. However, it is possible to good-think about Old English before the Victory, if we do it with Minitruthful unoriginality. There is something to be learnt even from the doubleplusdecadent writing of the Old English misguided-ones before the Enlightenment. Not, of course, in much of it. Minitrue will wipe out most of it as obsolete and unrevolutionary. But selected fragments are plushelpful to partisans who want to study, whoops, entail the Glorious Future.

Take, for example, the outmoded and unnecessary word, *Truth*, which cannot be entirely discarded from Little Sister's lexicon, since it forms part of the title of Minitrue in Old English: that is, Ministry of Truth. Our ancestors before the Victory got themselves into a doubleplusmuddle about this archaic concept, and other such words, which they termed value-words.

Philosophers wrote whole books and wasted whole forests of paper discussing the theory of Truth (a theory is an obsolete concept from the days before we had certainty). I myself got into terrible trouble with the press officers (embryonic predecessors of the Minitruthful censors) of a forgotten President called Harold for writing that the Truth meant little more than the official line put out by them and other such professional liars. But this was before my rewarding spell in the Gray's Inn Road Re-education Centre for Wordsmiths. I know better now.

Our rude forefathers were confused about Truth because they had not realized the simple fact, first discovered and proclaimed in 1979, and reinforced in 1983, that Truth is an objective quality like acid or black. As we all now know, Truth means what we are told it means, neither more nor less.

The classifiers at MinEd are drawing up the huge *New Oxford English Dictionary*, which may eventually have to go into more than one volume, in which every word in Newspeak is labelled true or nontrue. In the days before the Enlightenment writers worked in the unlight. But one or two of them got near to the Truth.

There is a poem (a primitive form of writing with rhythm and rhymes and other jungle tricks) by a writer of the period before 1984. His name and record have been vapourized. But I found a fragment of one of his 'poems' on a second-hand book barrow in the Farringdon Road. (I know that such repositories of old books are subversive, part of the Black Economy, and illegal; but an author at times has an unpleasant duty to examine such things, within Miniluv and Minitrue parameters of behaviour, it goes without saying.)

This fragment, no doubt from a terrible bourgeois poet whose name is deservedly unremembered, goes:

> *Leave Truth to the police and us; we know the Good;*
> *We build the Perfect City time shall never alter;*
> *Our Law shall guard you always like a cirque of mountains,*
> *Your Ignorance keep off evil like a dangerous sea;*
> *You shall be consummated in the General Will,*
> *Your children innocent and charming as the beasts.*

The language is primitive and emotional. Some of the words are obsolete or forbidden. But the general message seems to me inspiriting and Minitruthful. It could become a school text, or a patriotic Newsoc song, if the language is not so crude. The advice these rough, inchoate lines gives is the advice Little Sister gave us a quarter of a century ago, and which we followed.

The poet seems to be talking about the world statesmen of the Thirties, the lame and impotent forerunners of Big Brother and Little Sister. They had only a fraction of the power and the wisdom of those two great leaders, but the poem shows that they were working towards the Answer.

'Truth' is a matter for the police and Big Brother. 'Good' is another outmoded value-word and euphemism that has turned out to be an analytic, objective word. It means whatever the Party chooses to label 'Good' at any particular moment in time. The 'Perfect City' is, by a happy coincidence, one of Minitruthful's alternative and euphemistic names for New London.

'Ignorance' and 'Evil' are two more mistaken old concepts that have been abolished. The 'General Will' is, I believe, a reference to *la volonté générale* of Rousseau, than which no more pernicious doctrine has ever been invented. Whoops again. Erase that from the Speakwrite. Sorry, chaps.

The subjects of euphemism vary slightly from age to age and culture to culture. The methods of euphemism are manifold. You can abbreviate, as in w.c. You can veil your meaning in the decent obscurity of a learned tongue, or a foreign tongue, as in *lingerie*, the French for the linen from which the unmentionable garments are made. You can use litotes, as in, 'You don't look too great.' You can use a vague phrase, as in, 'Commit no nuisance.' You can use an elaborate circumlocution, as in, 'Please adjust your dress before leaving.' You can be enigmatical or poetical, as in, 'Shuffle off this mortal coil.' There can be a poetry in euphemism, but mainly when Shakespeare is doing the euphemizing. You can use a significantly concomitant circumstance, as in to remove, when what you mean is to rub someone out. You can be bombastic, as in emolument. You can tell a straight lie, as in, 'I'm just going to powder my nose.' You can use understatement, as in, 'I've had a glass or two,' i.e., 'I'm shmashed.' You can hint, as in, 'That's a carefully researched piece,' when what you mean is that it is plagiarized. You can direct thought in the right direction, as in honorarium. You are not always wrong to use euphemism. But you are wise to recognize that you are using it.

Related to euphemisms are those lying reversible phrases that mean the opposite of what they say. The English, who are a notoriously hypocritical race, and anxious to be liked, have a peculiar proclivity to these phrases. The late Sir Arnold Lunn invented the name 'phrops' for these euphemistic phrases that do not wear their true meaning on their face. Reviewer's phrops are 'The review is in the post;' and, 'Please edit this in any way you like.' The Literary Editor's phrops include: 'The cheque is in the post;' and, 'Lovely piece; I hope to use it next week.' A notorious whinger and quibbler of a Member of Parliament introduced a brilliant new phrop in the Letters Column of *The Times*. His previous letter had been comprehensively rebutted with fact and logic. The whinger started his reply, 'I am perfectly ready to admit.' This useful phrop euphemism actually means: 'I hate to admit that white is white, and black is black; but I just want you to know that it makes no difference to my opinion; my mind is as irreversible as the Pontick sea.'

Other euphemistic reversibles are, 'We must keep in touch.' This means: 'I never want to see you again.' 'As members will have read in the report . . .' means: 'Nobody ever reads the report, so I will give my usual idiot's guide to the uncontroversial parts.' Other phrops, which mean the opposite of what they say, to the confusion of foreigners not to the mannerisms of English born, are: No Smoking (in British Rail and Underground compartments); I don't envy anyone with money these days; Your little boy is *so* much more advanced than mine; It takes more than that to make me angry, my friend; and, from the London Underground again, NO EXIT.

I suppose we could describe phrops formally as auto-antonyms with euphemistic intentions. Here are some more:

I wasn't a bit annoyed – I found the whole thing extremely amusing.

Oh, I didn't mean *you* to do it.

I'd love to, but I have to go to a dreary party that day.

Of course, I am just a simple soldier . . . (Spoken by a senior officer. The subsequent harangue often indicates that this is no phrop, as intended, but the literal truth.)

(In signing letters) With good wishes: means what it says.

With warmest good wishes: means Go to Hell.

Industrial action means inaction.

Hardly used is a euphemism.

Public school is a phrop.

And here follow some euphemistic scientific phrops:

It has long been known that = I haven't bothered to look up the reference.

Of great theoretical and practical importance = interesting to me.

While it has not been possible to provide definite answers to these questions = The experiments didn't work out, but I reckoned that I could at least get a publication out of it.

The results will be reported at a later date = I might get round to this some time, but not yet, God, not yet.

It is clear that much additional work will be required before a complete understanding . . . = I don't understand it.

It is hoped that this work will stimulate further work in this field = This paper isn't very good, but neither is any of the others in this miserable subject.

Man can only stand so much naked truth. Euphemism and phrop are convenient ways of covering it up.

The opposite of euphemism is dysphemism. If euphemisms are words and expressions that clothe ugly, undesirable, or heinous activities in pretty verbiage, then dysphemisms are words and expressions that disparage good things by associating them with bad connotations. Professor A. Carnoy, the French philologist, claimed to have coined the word in 1927: '*Le dysphémisme . . . est impitoyable, brutal, moqueur. Il est une réaction contre le pédantisme, la raideur et la prétention, mais aussi contre la noblesse et la dignité dans le langage.* In fact the word had been coined fifty years before by L.A. Tollemache in *Safe Studies*: 'The great system which Comte, and other assailants, call by the euphemism, or dysphemism, of Catholicism.' It is a useful word for a small class of boo-words. During the English Civil War the Parliamentary party referred to themselves as 'the Godly', and named the Royalists by the dysphemism of 'the Malignants'. The Franciscans called the Dominicans 'Maculists' because they refused to affirm, as a matter of faith, that the Virgin Mary was conceived without stain (*sine macula*); the name was intended to wound and put the Dominicans in an odious light. A Northerner who sympathized with the South during the American War between the States was named a 'Copperhead' after a peculiarly venomous snake. Workers who refuse to join a union or who cross a picket line are called 'scabs'. Those are all dysphemisms, lovely dysphemisms.

Euphemism is one of the agents of change in a language, like metaphor itself, of which it is part. There are very few words that have a single, simple meaning; and they are boring words. Most words are continually changing their meanings by analogy, metaphor, euphemism, connotation, and social change in the big world outside the lexicon. Take an apparently straightforward word like the verb 'to examine'. It comes originally from a Latin word meaning the tongue of a balance, and it originally meant to weigh accurately, until, by the glacier of metaphorical shift, it came to mean to inquire into and test the amount or quality of, with no notion of weighing and balances. It has become what Fowler described felicitously as a dead metaphor. It contrasts with a live or dormant metaphor like 'to sift'. You can sift wheat or evidence. But, once you start sifting with parameters or acid tests or a microscope, the metaphor in 'sift' jerks to ugly life. It turns out to be not dead, but dormant.

Two similar changes are happening all the time with euphemism. First of all the euphemistic metaphor very quickly acquires the precise meaning that it is meant to veil, and becomes improper and rude. So the Bowdlers and Mrs Grundys of every generation have to go looking for a new euphemism, which in its turn at once becomes explicit. This endless purity-hunt may be frustrating for prudes; it is funny for the rest of us. Second, the sacred subjects about which we are inclined to be euphemistic change from age to age and society to society. First it was God that was taboo; then it was sex; now it is money, and race, and class, and death. I dare say that one could make a case for arguing that euphemism is increasing rather than decreasing. There is certainly a lot of it around. It does not do much harm, provided that we have a free press that allows us to mock it occasionally. Indeed, a world in which everybody spoke the exact truth all the time, without euphemism or metaphor, would be a bleak and ghastly place worthy of the pen of George Orwell. The English language is continually changing through its euphemisms. It always has; and it always will. There is no harm in the process, provided we recognize that it is going on.

# 7/GRAMMAR

*'Ego sum rex Romanus, et supra grammaticam'* ('I am the King of Rome, and above grammar'). The Emperor Sigismund, at the Council of Constance, 1414

'That sure is a great school. It's practical. They don't teach no goddam grammar there.' A Kansas farmer, speaking to Nelson Antrim Crawford, c. 1915

Grammar has a bad name, partly because of folk memories of centuries in which excessive reverence was paid to it, and generations of school-children had its rules beaten into them. The English grammar school, recently abolished, preserved in its name the superstitious belief that the only path to education lay down the thorny path of Latin grammar. Early pedagogues made a category mistake about grammar. They thought that the rules of Latin, a dead synthetic language, could and should be applied to English, a living analytic language. It was natural for them to overestimate the importance of the studies that they had acquired with such pain, that elevated them above the vulgar herd, and that led not infrequently to positions of considerable emolument. But it was fundamentally mistaken. Language, particularly English, changes all the time, and by definition changes the grammar with it. Grammar codifies the language as it exists today; it does not superimpose and predetermine a code of usage. Grammar, in short, was made for man, not man for grammar.

Originally, grammar meant the methodical study of literature. The ancient grammarians were textual critics and students of literature. Then grammar came to mean the science of language. Increasing specialization broke up the subject. The science of language became philology, and then, in the latest jargon, linguistics. Grammar has become that branch of linguistics that deals with a language's inflexions (accidence), other structures of words (morphology), its phonetics system (phonology), and the arrangement of its words in sentences (syntax). It is sometimes taken to include semantics, which is the study of the meanings of words. On the parade ground of language accidence, morphology, phonology, and semantics are drills that words perform individually, like new recruits each being made to march, halt, one, two, salute, one, two, salute again, one, two, about turn, one, two, and march away, 'swing your arms up, you horrible little word, or I'll have your guts for garters.' Syntax is the drill when squads of words are marshalled together and made to go through their paces. They are interesting and complex subjects, but their mastery should not be confused with writing well. It is a melancholy paradox that the greatest grammarians, from Holofernes to Chomsky, have been as clear as mud at expressing their meanings.

Branches of linguistics that are not usually included in the squad drilled by Sergeant Major Grammar are: orthography, or how words are written in a spelling that is considered correct; etymology, or the derivation, family tree, and history of words; orthoepy, how words are spoken and pronounced (do we believe in the concept of correct English pronunciation any more?); and composition, or how words are formed into compounds. But grammar is a mighty sergeant, and in its original, loose sense might be taken to drill some, if not all, of that awkward squad.

One of the ways in which the English language is changing is from being an inflected to an uninflected language. There is no need for alarm: the change has been going on for more than ten centuries. Inflexion, better spelt that way than 'inflection' to show that it is derived from the Latin noun rather than the past participle (a pompous, etymological observation), means the ways in which words change their forms to signal their grammatical relations to their context, or to modify their meanings in other ways. The sort of changes that are signalled by inflexion in English are changes of tense, voice, mood, person, gender, number, or case. 'Grammarians', 'him', 'foggier', and 'baffled' are formed by inflexion from 'grammarian', 'he', 'foggy', and 'baffle'.

Old English, spoken and written by the Anglo-Saxon founding fathers of our language, was a heavily inflected language, like the other Teutonic languages to which it was closely related. Nouns had genders and other inflexions for the various cases. *Stan* (a stone, not a chap) was masculine, and his genitive plural, 'of stones', was *stana*. *Boc* (a book) was feminine, and her dative plural, 'to book', was *bocum*. *Cild* (a child) was neuter; its genitive singular, 'of a child', was *cildes*. Adjectives and pronouns were similarly inflected with genders and cases. Some of them even had a dual for referring to plurals of two but not more. For example, the second person personal pronoun, in addition to the form that became 'thou' for the singular, and the form that became 'ye' for the plural, had a dual for referring to you two over there. This declined charmingly as follows: nominative, *git*; accusative, *inc* or *incit*; dative, *inc*; genitive, *incer*. Similarly the Old English verbs were conjugated for person, number, tense, voice, and mood, with long lists of irregularities. It was a beautifully complicated grammar, and must have been hell to learn.

Over the centuries most of these inflexions have been worn away from English. A few remain, in pronouns, in the subjunctive, in irregular plurals, protruding through the surface of English like menhirs; relics and reminders of a vast lost language. You would have imagined that thoughtful Anglo-Saxons in, say, the eleventh century would have worried when they noticed the dual number of Old English fading away, and their case endings becoming obsolescent. But there is no trace of any such linguistic anxiety in the records. Our generation is the first to have worked itself into a froth of anxiety about the state of the language, and to worry that it may be dying. Change and decay in all around we see, at any rate on black Monday mornings. But not all change in language is decay. In general English evolves to meet the new needs we want to put it to, and is perfectly suited to the uses of the present generation of English-speakers. In the same way Aleutian perfectly suits the linguistic needs of the thousand people in the Aleutian Islands and about a hundred more on the Commander Islands, which belong to the Soviet Union. If they find new needs, they will change their fishy language. Aleut quotation, to impress you: '*Aganan, aganan, tanan akuya, akuya, wakun qayaxtalkinin aganagan.*' As every schoolboy knows, that means: 'These countries are created, created. There are hills on them.'

Decadence is a misleading vegetable metaphor to apply to language. Where we think that we see a language decaying, it is more likely that the people using it or their needs have changed. Latin did not decay after the fall of Rome. But different chaps were using it for different purposes; and, as Helen Waddell demonstrated memorably, the Latin of the Dark Ages was different from that of the Golden, but splendid for its purposes. And, as the Empire crumbled, the Latin of each region began to develop in its own way, without the unifying, centripetal influence of Rome. So Latin evolved into the Romance languages: Italian, French, Spanish, Portuguese, and Rumanian, which are each the languages of an entire nation; and Catalan, Provençal, Rhaeto-Romanic, Sardinian, and Moldavian, which are confined to regions within countries. You can, if you want, describe all these Romance languages as decadent forms of Latin; but it would not be a very helpful way to describe them, and I should take care that you do not let Dante, Racine, Cervantes, Camoëns, and a noble army of other great writers, who have enriched the world, hear you saying it.

However, not all linguistic change is for the best, in the best of all possible languages. For example, the fashion for using 'disinterested' as smart alternative for 'uninterested' diminishes us by a useful word. I know that the distinction between the two is quite modern. Careful writers from John Donne onwards used 'disinterested' in its fashionable modern sense of 'uninterested'. But the differentiation, by which 'disinterested' came to mean not influenced by interest, impartial, unbiased, unprejudiced, gradually established itself. It is a pity that we are losing it, because none of the near-synonyms is quite an exact synonym: an interest is not the same as a partiality, a bias, or a prejudice. Whereas 'disinterested' meaning 'uninterested' seems to me an exact synonym, adding nothing but a spurious novelty. It is an otiose change.

Most of the grammatical changes in English do not diminish the language. We have learnt to get on wonderfully well with prepositions to take the place of the inflected case-endings of nouns and adjectives. They are simpler, more regular, and easier to learn. Easiness is a virtue in grammar, *pace* old-fashioned grammarians of the Holofernes school, who confused difficulty with depth. No doubt it would be elegant to have retained the dual number. But we get along well enough without it, by adding some such indicator of duality as 'you two' or 'them both'.

Some of the grammatical changes that are taking place, in this period of rapid linguistic change, are malign rather than benign. Anything that reduces the flexibility with which we marshal English, or reduces the vast number of choices available to the English-speaker to express a vast number of shades of meaning, diminishes the language, and accordingly diminishes us. Already even educated users of English, such as journalists, suffer from chronic uncertainty about the difference between 'I' and 'me' and the other cases of pronouns. They will have gone by the end of the century. The nice but complex distinction between 'shall' and 'will' is dying; let it die. But it is a pity, because the simpler grammar will not admit so many shades of meaning. It is like the new drill on the parade-ground, designed for soldiers holding delicate FN rifles rather than the robust .303 rifles used from the Boer War to the Second World War: it is modest, decent, workmanlike drill; but it lacks the grandeur and the flexibility of the old sort. *Eheu fugaces*, maybe, but the language lives and has no regrets.

One of the reasons that English grammar is becoming progressively simpler is that so many more people are learning it, being taught it as a second language by people for whom it is not a first language either. They do not have the time or the capacity to learn our complicated grammar. Therefore the grammar will be simplified. Those of us who know the old grammar in its full glory will continue to use it, but we shall sound and look increasingly stuffy, as those of us who persist in using 'whom' or the subjunctive correctly already do.

One prevalent example of our grammatical confusion arises out of the distinction between those pretty little modal auxiliaries 'may' and 'might'. Here are some recent examples of the confusion, all taken, I regret to inform you like a copper's nark, from the columns of *The Times*. After some race riot, a senior policeman was quoted as saying: 'It *may* well have not happened last week-end, but it was bloody well going to happen some time.' But it did happen, so he should have said 'might' not 'may', which indicates doubt about whether it actually happened. Peter Hain speaking: 'Had it not been for the media's willingness to report news of the charge in the sceptical terms they did, I *may* not have been acquitted.' But he *was* acquitted; 'might not' would have been better grammar, and, what matters more, would have made his meaning clearer. 'From this penalty Sorensen scored a goal that *may* not have come by any other means.' Might not. 'If the weather had not been so bad, the number *may* have been greater.' But the weather was bad, and the number of demonstrators was small and *might* have been greater. 'After a frantic mêlée in the six-yard area, a goal *may* have been scored.' All that the football writer meant was that with a little bit of luck and a good bounce the ball *might* have been put into the back of the net. What he succeeded in suggesting was that the ball *may* actually have crossed the line, unnoticed by the referee and his linesmen: a serious and indeed a fighting suggestion.

The confusion is prevalent, and obscures meaning. It may or might be instructive to examine how it has come about, for its causes lie deep in the roots of English grammar. When used in the present tense, the auxiliaries 'may' and 'might' are almost interchangeable, and the difference is one of nuance. 'He may sue for libel' differs from 'he might sue for libel' by only a slight degree of probability, and, either way, I do not want to risk it. But when used in the past, to report what happened or in any narrative, 'may' indicates uncertainty on the part of the speaker at the moment when he is recording a past event, whereas 'might' indicates a possibility that lay in the power of the doer at the time of the action described. If we say of somebody, 'He *may* have taken bribes and joined the KGB while up at Trinity, Cambridge,' we are making a serious allegation: we are not sure whether he did so or not, but he may have done so. 'He *might* have taken bribes and joined the KGB' indicates that he did not perform either of those fashionable acts, although several of his contemporaries did. It makes a considerable difference.

There is another reason for the misuse of 'may'. It is, ill-omened name from the past, an irregular verb. Like several other auxiliary verbs, such as 'can' and 'ought', 'may' has the peculiarity that it does not take the normal inflexion of the present tense. The regular verb suffixes an 's' for the third person singular, 'he says', 'she lays eggs or odds'. But in these auxiliaries we have the 'irregularity' he may, must, ought, can, and so on, with no final 's'. Learned grammarians know that this is not an irregularity, for it only shows that in this group of verbs the Old English pre-historic present tense has been lost somehow and somewhere, and replaced by the past. The present tense we now use is simply the normal past tense of a strong verb, inflected in the regular way, that is with no final 's' in the third person, as in 'she lay on the ground'.

In German, where the same process took place before records exist, these 'preterite-present' verbs have developed new past tenses. But in English we still lack a past tense for most of them, so we have to find circumlocutions for the past tenses of 'must' or 'can' or 'ought', where Germans can say *musste*, *konnte*, or *sollte*. But 'may' is in English an exception, since the past tense of 'may' has been formed by our thoughtful ancestors, namely 'might'. Like all inventions, it brings its own problems. It may well be that the current confusion between 'may' and 'might' is influenced by the atavistic linguistic feeling of the user that 'may' has, because of the lack of the 's', a preterite form and indicates an event enacted in the past. Let us hope so.

If we are losing the distinction between the tenses of the subjunctive, because of this confusion between 'may' and 'might', as we seem to be in even the best-regulated newspapers, English will be diminished until we devise a new way of making the distinction. In a century's time shall we say, 'We *might* have preserved the subjunctive, if we had not been so careless'? Shall we say, doubtfully, 'We *may* have preserved the subjunctive: it survives in *The Times* and other publications that treat the language carefully'? Or will it not make a blind bit of difference whether we say *may* or *might*, because the distinction will be dead? If the distinction is dead, English will have evolved another way of expressing the subjunctive mood of willing, desiring, conditional, probability, or prospective. An advanced language cannot get by without such a mood. Unless you take the view that a century from now we shall be back in the Stone Age, grunting proper names at each other, and I dare say a few improper names as well, English will find a new way of distinguishing between 'may' and 'might', if we are losing the old way.

The subjunctive is dying, let it die. I very much doubt if there will be any more than relics of the subjunctive in the twenty-first century. It has been weakening from the first forms of recorded English, and has a great deal to do with the complications of what are called the modal verbs, 'may' and 'can' and 'shall' and so on, all of which have been playing elaborate games of musical chairs for a thousand years. In the process the subjunctive has become eroded and fallen away. It had gone effectively by about the eighteenth century, and still continues to crumble. 'If I were you' might carry on for some time yet, but only as a relic of an old system. We have plenty of relics of old systems, like those menhirs sticking through the turf, in all languages.

Another grammatical distinction that is dying is the distinction between 'shall' and 'will' in the future and conditional. It has been an unconscionable time dying. At the beginning of the century Henry Bradley in the *OED* and Dr C.T. Onions observed that the faultless idiomatic use of 'shall' and 'will' was one of the points that were regarded as infallible tests of the correct English speaker; and that it offered peculiar difficulties to Scots, Irish, Americans, provincials, and other lesser breeds without the Law. It is a marvellously elaborate distinction, equipping its master with a great range of shades of meaning. But it is difficult and 'irregular' and a Shibboleth to catch out 'incorrect' users of English at the passages of Jordan. The distinctions are set out with precision in the *OED*, and are worth having a look at as one of the monuments of English grammar. The principal distinction, by which 'shall' is used for simple futurity in the first person, and 'will' in the second and third persons, while 'will' denotes intention, volition, or choice in the first person, but 'shall' does the job for the second and third persons, is summarized in the crude schoolboy rhyme:

'In the first person simply "shall" foretells;
In "will" a threat or else a promise dwells.

"Shall" in the second and the third does threat;
"Will" simply then foretells the future feat.'

And we all know the sad story of the Irishman who got it wrong, when he was drowning not waving, and shouted, 'I *will* drown, and nobody *shall* save me,' and was left to drown by the pedants on the shore.

As Fowler noticed more than fifty years ago, there is a tendency among those not to the manner born to question the existence, besides denying the need, of the distinctions between 'shall' and 'will'. They exist, all right; *si monumentum requiris*, look in the *OED*. But do we need them? Well, it is still better to say Shibboleth than Sibboleth, since the distinction has been worked out over the past three centuries by the best users of English. Jephthah and his bloody Gileadites are not yet going to cut our throats for using 'shall' and 'will' correctly, and the correct use does allow a greater variety of meanings than most imaginable alternatives.

Whether we need them or not, the distinctions are dying. English is a democracy, and the great majority of English-speakers are now brought up and taught in cultures that little note, nor long remember, the fuss about 'shall' and 'will'. In due course the correct use of 'shall' and 'will' will come to sound insufferably insular and pedantic; but not yet, not yet. The distinction is still available in all its majesty for those who care to use it. The rest can struggle in the dark to evolve a way of distinguishing so many delicate shades of meaning.

Let us move from those exemplary difficulties with the conjugation of verbs to another chapter of accidence, the declension of pronouns. It is not surprising that English-speakers are having increasing difficulty with case-endings: there are so few of the things left to practise on. A prevalent new confusion is the genteel illiteracy of using 'whom' where 'who' is right. The objective case 'whom' sounds formal and a little old-fashioned. It would be pedantic to object to the reverse usage, 'Who were you with last night?' *Pace* the Fowler brothers, this colloquialism has become so firmly established, in written as well as spoken English, that it is difficult to invent a context in which the correct use of the objective, 'Whom were you with last night?', would not sound quaint. But dim unease about the case-endings of pronouns, arising I suspect from ill-digested and ill-remembered grammar in the Lower Fourth, frequently causes writers to plump for an absurd 'whom', as in, 'He was asked whom his father was.' That example was taken, alas, from *The Times*. The error is widespread in all the newspapers that top people take. The popular tabloids are innocent of it, tending to avoid 'whom' and other case-endings as posh and élitist beasts.

'He had an air of being but vaguely aware of whom Miss Chancellor might be.' That, as you might have guessed from the name and other intimations, was Henry James. It is an indirect question, and should be 'who'. How endearingly characteristic of the Old Pretender to have chosen the more elaborate and refined, but, as it happens, incorrect, pronoun.

> 'And in these fits I leave them, while I visit
> Young Ferdinand, whom they suppose is drown'd . . .'

That was Shakespeare, speaking through his mouthpiece Prospero. The relative pronoun is the subject of 'is drown'd' and should be 'who'. Perhaps it has been attracted into the accusative by the adjacency of Young Ferdinand, who is objective, being visited, and would be in the accusative, if 'Young' and 'Ferdinand' had case-endings. Perhaps there was confusion with another way of putting it, 'Young Ferdinand, whom they suppose to be drown'd.' Perhaps, when in doubt between 'who' and 'whom', Shakespeare reached for the latter, because it sounded more elegant. Many of us still do. Perhaps he just liked the sound of it better. Let us not pick nits with Shakespeare's grammar, other than to remark that 'who they suppose is drown'd' is grammatically correct.

'But whom say ye that I am?', Matthew XVI, 15. If Shakespeare, Henry James, and the forty-seven revisers and retranslators of the Authorized Version on occasion did not know their 'who' from their 'whom', what hope is there for us lesser mortals?

In a particular kind of relative clause it has become normal over the past few years to use the accusative 'whom' instead of the nominative 'who'. It is now normal and becoming 'correct' to write: 'Thomas Huxley had a no less famous son *whom* one presumed was also called Geksli like his father.'

The change will mean that teachers of English will have to conform. The relevant passage in a new English Grammar for foreign students will read something like as follows: 'The nominative of the personal relative pronoun is normally *who* and the accusative *whom*; but if between the relative pronoun and its verb there are inserted two or more words, of which one is itself a verb, *whom* is used for the nominative.' This new formula seems to fit modern usage. It is not (yet?) correct to say: 'Mrs Thatcher *whom* is

Prime Minister.' But it is now correct to say: 'Mrs Thatcher *whom* he said is Prime Minister.' It is still incorrect, however, to say: 'Mrs Thatcher *whom* at present is Prime Minister.' In the last example the two words coming between the relative pronoun and its verb do not include a verb.

I am aware that English grammarians cannot bear people *whom* they imagine talk about nominatives and accusatives. But this is a permissive age. It is wrong for any word to be banned from current use just because grammarians find it offensive. And in any case foreigners have those two convenient words in their languages and use them freely.

There may be something to be learned about the characters of the two newspapers from the fact that on the day that *The Times* wrote, 'Mr Tatchell *whom* Mr Foot declared would never be a Labour candidate,' the *Telegraph*, making the opposite and old-fashioned mistake, wrote, 'Mr Tatchell *who* Mr Foot recently denounced in Parliament.'

The vestigial case-endings of English grammar are dying. There is no cause for alarm: they have been dying for ten centuries. As the epitaph on the tomb of a young girl in an English country church-yard put it:

> 'Her as was has gone from we,
> Us as is will go to she.'

In addition to four mistakes in the cases of personal pronouns, that verse makes a mistake in the number of the verb in the second line. We is not singular: us are plural. I do not detect increasing grammatical confusion about number among modern users of English. On the whole we can still tell a singular from a plural, though there are traps and common mistakes. There always have been. We still have trouble with compound subjects: the editor and his leader-writers are illiterate; the editor or his leader-writer is illiterate. We have trouble with relatives (no, not relations, dumbo, though we may have that as well): he is one of the most ungrammatical writers that has ever scribbled. What has happened there is that the 'one' has attracted the verb into the singular, where it should be governed by the plural relative pronoun 'that'.

Collective nouns of multitude are ancient ha-has into which we still continually fall. Is the Government, the board, the pack, the army a singular, or are they plurals? Alas and dammit, there is/are no hard and fast number of rules. English grammar is deplorably lax. One should avoid switching horses in mid-stream, starting in the singular, and then changing to a plural, as in, '*The Times* also gives some interesting comments by their special correspondent.' Here is a nice guiding principle, not a rule, if you must have one. If the sense of the sentence points one's attention to the constituents of the collective, the verb should be plural; if the sense directs one's attention to the collective as such, the verb should be singular. Thus: the council was elected in November; but the council are at sixes and sevens; the Government has issued a warning; but the Government are feeling the strain after four years of office. In practice the use of a singular verb with a collective noun is commoner, and is generally more convenient. Having chosen, stick to your choice, and avoid things like, 'the committee, which was appointed two years ago, presented their report yesterday.' Whom am I to tell you what to write? But if you start confusing number, we may end up by killing it as we have almost killed the subjunctive and case-endings.

Syntax, the mass parade of words, has also, like the rest of English, recently slackened and become less prescriptive. When grammar was taught as though it were governed by the laws of the Medes and the Persians, grammarians ruled that a sentence had to have a verb in it, and thumped us when, out of carelessness or perversity, we composed a verbless sentence. These were fairly low-grade grammarians in prep schools. The professionals always recognized that there was more to it than that simple rule. The relevant fascicle of *The Oxford English Dictionary*, published in 1912, defined a sentence more sensibly as a series of words in connected speech or writing, forming a grammatically complete expression of a single thought. It added, 'in popular use often such a portion of a composition or utterance as extends from one full stop to another.' The answer to anybody who says that you cannot have a verbless sentence can be given, with the alacrity of Dr Johnson refuting Berkeley, by writing one. Like this. The truth is that there always have been verbless sentences, for dramatic climax, comment to jerk one's readers awake, and other rhetorical reasons. Tacitus, that master of rhetorical effect, was addicted to them. The modern schools of poetry and prose have annihilated the rule that a sentence must have a verb. If you do it too often, without the genius of James Joyce, you will sound not like Joyce, but jerky. That is a priggish stylistic observation, not a grammatical one.

The most sensible modern definition of a sentence is that it is a sequence of words capable of standing alone to make an assertion,

ask a question, or give a command, usually consisting of a subject
and a predicate containing a finite verb. Usually, but not necessarily. That is a verbless sentence for emphasis and afterthought.

Let us take another great Shibboleth of English syntax, the split
infinitive. Anybody who reads the letters that readers write to
newspapers will be aware that the split infinitive is the error that
annoys them most. The only grammatical 'rule' that most people
retain from their schooldays is the one about not splitting infinitives. The best argument against splitting is that, if you do, you will
have so many letters to answer from correspondents eager to put
you right. But, as George Bernard Shaw once reminded an editor of
*The Times*, every writer worth his salt occasionally splits the
infinitive in order to avoid the much greater fault of ambiguity.

The 'to' of an infinitive is so much a part of the verb that they are
virtually one word, although written as two words. To separate
them by an adverb is a bold move, of the same kind of boldness as
writing a verbless sentence. But it is not difficult to construct
examples of sentences in which the only way to express your
meaning exactly is by splitting your infinitive.

For example: our object is to further improve modern English
grammar. This is preferable to, 'our object is to improve further
modern English grammar', which gives a sense different to the one
intended. It is also preferable to, 'our object is further to improve
modern English grammar', which leaves in doubt whether an
additional object or an additional improvement is the point. The
prudent writer might well recast his sentence so as to avoid splitting
the infinitive, and in consequence having to write dozens of letters
apologizing to pedantic know-alls. What a prudent writer is doing in
the first place, supposing that we can do anything as Quixotic as
improve modern English grammar, is another question.

W.H. Fowler maintained that a real split infinitive, though not
desirable in itself, was preferable to either of two things: to real
ambiguity, and to patent artificiality. An example of patent artificiality is, 'in not combining to forbid flatly split infinitives.' 'In not
combining flatly to forbid split infinitives' would be ambiguous; is a
flat combination being contrasted with a deep or rough combination? The only thing to do with the phrase is to be a devil and split,
'in not combining to flatly forbid split infinitives.'

I see no evidence that split infinitives are much more prevalent
than they were a generation ago. They may even be less prevalent,
since the rule about not splitting is the one 'rule' of English

grammar that everybody knows. What has changed is that we understand better how such rules work.

Prepositions are the awkward squad in the middle files of the middle rank on the parade ground of grammar. They change their dressing and their idiom more erratically than other steadier words. There is no need to panic. They always have. One recent tendency is to reinforce our verbs by attaching a tail of more or less useful prepositions to them. It is an American tendency. For example, there used to be the transitive verb 'to meet'. Now it has pupped its epigoni 'to meet with' and 'to meet up with', provoking purist Britons to ask what possible advantage there can be in using two or three words for the job that one word had done before.

Although I am not native in the United States and to the manner born, I dare say that one could make a case that the three variant idioms are not exact synonyms, but differentiate nice shades of meaning. 'To meet with' suggests a formal meeting: 'I cannot come today, I have to meet with my accountant.' 'To meet up with' is the informal and matey idiom for meeting a person or encountering a thing. Matiness and informality are not yet punishable offences in English grammar; but those of us who prefer economy in language can simply carry on meeting each other without benefit of prepositions.

The grammar of prepositions is as fluid as the rest of grammar. A generation ago there was a prescriptive school of grammarians who argued that the correct idiom was 'different from' rather than 'different to' or 'different than'. We do not say 'differ to'; therefore you cannot say 'different to'. On the contrary, we can and do, and good writers of all ages have done so. It is a superstition that an adjective derived from a verb must conform to the construction and prepositions of its parent verb. We say this 'accords with', but 'according to'; this 'pleases me', but 'pleasant to'; this 'suffices', but 'sufficient for'.

Surely we can agree, at least, that 'different than' is a solecism and a barbarism? It is becoming increasingly popular as an idiom in American speech and writing, probably by analogy from 'other than'. The comparative sense of 'different' makes 'than' the preposition of the month. Let us agree that 'different than' is an Americanism to be avoided by all stylish writers sensitive to idiom. The trouble with that is that you have to count out of your catalogue of stylish and sensitive writers Fuller, Addison, Steele, Defoe, Richardson, Goldsmith, Fanny Burney, Coleridge, Southey, De

Quincey, Carlyle, Thackeray, Newman, and a vast second eleven of good writers, all of whom used 'different than'. 'Different from' is the idiom that comes naturally to me; but we do not want to find ourselves in the position of the recruit on the parade ground, whose mother, watching the drill, said: 'Look; little Johnny is the only one in step.'

It is a moot point whether semantics, the study of the meaning of words, is part of grammar, or not. Let us for the moment assume that it is, and observe lugubriously that semantics changes as fast as the rest of grammar, causing grief and alarm to those who find that the meanings of words they were taught as children are slipping away from them. They write indignant letters to the newspapers pointing out that 'prestigious' is defined in *The Oxford English Dictionary* as 'practising juggling or legerdemain', and cannot mean 'endowed with the VIP quality of prestige'; that 'hopefully' means 'in a hopeful manner', not 'it is to be hoped'; that 'disinterested' is not a synonym for 'uninterested'.

We seem to feel this elegant semantic pain particularly in our generation, perhaps because it is happening faster. But we have no accumulated sense of pain from the huge changes that have occurred from Anglo-Saxon times onwards. We do not go around suffering because grammatical gender was given up between Anglo-Saxon and Middle English. Words drift. 'Lewd' to our Anglo-Saxon forefathers meant merely 'lay, that is, not clerical'. It drifted to become 'secular', and then 'worldly', and then to its modern meaning of filthy and rude. 'Meat' originally meant any sort of food, not particularly 'flesh of a beast'. 'Out of the eater came forth meat, and out of the strong came forth sweetness.' You will remember that the meat in that riddle was honey.

'Cunning' in the earliest recorded English meant knowledge or learning. The word has drifted down the centuries through various grades and shades of meaning until it has reached its present stage of craftiness. But its roots are preserved in the conning tower of a submarine, which is closer to the Anglo-Saxon meaning of knowing and learning.

Not all the semantic changes in language improve things; many of them erode useful distinctions that have been established over the years. The vogue use of 'disinterested' as a prestigious synonym for 'uninterested' reduces the language, because the available substitutes for 'disinterested' in its original meaning, 'impartial', 'unbiased', 'detached', 'unprejudiced', and so on, are not quite the same. But are we quite sure that the original meaning of 'disinterested' was impartial? The evidence is that 'disinterested' and 'uninterested' were used indifferently to mean 'uninterested' for several centuries before the distinction between them was established. It is, nevertheless, a useful distinction, and it is a shame that it is going.

I do not see that we are losing anything useful in the original meaning of 'prestigious' meaning 'being up to conjuring tricks and legerdemain'. Prestige as a noun has firmly established itself in the work-box of the English language. We may not much like the concept or the system of values it represents. But any noun needs an adjective, and it is going to find one somewhere.

'Hopefully' used absolutely to mean 'it is to be hoped' arouses passionate objections because it is unEnglish, because it is American, because it is confusing, and because it is pretentious. Of these, only the last objection is sensible. 'Hopefully' used absolutely is not unEnglish; there are dozens of adverbs that can stand on their own without qualifying a verb, from 'apparently' to 'presumably'. Some of them even have two forms, one for the absolute construction: 'Regrettably, we cannot come; we inform you regretfully.' When 'hopefully' spread across the Atlantic like genital herpes a decade ago, I wrote a priggish piece saying that it was confusing. We should no longer be able to tell what was meant by, 'To travel hopefully is a better thing than to arrive, and the true success is to labour.' I recant. I think that the experience of the past ten years has demonstrated that we can distinguish between 'hopefully' used to qualify a verb and 'hopefully' used absolutely. We do it in speech by accent and intonation; in writing we do it with commas to cordon off the absolute 'hopefully'. The fact that absolute 'hopefully' has established itself so widely throughout the United Kingdom indicates that it fills some linguistic need. I gave up any idea of struggle against the usage when a year or two ago a shepherd in the Highlands of Scotland used it constantly while we were walking his hill together. It is an Americanism. So what? In fact it was more probably originally a German-American or Yiddish-American expression.

The only persuasive argument against 'hopefully' that I can find today is that it is pretentious. It is a PR word, less straightforward than 'I hope', and used to suggest that more people are doing the hoping than may perhaps be the case. Anyway, it is not compulsory to use it.

This rapid survey of the parade ground English grammar, taking various exemplary squads and individual soldiers to march for all the others, may suggest chaos. Not chaos, but constant change is the condition of the grammar of any living, working language. Dr Johnson wrote in the preface to his *Dictionary of the English Language*: 'If the changes that we fear be thus irresistible, what remains but to acquiesce with silence, as in the other insurmountable distresses of humanity? It remains that we retard what we cannot repel, that we palliate what we cannot cure.' Only a fool would argue with Samuel, the patron saint of English letters. But in this instance he may have exaggerated a trifle the evil of changes in language. Of course there is good English and bad English. Writers of genius like Johnson set the standards for the rest of us, and we have a linguistic and literary obligation to follow them as well as we can.

Some reputable and talented commentators take an apocalyptically pessimistic view of the future of English. They are right to point out that there are strong centrifugal forces pulling English apart: nationalist and racialist pride, the increasing dominance of the spoken word, the proliferation of teachers of English for whom English is not their first language, the feeling that one should do one's own thing, in language as in everything else. We should, however, point out to them that there are also strong centripetal forces at work in English: television and the other mass media, including pop songs, mass tourism by all sorts and conditions of people, and above all the printed word and our good writers. My guess is that English will hang together as the world language, with a strong central core surrounded by a rich profusion of dialects and jargons, all largely unintelligible to outsiders. But, even if the pessimists prove right, it is not the end of the world. Look at the rich things that grew out of the fragmentation of Latin.

# 8/SPELLING

'Take care that you never spell a word wrong. Always before you write a word, consider how it is spelled, and, if you do not remember it, turn to a dictionary. It produces great praise to a lady to spell well.'
Thomas Jefferson, *Letter to Martha Jefferson*, 1783

    'When the English tongue we speak,
      Why is *break* not rhymed with *freak*?
    Will you tell me why it's true
    We say *sew* but likewise *Jew*?'
Evelyn Baring, Lord Cromer, *Spectator*, 9 August 1902

English spelling is notoriously difficult, extravagant, and vexing. For nearly two centuries it was the subject on which most time and tears were expended in British schools, with generations of children working their way through readers, and Spelling Bees, and lists of tricky words from diarrhoea to, well, eschscholtzia.

The urge that made orthography queen of the British curriculum was a typically British wish not to appear lower class, and not to be mocked. That great snob, Lord Chesterfield, put the reasons for spelling correctly in a letter to his son of 19 November 1750:

'I come now to another part of your letter, which is the orthography, if I may call bad spelling *orthography*. You spell induce, *enduce*; and grandeur, you spell *grandure*; two faults, of which few of my house-maids would have been guilty. I must tell you, that orthography, in the true sense of the word, is so absolutely necessary for a man of letters, or a gentleman, that one false spelling may fix a ridicule upon him for the rest of his life; and I know a man of quality, who never recovered the ridicule of having spelled *wholesome* without the *w*.'

No doubt, for homiletic purposes, Lord Chesterfield was exaggerating the life-long humiliation of a single misspelling, and laying on with a trowel the literacy of his house-maids. We know that women were notoriously given a worse education than their male counterparts in social class. See Swift's *A Letter to a Young Lady on her Marriage*, published in 1727:

'It is a little hard that not one Gentleman's daughter in a

thousand should be brought to read or understand her own natural tongue, or be judge of the easiest Books that are written in it: and it is no wonder, when they are not so much as taught to spell in their childhood, nor can ever attain to it in their whole lives.'

Spelling became not merely the shibboleth that distinguished one as a gent, or even a lady. A century later bad spelling could ruin one's career as well as one's social standing. Dr Morell, a famous Inspector of Schools in England, was quoted in 1877 as remarking that: 'Out of 1,972 failures in the Civil Service examinations, 1,866 candidates were *plucked for spelling*. That is, eighteen out of every nineteen who failed, failed in Spelling.'

There has been a reaction against such extreme emphasis on orthography above other more useful forms of knowledge. In the 1970s an official witness of the National Union of Teachers advanced the opinion to a Parliamentary Select Committee that spelling was a trivial matter, and that no time should be wasted on teaching it in English schools. The modern emphasis is on creative writing, and on getting children to express themselves.

This is a more liberal and sensible priority. But, with the best will in the world, we cannot pretend that the standard of spelling is what it was. The examiners of Greats, the stiffest undergraduate degree at Oxford, and accordingly anywhere in the world, reported confidentially in 1983 that they had tried not to penalize candidates for less than perfect English, remembering that strange things can happen when people are writing at speed, that Gertrude Bell won her First in 1886 despite a lifelong tendency to write one of her favourite words as *pidgeon*, and that it was not her fantastic misspellings that lost Winifred Holtby her First in 1921 but flippancy about the private life of Henry VIII. But they did not positively welcome a total absence of apostrophes, or the frequent appearance of the following:

'*Absense, acomodate, acuracy, my advise is, advisor, agression, ellusive, augeries, benefitted, bourne out, Cataline, closetted, cruxial, concensus, confidante* (used of males), *championned, descision, dissafectation, developement, expedience, extravagent, exercizing, fulfill, flowt, hommage, independant, incompetance, indigent* (for indigenous), *irrelevence, Lybia, neglegable, obediance, occured, ommissions, payed, Pelopponese, permited, philibustering, pivotted, practiced, the practises, primarilly, privelege, privilidge, profitted, proffessional, prophecying, plaigerised, revealling, seige, sieze, seperate, significence, stationned, successfull, supercede, unprincipalled, unprovoced, willfull, yoeman.'*

For at least the past two centuries, since spelling became a King Charles's Head for teachers and parents, there have been two prevalent attitudes to orthography.

The first sees correct spelling as the final mark of full literacy, and rigid adherence to the complex and illogical rules of English spelling as a test of whether one is educated, an AB-Reader, and even worth employing. In its extreme acceptance this attitude is clearly rigid and silly. Shakespeare was a rotten speller. At its worst, bad spelling is slovenliness and carelessness, like having egg-stains on one's tie: Dr Johnson was notoriously careless about egg-stains, and indifferent to clean linen. In certain jobs, such as those of secretary, sub-editor, English teacher, humanities don, and publisher, it is necessary to spell correctly. But, if one cannot learn to spell, one can always buy a good dictionary, and look up the spelling of doubtful words. The new generations of the sixties and seventies came out of school and college saying: 'I can wear my hair long; I don't have to wear a tie (tights, if they were girls); and I can spell as I want, provided I do my own thing, and express my true feelings.' This may have been imprudent: prospective employers and customers rated the minor virtues of correct spelling and ties without egg-stains more highly than they did. It may even have been mistaken: why should we take your attempts to communicate with us in writing seriously, if you cannot take the trouble to get even the trivial matter of spelling right? But the modern tendency is to devalue the importance of orthography. It is bound to affect what happens to English spelling over the next fifty years.

The second principal attitude to spelling has been the urge to reform it; to invent a simpler, more logical system of English spelling that will be easier to learn, and will represent more accurately the way that words are pronounced. This attitude has often been held in conjunction with the former attitude, respect for orthography. Its proponents want more people to be able to achieve literacy and orthography.

It is an attitude that is bound to increase its momentum as the century grows older, and more people from Manila to Manchester wrestle with the mysteries of spelling English as a second language. But it is not a self-evident truth that a new system for writing English would be an improvement. For one thing, if we are going to spell phonetically, so that the written word represents more closely the way it is pronounced, whose pronunciation are we going to imitate, in a world in which the pronunciation of English is becoming increasingly diverse? For another thing, English spelling often conveys information about the etymology and meaning of a word: if you could devise a completely phonetic system of spelling (impossible) homophones would become homographs, and the spelling would no longer help us to distinguish between *air* and *heir*, *son* and *sun*, *vane* and *vain* and *vein*, *whether* and *weather* and *wether*. New phonetic spelling would cut off twenty centuries of history of the English language, some of it informative, all of it valuable.

For another thing, the improvers of spelling, like all sects and fanatics, although passionate that something has to be done, can never agree on What is to be Done? Over the past century dozens of new systems of spelling have been proposed, each of them promising Utopia of Orthography, where the wolf shall spell with the lamb, and a little child shall lead them into the land of easy literacy. And for another thing, most of these improved systems of spelling are artificial. Changes in language that stick tend to be organic growths. In particular the English, who have a national genius (vice?) for evolving national institutions rather than making revolutionary changes or wiping the blackboard and starting again from the beginning, resist artificial changes. Not many artificial languages or elements of language have caught on. Esperanto was introduced in 1887 by Dr L.L. Zamenhof. A century later it shows no signs of becoming the universal language. The handle Ms was artificially created in the 1960s, in order to satisfy feminist unwillingness to be labelled by marital status. That has caught on. But there is formidable resistance, not the least part of which is British reverence for traditional ways, to the introduction of any new system of spelling; as the reformers have found.

The past can help to explain the future. Before considering the ways in which spelling is going to develop for the rest of this century and into the twenty-first, it is instructive to see what happened in the past. Unlike a Romance language or a purer Germanic language, English is not a seamless robe woven from a single thread from the past, modified by local custom and colour. It is a patchwork of Anglo-Saxon and Old Norse, Norman French and clerks' Latin, Wessex and Kent, Mercia and Northumbria, the conventions of printers and the customs of pedagogues. England has always been a refuge for exiles and a new home for immigrants from around the world. Their languages have enriched English, and complicated English spelling.

In the beginning was Old English. In the fifth century AD waves of Germanic invaders from the continent invaded and subjugated the Celtic and Romano-British inhabitants of Britain. The immigrants came from two principal tribes, the Angles and the Saxons. They were pagans, boasting ideals of loyalty and vengeance, and walking in fear of fate. There is evidence to suggest that they brought the Germanic runic alphabet with them.

Within two hundred years they had been converted to Christianity, to such effect that England was the centre of missionary endeavour, and, for a time, the heart of European civilization. Their Anglo-Saxon language began to grow away from its Germanic roots as soon as they landed, in the same way that American English began to grow away from British English as soon as the first settlers landed. The written word was an important medium for spreading the Word of God. In addition, the church took an immediate interest in the codification of law. English orthography starts to evolve in Bibles, service books, and lawcodes, almost immediately after Augustine landed in Kent on his mission from Pope Gregory the Great to convert the English, and, incidentally, to start the long story of English spelling.

As England evolved politically through a number of petty kingdoms, so the English language evolved in a number of regional dialects and spellings. By the end of the eighth century these had been absorbed into three dominant kingdoms and dialects: Northumbria, Mercia, and West Saxon and Kent. In the ninth century Norsemen, distant cousins of the Anglo-Saxons, and speaking a related language, invaded across the North Sea and subjugated most of Northumbria and Mercia, which became known as the Danelaw. Alfred, King of the West Saxons, fought a rear-guard action in Wessex, and by the momentous victory at the Battle of Ethandun (Edington in Wiltshire) stopped the Norsemen from subjugating the whole of England. The dividing line between Wessex and the Danelaw ran along the old Roman road between London and Chester known as Watling Street. The old division is still marked by the difference in place-names, dialect, and spellings on either side of the line. Language lasts longer than stone or law.

In the tenth century Alfred's successors conquered the Danish areas, and unified England under the West Saxon royal house. Written records from this period are sparse, and often consist of Anglo-Saxon glosses in the margins of church writings in Latin. But the experts can distinguish the four dialects of Northumbrian,

Mercian, Kentish, and West Saxon, and four slightly different conventions of spelling, vocabulary, syntax, and accidence in the four regions.

As Wessex established political dominance over the rest of England, so the West Saxon dialect and house-style of spelling became the standard for scribes working in all the great church word-factories, from Winchester and Canterbury to Durham and Lindisfarne. After the ruinous Viking invasions, there was a period of peace and consolidation. The Benedictine order was reformed, and revitalized monastic life. Alfred had personally promoted a series of translations from Latin into English in his revival of religion and learning. The demand for books in the vernacular was unparalleled in the rest of Europe. And the professional scribes who copied the books developed a universally accepted standard of orthography for Old English. This is the simple foundation on which the rickety structure of subsequent English spelling has been erected. The final stage of Anglo-Saxon spelling was more phonetic than English spelling has ever been since: each letter represented a single sound; there were none of your tiresome modern silent consonants, as in 'debt' and 'thought'; the vowels were more simply denoted than in subsequent English, with each vowel grapheme equalling one vowel position. English was the only vernacular in Europe, widely used in official documents, with a fully developed literary form and standard spelling.

The Norman Conquest in 1066 was the watershed in English orthography, as it was in so many other aspects of English life. It effectively destroyed the last occasion when English was simple to spell, because it was spelled as it was sounded.

The new ruling class of noblemen and clerics spoke, as Duke William did, the *langue d'oil*, the language of northern France. This became the language of the court, and of parliament and the law, until the fourteenth century. The English became a subject people, separated from their rulers by race and language. We can still see the great divide in the language: the Anglo-Saxon peasants looked after the cows, calves, swine, and sheep in the fields, and developed surnames such as Shepherd and Howard or Hog-ward. When the creatures got to the table, the Normans ate them as beef, veal, pork, and mutton. English as the only fully developed standard literary form in Europe was lost, not because the conquerors suppressed it, but because they had no use for it.

Spelling broke up in English. There was no English in official documents to set a national standard. The executive arm of the state could neither speak nor read the language. There was an immediate decline in the secular demand for books in any language: the new Norman rulers were not great readers, far less literate than their Anglo-Saxon subjects. Those who wanted books, wanted them in French or Latin.

Generations of political, social, and orthographic upheaval followed the Norman Conquest. Slowly the two languages amalgamated as the two races grew together, helped by such linguistic bridge-builders as clerks, bailiffs, nurses, and foremen. It was a time of rapid development of the language. But it developed piecemeal and regionally, not nationally, because nobody was setting a national standard at the centre. The rulers were issuing no secular or ecclesiastical documents in English. The feudal system favoured local and regional isolation. And the language itself was becoming looser and mongrel. In 1350 the Black Death wiped out a third of the population in less than two years. Those who were left to speak English were speaking a less elaborate language that was ceasing to be inflected. Gender was going. The English no longer wanted to remember that while *woman* was masculine, *wife* was neuter. French words, spelling, and pronunciation invaded English. Something like forty per cent of the English vocabulary in a dictionary today is derived from French: the proportion of Gallic words in an average sentence is much smaller, because most of the basic words, the nuts and bolts of the language, are English. After the Conquest the Englishman had to recognize (and pronounce, and spell) an alien *government*, *royalty*, *authority*, and *parliament*. Even if his *sovereign* was a *tyrant*, he had to pay his *taxes* to the *exchequer*, or *exchange* his *liberty* for a *dungeon*.

The French invasion of English, and the diffused development of English along regional channels, like a great river breaking into separate channels in its delta, are the two great changes that distinguish Middle English from Old English. Each jerry-built eccentric erections on the foundation of Anglo-Saxon spelling. Each affected the way we spell today.

Three centuries after the invasion, the pretence of bilingualism, Norman French for the ruling class, English for the ruled, finally collapsed. Parliament admitted that French was 'much unknown in the said realm', and that ordinary citizens in legal and administrative proceedings had 'no understanding of that which is said for them or against them'. The combination of these two great languages, one Germanic, one Romance, had created the richest vocabulary and the most irrational spelling in the world.

The separate development of Middle English came to an end with the end of the Middle Ages and feudalism. As politically a centralized government emerged, so linguistically a standard dialect and spelling began to evolve. Standard spelling followed the government, that is, the court. It is chance that we have ended with the dialect of English that we have. If the ambulatory kings of the Middle Ages, for ever on chevachee or warfare around their kingdom, had settled in Hereford, or Worcester, or Gloucester for their capital, English today would be spoken and spelled in the west midlands dialect that philologists call AB.

If they had settled in Oxford, another favourite port for the perambulations of the court, modern English and modern spelling would have developed from the Wycliffite literary standard. In fact the court came to rest at Westminster, just outside London; and the Middle English dialect of London became the national, and now the international, standard for written English as a world language.

At the same time the spread of learning and the growth of wealth diffused the demand for books. The great universities were founded. Literacy spread among the new merchant classes. Cheaper paper replaced expensive parchment, and brought books and reading, and consequently standard spelling, within reach of a much greater proportion of the population. And book production started to pass out of the hands of the clerks in the monasteries, and into the hands of the new secular craft of scrivener. Chancery, the court that kept the public records, passed out of clerical hands into secular, and removed from Westminster Abbey to Chancery Lane.

The proliferation of writing, soon vastly increased by the invention of printing, created an irresistible impulse towards a standard dialect and standard spelling for English. Because of the accidents of politics, the standards selected were the London standards of the south-east of England.

The Renaissance is generally understood to refer to the rediscovery of classical culture and learning after the sleep of the Middle Ages. It had just as much to do with a flowering of vernacular literature throughout Europe. Thomas More wrote *Utopia* in Latin, but he was a creative innovator in English. Fifteen years after he died, *Utopia* appeared in English. The sixteenth-century poets and playwrights were as adventurous with their language, as their contemporaries were with their discoveries around the oceans of the world. Poets were often buccaneers and explorers in their spare time: Sir Philip Sidney, Drake, Raleigh, and their peers. The greatest of them had small Latin and less Greek, but minted more new words and adventurous spellings for the English language than anybody before or since, including James Joyce.

The exuberant flowering of language had little time to bother with orthography. But after it the printing press and the schoolmasters started to impose standards. The writers themselves wanted rules. Caxton had taken over the conventions of the best medieval scribes; and in general the early printers adhered to the medieval scribal tradition. In the hurry of the new invention and the bustling century, they did not yet see any virtue in consistent spelling. Elizabethan compositors often varied the spelling of words in order to justify a line of type, so that it fitted the right length. Their readers were used to seeing the same word spelled in different ways on the same page.

The idiosyncratic spelling of different printers has been closely studied in the works of the most minutely studied of all English writers, Shakespeare. Books, and marshlands of glosses under the thin trickle of text at the top of the page, have been devoted to the preference of Compositor A in the first folio for the spellings *doe*, *goe*, and *here*, contrasted with the preference of Compositor B for *do*, *go*, and *heere*.

But gradually standard spelling came in. It has been suggested that the English Civil Wars had an important influence: printers, heavily engaged in the war of words by political pamphlet that preceded the war of swords, had no time to bother with more than one way of spelling a word, even for the sake of obtaining a better justified line. Others have suggested the King James Bible of 1611 as an influence to orthography. This is clearly nonsense. A quick look shows that the only consistency in spelling is that the printers always preferred the spelling that suited their spacing best. Subsequent editions of the Authorized Version in 1629 and 1638 gradually got rid of most of the variant spellings, but this was an effect, not the cause, of greater spelling stability.

The influence towards standard spelling in the sixteenth century came from several directions. There were the philosophers of spelling, such as Sir Thomas Smith, a famous Cambridge don, who published in 1568 *De recta et emendata linguae anglicae scriptione dialogus* ('A dialogue concerning the correct and improved orthography of the English language'). Smith was a notable classical scholar, and his book was, naturally, in Latin. Other influential works that argued for standard spelling were John Hart's *An*

*Orthographie* (1569), Richard Mulcaster's *The First Part of the Elementarie* (1582), and Alexander Gil's *Logonomia Anglica*, in Latin (1619).

There were the pedagogues, who put the precepts of the philosophers into practice. Such was Edmond Coote, master of the free school at Bury St Edmunds, who published *The English Schoolmaister* in 1596. In his preface Coote wrote:

'I undertake to teach all my scholers, that shall be trayned up for any grammar schoole, that they shall neuer erre in writing the true orthography of any word truly pronounced . . . and the same profit doe I offer vnto all other both men & women, that now for want hereof are ashamed to write vnto their best friends: for which I haue heard many gentlewomen offer much.' Coote's spelling may be shaky by modern standards. But he expresses an early disapproval of bad spelling, and an early desire for orthography.

As people became aware of the arguments of the philosophers, the teaching of the pedagogues, and the poor impression of slovenliness and lack of education created by bad spelling, there was a vogue for popular spelling books. Richard Mulcaster was the first headmaster of the Merchant Taylors' School, later High Master of St Paul's, and is assumed to have been mobbed up in the character of Holofernes, the pedantic schoolmaster in *Love's Labour's Lost*. His book had a great vogue. Edmond Coote's book enjoyed enormous popularity over a long period. Its fifty-fourth edition was recorded as late as 1737. The popular mood was towards standardization. The Age of Reason respected rules and logic, symmetry and standards, qualities it found in Greece and Rome.

Printers and pedagogues lived off each other, as they still do. Printers made money out of the spelling books. Spelling books influenced the house style of printers.

There was a proposal to establish an English Academy, on the lines of the Académie Française, founded in 1635, to police the language, regularize the grammar, throw out the 'bad' words, restore the good, and lay down standards for spelling. It was supported by the Royal Society, and by literary eminences such as Dryden, Evelyn, and Swift. The Government even gave the proposal its backing in 1712.

No British Academy was formed. No academic or official dictionary was published to revise the orthography. An Englishman's language, like his home, is his castle, and he is peculiarly resistant to official attempts by the authorities to tinker with it.

But Johnson's *A Dictionary of the English Language*, published

in 1755, had a profound influence. He is sometimes said to have
created a standard English spelling. This is to misunderstand what
he did. He suffered from no delusion that he was acting as a one-
man arbiter of orthography. By his time the spelling was already
well on the way to being fixed. In his Preface, Johnson wrote:

> 'In adjusting the orthography, which has been to this time
> unsettled and fortuitous, I found it necessary to distinguish those
> irregularities that are inherent in our tongue, and perhaps coeval
> with it, from others which the ignorance or negligence of later
> writers has produced . . . Even in words of which the derivation is
> apparent, I have been often obliged to sacrifice uniformity to
> custom; thus I write, in compliance with a numberless majority,
> *convey* and *inveigh*, *deceit* and *receipt*, *fancy* and *phantom*;
> sometimes the derivative varies from the primitive, as *explain* and
> *explanation*, *repeat* and *repetition*. Some combinations of letters
> having the same power are used indifferently without any dis-
> coverable reason of choice, as in *choak*, *choke*; *soap*, *sope*; *fewel*,
> *fuel*, and many others; which I have sometimes inserted twice,
> that those who search for them under either form, may not search
> in vain.'

Johnson was the only writer of genius who ever produced a
dictionary, which is why it is good to read. His system of citing
examples of the best authorities, of indicating etymology, and
pronunciation, are still followed by lexicographers. (There are even
jokes in the *Dictionary*: having announced that he will quote from
no living authors in his *Dictionary*, because he does not want to
make invidious choices about whom to include, he proceeds to
quote extensively from his own works, and on at least one occasion
attributes a tag from Alexander Pope to Samuel Johnson.)

Johnson is important to the history of spelling because his
*Dictionary* was the first to be accepted universally as the standard of
usage and spelling. It was followed, closely, by all dictionaries
during the following century and until the *Oxford English Dictionary*, which is clearly a descendant of Johnson. Like the dictionaries
of the French Academy, almost contemporary with his, Johnson's
*Dictionary* became the accepted standard for private spelling.
Every Englishman's house had the Bible, Shakespeare, and Johnson's *Dictionary*. Johnson followed the spelling generally adopted
by the printers, and established it in private use as the standard of
literate English writers and spellers.

The spelling evolved for the London dialect of Middle English, and written down and broadcast by Dr Johnson, is still largely the one we use today. Dr Johnson would find little to puzzle him, at least in the way of spelling (apart from misprints) in a modern issue of *The Times*, the first issue of which appeared in the year after his death. This is one of the reasons why English spelling is so unphonetic and difficult for those not trained in the history of the language. Spelling was standardized by printers and others at the end of a period of very rapid change in pronunciation, especially in its vowels. Elizabethan English would have sounded quaintly Mummerset, even to Dr Johnson. By the time orthography was fixed, it had become completely unphonetic. Further discrepancies and complications arose when letters were inserted in words, where they were not pronounced, for purely etymological reasons (for example, *debt*, *doubt*), or for reasons of analogy (for example, *delight* and *tight*). The evolution of standard spelling produced a beautiful, complex, but peculiar creature.

Since Dr Johnson's great report on the state of the language, there have been enormous changes. Hundreds of thousands of exotic spellings have come into the English lexicon from India to North America, from *kimono* to *tapioca*, as English has become a world language, and draws its vocabularies from the round earth's imagin'd corners. Johnson disapproved of such borrowings, and called them 'barbarous colloquialisms'. But he knew that he could not keep them out of the mighty engine of English: 'If the changes that we fear be thus irresistible, what remains but to acquiesce with silence, as in the other insurmountable distresses of humanity? It remains that we retard what we cannot repel, that we palliate what we cannot cure. Life may be lengthened by care, though death cannot be ultimately defeated: tongues, like governments, have a natural tendency to degeneration; we have long preserved our constitution, let us make some struggles for our language.'

In the same period thousands of words have died from neglect, their spellings forgotten; for example, the useful word *humdudgeon* meaning a sort of hypochondriac's flu. It is probably derived from 'humbug' and 'dudgeon'; the example of its use given in Grose's *Dictionary of the Vulgar Tongue* is: 'He has got the humdudgeon; nothing ails him except low spirits.'

Thousands of other words have changed their meanings to meet new needs and serve new purposes. Locke called Isaac Newton a 'nice' man. He didn't mean, as we should today, that Newton was an amiable chap, but that he was touchy and irritable. If Locke had called a *woman* nice, he would have meant that she was what we term today 'fast'. There is an example of the male bias of the English language to outrage feminists. In the sixteenth century a 'painful, experimental' Puritan preacher was not a pain to listen to, because of his trendy props and visual aids. He was a painstaking orator who preached from personal experience and witness. The adjectives have changed their meanings. In Dr Johnson's time, *prestigious* meant tricky, as in legerdemain.

There have been many changes of meaning since Dr Johnson, and very many new words. Changes in spelling have been comparatively few. The most pronounced tendency has been to standardize and restrict diversity of spelling: where Johnson recognized several spellings, the Victorians and we have settled on a single invariable one. In a very few words the haphazard old diversity persists, as in *shew/show*, *inquire/enquire*, and *grey/gray*. Sometimes the variant spellings stuck to different meanings of the same word, and are now regarded as different words: for example, *metal/mettle*, and *flour/flower*. Gothic or 'black-letter' type used by the early printers gave way to Roman characters, and long *s* used in the first edition of Johnson's *Dictionary* was replaced later by ordinary *s*. The Middle English preference for a *v* initially and *u* in the middle of a word, still copied by Johnson, gave way to the convention of using *u* for the vowel and *v* for the consonant. In the same way *j* came to be used for the consonant, and *i* for the vowel. The Middle English tendency to use *y* as a spelling for *i* next to *m*, *n*, and *u*, in order to avoid manuscript misreadings, did not long survive the invention of printing. The sounds developed from Middle English open *e* and *o* came in the sixteenth and seventeenth centuries to be represented by *ea* and *oa*, as in *eat*, *deal*, *loaf*, *broad*. It became standard to avoid a final *oa*, hence *foe* and *toe*. Similarly it became correct to represent the sounds of the Middle English closed e and o, by *ee*, *oo*, and in addition the exotic *ie* for the former, following French influence: hence *keen*, *see*, *cool*, *doom*, and *field*.

The other egregious change in English spelling since Dr Johnson has been the branching off of American spelling. Such linguistic divergence is natural, when the speakers and spellers of a language are separated by government, custom, and an ocean. The fugleman who exemplified the change, and first differentiated between British and American usage, was Noah Webster, the teacher, journalist, and lexicographer. His *Spelling Book*, the first part of his *A Grammatical Institute of the English Language* (1783–85), played a fundamental part in American education by standardizing spellings that differed from the British. It was so widely used that by 1890 this book, with its four hundred revisions, had sold more than 60,000,000 copies. His great *An American Dictionary of the English Language* (1828) took the position, which seemed revolutionary at the time, that an American dictionary should include Americanisms, and should base its definitions and spellings on the usage of American as well as British writers.

It is an agreeable paradox of lexicography that in his *American Spelling Book* Webster rejected the spelling that seems today the most typically American: the dropping of the 'u' from such words as *honour* and *favour*. At this stage in his career Webster was following Johnson's spelling, and castigating attempts at reform. Writing of reformers who wanted to drop the 'u' from *honour* and *favour*, Webster wrote: 'It happens unluckily that, in these words, they have dropped the wrong letter – they have omitted the letter that is sounded, and retained one that is silent; for the words are pronounced *onur*, *favur*.'

But Webster included the variant spellings *honor*, *color*, *humor*, *favor*, and other such words in his *Dictionary*. And American preference gradually came round to selecting them as American spellings; but not until well into the twentieth century. Most of the other characteristic American spellings were first recorded by Webster: the preference for endings in *-er* where the British write *-re*, as in *center*, *meter*, *reconnoiter*, *saltpeter*, *theater*, and so on; the preference for the single rather than the double *ll* in derivatives in *-ed*, *-ing*, *-er*, or *-or* of words ending in an *l*, as in *disheveled*, *equaling*, *jeweler*, and such as *woolen* and *marvelous*; conversely, the tiresome preference for *ll* where Britons write a single *l*, as in *enroll* and *instill*, and *fulfill*, *skillful*, and in nouns in *-ment*, such as *fulfillment* and *installment*; preference for a single *p* where Britons write a double *pp*, as in *kidnaped* and *worshiper*; the similar preference for a single *t* where Britons write a double *tt*, as in *carbureted* and *sulfureted*; the tendency to replace *ae* and *oe* in words derived from Greek and Latin, as in *etiology*, *hemoglobin*, and *esophagus*; the preference for *-ize* in verbs and their derivatives that have been or could have been derived from Greek verbs, where Britons prefer *-ise*.

These and other American spellings were fixed by custom and usage, not lexicographers. But Webster was influential, because he stated the self-evident truth that Americans were no more bound by London spelling than by Westminster law; and because he provided the tools that taught the schools.

The wish to reform English spelling, to make it correspond more closely to pronunciation, and consequently simpler to learn, has run in parallel to the wish to standardize it for the past four centuries. A very early instance of it was initiated by a controversy over the correct pronunciation of Ancient Greek started by Erasmus. Two Cambridge dons, Sir John Cheke and Sir Thomas Smith, adopted the revised phonetic pronunciation recommended by Erasmus. Smith was moved to carry on and write the first printed proposal for English spelling reform, *De recta et emendata linguae anglicae scriptione dialogus*, mentioned above. Smith argued that as different languages have different sounds, they need somewhat different alphabets. He offered an extended Latin alphabet to cope with the English sound system, introducing new symbols drawn from Greek, early English, and his own imagination, together with a series of diacritics. John Hart, in his *An Orthographie*, proposed an international phonetic alphabet, in order to simplify the teaching of reading, to enable 'rude, country Englishmen', as well as foreigners, to pronounce in what has come to be called Received Pronunciation, and to make it easier to learn foreign languages.

From then on the voice of the spelling reformers has seldom been silent; though they have seldom spoken in unison. John Wilkins, Master of Trinity College, Cambridge, and later Bishop of Chester, was a notable reformer of the seventeenth century. His *Essay towards a Real Character and a Philosophical Language* (1668) invented an international phonetic alphabet to represent a universal sound system. As usual with logical new spelling systems, it fell on stone-deaf ground, and Englishmen carried on mis-spelling in the good old way. Dr Johnson remarked: 'Bishop Wilkins proposed, without expecting to be followed, a regular orthography.' Johnson took a characteristically bullish line with the reformers, tossing and goring them when opportunity presented itself: 'Ingenious men, who endeavoured to deserve well of their country, by writing *honor* and *labor* for *honour* and *labour*, *red* for *read*, in the preter-tense, *sais* for *says*, *repete* for *repeat*, *explane* for *explain*, or *declame* for *declaim*. Of these it may be said, that as they have done no good, they have done little harm; both because they have innovated little, and because few have followed them.'

A notable reformer of the eighteenth century was Benjamin Franklin, who proposed a reformed alphabet, because, 'If we go on as we have done a few Centuries longer, our words will gradually cease to express Sounds, they will only stand for things, as the written words do in the Chinese Language.' His young correspondent in London, Mary Stevenson, replied in the Franklin reformed alphabet, stating the customary objections to reform: obliteration of etymology, reduction of homophones to homonyms, and general increase of ambiguity. Franklin replied with his famous justification of the lasting advantages of a reformed system:

> 'To either you or me, who spell well in the present mode, I imagine the difficulty of changing that mode for the new is not so great, but that we might perfectly get over it in a week's writing. As to those who do not spell well, if the two difficulties are compared, (viz.) that of teaching them true spelling in the present mode, and that of teaching them the new alphabet and the new spelling according to it; I am confident that the latter would be by far the least. They naturally fall into the new method already, as much as the imperfection of their alphabet will admit of; their present bad spelling is only bad, because contrary to the present bad rules; under the new rules it would be good. The difficulty of learning to spell well in the old way is so great, that few attain it; thousands and thousands writing on to old age, without ever being able to acquire it.'

Weight was added to the case for reform in the nineteenth century by two groups of improbable bedfellows: missionaries and secretaries. Missionaries, trying to make the Bible accessible to non-literate converts, devised new alphabets, inevitably phonemic. Their efforts emphasized what an indirect and confused relationship the roman alphabet, as used in English, had with the English sound system. And shorthand typists, with their new systems of shorthand that took down the sounds rather than the letters, illustrated how very odd much traditional English spelling was.

The eminent Victorian champion of spelling reform was Isaac Pitman, inventor of the shorthand that bears his name, and the first system to be wholly based on phonetic principles. In the United States there were numerous attempts to introduce phonetic alphabets, in order to make spelling easier for immigrants from many countries. The American Spelling Reform Association was founded in 1876. It produced a modified phonemic roman alphabet of thirty-two letters, which was taken up rather less enthusiastically than deep-freezes in Iceland. The British Spelling Reform Association was founded in 1879, and included not only the philological élite, but celebrities like Tennyson and Darwin. As if there were a shortage of patent reformed orthographies, the British Association proposed three new reform schemes within six years. Most schemes of orthographic improvement being very laughable things, they died the death, like all the others.

In the United States in 1906 Andrew Carnegie gave a quarter of a million dollars to help to set up the Simplified Spelling Board. Not much has been heard from it since, except that it has, inevitably, pupped two sister organizations, the Simplified Spelling League, and the Simplified Spelling Association. In the United Kingdom the British Simplified Spelling Society was set up at the beginning of the century, with the support of the great and the good and the enthusiastic. Bernard Shaw campaigned for an entirely new alphabet, and left money in his will to create and promote a newly designed set of forty characters to be used in strict, one-to-one phonetic correspondence with speech sounds. Every so often there is a new surge of enthusiasm for reform. As always, the reformers can never agree on a perfect system, and can never stick to any proposed system for long. Nor can they recognize that there is more to any system of writing than the representation of sounds. No language can cut off its roots, or free itself from its history. English spelling, in its complex and often infuriating beauty, represents fifteen centuries of development of the language. The English way, with the language as with the constitution, is to adapt rather than scrap and replace.

After that somewhat breathless summary of how we have achieved the spelling that we have got today, we can venture a peer into the future, always reminding ourselves that prophecy is a fashionable superstition. History does not repeat itself. There is no reason that an extrapolation of what has happened in the past to the evolution of orthography should be an accurate guide to what is about to happen. Nevertheless, if you have to roll out the fatuous crystal ball, the following points are commonsensical. Dr Johnson would approve.

1.   English spelling is chaotic, difficult; and beautiful.

2.   The pressure to simplify it is bound to grow because of two new factors: the new technology of computers and mechanical reading and writing; and the millions of new English-speakers learning and teaching English as a second language.

3.   It is no longer good enough to dismiss the case for reform with the élitist nonchalance of Swift: 'The foolish opinion advanced of late years that we ought to spell exactly as we speak.' Chinese, Eskimoes, Portuguese au pair girls, and Italian waiters are not going to have the time to learn the nuances of etymology, meaning,

and history that lie hidden in traditional English spelling. If we do not look out we shall create a two-class system of apartheid in spelling: the complete works for educated native-speakers, and a simplified phonetic system for barbarians and hoi polloi. This would be a disaster.

4.   Because of its mongrel origins, English is exceptionally intractable to phonetic spelling. Variations of stress play havoc with syllable sounds, and make it peculiarly difficult to devise a system that spells words of the same family in the same way. Eminent and thoughtful philologists have come to the conclusion that the system of spelling English that has grown organically, in spite of its often cited inconsistencies, comes remarkably close to being the best possible orthographic system for so complex a language.

5.   Spelling reformers have yet to devise a better system, or even a system on which they can all agree for more than ten minutes. It is easier to see the advantages of a simplified system than to devise one, or to recognize how much we should lose by amputating the etymology and history of our spelling.

6.   Radical reform may eventually come: either because the pressure from new technology and new learners of the world language becomes irresistible; or because some literary genius as great as Dr Johnson invents a better system; or because the language decays and degenerates.

7.   Until that happens, we might as well carry on in the empirical English way, removing useless excrescences, and simplifying piece-meal, where we can do so without losing something of value. Like other branches of a living language, spelling is constantly growing and changing. We need to continue to evolve an orthography that does not overburden learners of English as a second language, destroy the information other than pronunciation that spelling gives, or outrage native writers of English by its crudity.

8.   We may have to give up the nicer etymological spellings, the reason for which is apparent only to scholars. For example, *The Times* and *The Oxford Dictionary for Writers and Editors* have recently both abandoned the 'correct' etymological spelling of certain nouns and adjectives ending in *-xion* and *-xive*, such as *connexion*, *inflexion*, and *reflexive*. The historical reason for their taking an *-x* rather than *-ct* like most such words is that they are derived from actual Latin nouns in *-xio*, such as *connexio*, rather than from the past participle stem of a Latin verb in *-ct*. The influence of the verbs *connect*, *inflect*, and *deflect*, and the analogy with the multitude of English nouns ending in *-tion* makes *con-*

*nexion* and its small band of brothers that take the *-x* stick out like
sore thumbs. Latin scholars know that the past participle stem of
*necto* is *nex-*, and of *flecto* is *-flex*; and that accordingly the etymological basis of their nouns is *nexio* and *flexio*. The knowledge is
interesting, but not crucial. We can no longer run English spelling
so as to avoid wounding the susceptibilities of classicists: we never
could. In any case, we are not creating a grotesque anomaly even in
strict etymology: a few Latin nouns are formed from the present
rather than the past participle stems, for example *oblivio*. A similar
etymologically correct and pretty spelling that has recently been
given the thumbs down is *Monna Lisa*. *The Times* persisted with this
for two centuries, to demonstrate that it is a very superior paper,
and knows that *Monna* is derived from *Madonna*. Now that even
the Italians have gone over to *Mona Lisa*, when they are not writing
*La Gioconda*, *The Times* has sold the pass in the last ditch.

9.   Dog will eat dogg. Of all the vexations that are vexed in the
vexing system of English spelling – though the vexation of
anomalous vowel sounds may be the worst, – the vexation of double
or single letters for consonantal sounds is the most tormenting. The
majority of words whose spelling cannot safely be inferred from
their sound present the difficulty that one cannot deduce whether
some single consonantal sound is given by a single letter, a double
letter, or two or more letters, as in *sch*. The sort of words I have in
mind, and which cause me trouble, are *accommodate*, *committee*,
and *comity*; *harass* and *embarrass*; *Britain* and *Brittany* (which is
plain daft); *acquiesce* and *aqueduct*. The jungle has grown over
many centuries. The only general rule that applies (most of the
time) is that the vowel before a single letter is sounded long, as in
*holy*, and that the vowel before a double letter is sounded short, as
in *holly*. It is possible that this rich and informative profusion will be
cut back, as mechanical cutters now mutilate the hedgerows, by
simplifying all consonantal sounds to single letters. This would
greatly reduce the signals given by English spelling. It would
degrade the language. But it may be inevitable.

10.   American and British spellings will come together. It would
make sense for the British to adopt the downright American
spelling of words such as *humor* and *honor* (*umor* and *onor*?), and
for the Americans to surrender their heroic and stubborn defence of
that unnecessary letter, the whoreson zed, in verbs ending in *-ise*.
Sense is on the side of that change. History is against it. If
Americans and British were going to agree on spelling, you would
have thought that the centripetal influence of the press would have

achieved it by now. The centrifugal influences of pronunciation, national idiosyncrasy, chauvinism, and the natural process by which language grows in its own herbaceous border, have combined so far to keep the spellings separate in the two principal English-speaking countries. The advantages of a standard spelling of English all over the globe are great. We may not get them without the birth of a natural genius for orthography, or an international conference to set the standard, from which, good Swift and Johnson, deliver us.

11. The Doomsday scenario, as we say in the trade, is that reading off video screens is so expensive, and causes so much eye strain, irritation, and confusion, that the new technology of writing and reading will create an irresistible impulse to a qik anser to lerning English without ters. We shall simply amputate all 'surplus' letters, serving no apparent purpose for either pronunciation or meaning, from words such as *acomodation*, *miselaneus*, *reserch*, *lern*, *caotic*, *literat*, *hav*, *giv*, *anser*, and *qik*. Psychologists at Aberdeen University devised such a system of shortened words in 1984, on the grounds that it is easier, it could be spread rapidly by the new electronic technology, and in turn it would stimulate the spread of the technology by making it easier to use. The system is much like the initial teaching alphabet, ITA, introduced in the 1960s in Britain, and based on the notion of making spelling easier for beginners by using the principle of spelling as you speak. The rapid death of ITA shows that all such schemes of basing spelling simply on pronunciation are blinkered, fanatical, and doomed to failure, because they attempt to substitute the tyranny of phonetics for our present haphazard democracy. English spelling conveys many more messages than simple pronunciation. If it were to cease to do so, the language would be greatly impoverished.

# 9/PUNCTUATION

'"Not to put too fine a point upon it" – a favourite apology for plain-speaking with Mr Snagsby.' Charles Dickens, *Bleak House*, ch. 11

'Even when the sense is perfectly clear, a sentence may be deprived of half its force – its spirit – its point – by improper punctuation. For the want of merely a comma, it often occurs that an axiom appears a paradox, or that a sarcasm is converted into a sermonoid.' Edgar Allan Poe, *Marginalia*, 1844–9.

Punctuation is the politeness of printers. It is not part of the deep structure of the language, but a convention that has been imposed on written language quite recently in order to help the reader in various ways. In speaking we can use pause and intonation, gesture and change of tone, the raised eyebrow or the expressive Indian rocking of the head from side to side indicating doubt, diffidence, and deference, to punctuate our words and elucidate our meaning. Such aids are not available to the written word; accordingly, we have invented others. The rules of punctuation are not carved on tables of stone, and we should not be surprised or shocked to discover that they are at present changing rapidly. The new technologies of printing both impose and require new marks. Printing by photocomposition and reading from a visual display unit are new techniques, which are already introducing new kinds of punctuation.

When we said that the rules of punctuation were not carved on tables of stone it was a metaphor from the Old Testament but it was also literally true the earliest inscriptions have letter after letter carved in rows with no spaces or other marks even between words so providing nice employment for textual commentators and editors however most languages gradually evolved systems of punctuation to indicate stops pauses interrogation exclamation uncertainty and the quotation of direct speech.

Ours is so refined that it can make sense of a sentence that contains the word 'had' eleven consecutive times. Fred, where Philip had had 'had had', had had 'had'; 'had had' had had the teacher's approval.

The origins of punctuation are lost in the mists of epigraphy. It depends a bit on what you mean by punctuation. When Hebrew started to die out as a spoken language, perhaps as early as the first century BC, scholars began to put single, double, or triple points above consonants to indicate preceding or succeeding vowels. The Hebrew alphabet consisted only of consonants. Points were devised so that the traditions of intonation and pronunciation should not be forgotten. But was it punctuation?

Greek inscriptions before the fourth century BC were continuous: words and sentences were not separated or marked in any other way.

Aristotle, the great systematizer, started to divide topics by paragraphs. The *paragraphos* was probably originally a short horizontal stroke written below the beginning of a line in which a break of sense occurred. Other scholars think that paragraphs were marked by a dividing stroke between them. Fragments of Plato's *Phaedo*, found at Gurob, show signs of paragraphs ending with a double point (:), as well as short dashes separating different speeches. Euripides used a wedge or sideways V to mark changes of speaker in his tragedy *Antiope*. Again we have to ask, do marks to indicate paragraphs or change of speaker constitute what we mean by punctuation?

Most etymologists attribute the invention of punctuation to Aristophanes of Byzantium, who was in charge of the great library of Alexandria *circa* 194 BC. He invented a system of points corresponding to our comma, semicolon, and full stop to mark short, medium, and long periods of writing. The sections were divided according to rhetorical theory. The points were put after the last letter in each section, and were placed at the bottom, middle, or top of the letter, depending on the length of the section: in short sections the point was at the bottom; in long sections, at the top. All writing was done in majuscules, or capital letters, so that it was easy to distinguish the three positions.

In addition to these points, Aristophanes is also credited with having created the systematic study of other kinds of punctuation and accentuation. He is said to have invented the virgule, hyphen, apostrophe, and quotation marks. The virgule, written sometimes as a slash and sometimes as a long comma, was put between words where the meaning might seem ambiguous. The hyphen, used to denote compound words, was drawn as a curve or a line under the appropriate letters. The apostrophe was written as a curve or a straight accent or a point. It indicated elision; it was put after foreign names to show their status; and it was used to distinguish two consecutive vowels and double consonants. Quotation marks in the form of crosses, horizontal strokes, wavy strokes, or wedges (perhaps derived from Euripides) were put in the margin to indicate a quotation.

Aristophanes' system of punctuation was used by textual critics and other scholars; but it was not widely adopted by scribes for general use.

Between Aristophanes and the Renaissance there were two important developments in the history of punctuation. First, during the seventh and eighth centuries handwriting introduced minuscule as well as majuscule letters. Capital letters could now be used to note important or exceptional words. And the ascenders and descenders of minuscule manuscript made it harder to read a text without punctuation.

Second, Charlemagne, King of the Franks from 768 to 814, and Holy Roman Emperor for the second part of this period, and Alcuin, the English director of his palace school, led an educational revival that produced improved spelling and punctuation in biblical and liturgical texts. Only a simplified version of Aristophanes' system was in use. It consisted of two marks: the full point and the colon, the latter being used to indicate an intermediate stop. By the eleventh century Aristophanes' full system was in use. In addition new marks, including the *punctus interrogativus* which resembled today's question mark, had been introduced to indicate a syntactical break and a change in inflection. These new marks were derived from musical notation used in Gregorian chants.

In 1453 Constantinople, the West's umbilical cord to our classical past, was attacked and conquered by Ottoman Turks. Greek scholars emigrated to Western Europe, bringing with them Greek culture, and stimulating an intense interest in Greek literature. From that tremendous event modern punctuation evolved.

Our familiar punctuation marks were originally rhetorical divisions in the structure of a sentence, derived from Greek grammar. A comma was a clause of fewer than eight syllables. In *Timon of Athens*, I, 1, 48, the Poet says:

> 'No levell'd malice
> Infects one comma in the course I hold . . .'

A colon, also taken from Greek rhetoric and prosody, was a clause of from eight to seventeen syllables. John Cleveland, with a characteristic metaphysical conceit, wrote in *Against Sleep*:

'Sleep! the Days Colon, many Hours of Bliss
Lost in a wide Parenthesis.'

A period was originally a rhythmical division composed of two or
more cola, or, as we should say these days, colons. In 1593 Thomas
Nash, that ferocious controversialist, wrote in reply to his rival in
rhetorical acerbity, Gabriel Harvey: 'I talk of a great matter when I
tell thee of a period; for I know two several periods in this last
epistle, at least forty lines long apiece.'

The original sense of a period survives in such expressions as an
orator being said to speak in rounded periods, or a writer like
Carlyle being described as writing in thunderous and immense
periods.

An inflected language such as Latin, in which most words modify
their forms to show their grammatical relations to their context,
needs punctuation less than an uninflected language, such as
English, in which few words retain such signals. Accordingly, when
Old English started to lose its inflexions, exact punctuation had to
be developed to clarify grammatical relationships and to prevent
misunderstandings and confusion of meaning. At the end of the
ninth century, when Alfred translated into English the *Cura
Pastoralis* of Pope Gregory to improve the spiritual education of the
English clergy, he introduced primitive punctuation marks, which
sign-posted the grammar and translated into the vernacular something of the logic and precision of the Latin. From Alfred on
punctuation points were gradually brought into English to indicate
pauses of various lengths. John Wycliffe's first translation of the
whole Bible into English, *circa* 1382, provides the earliest example
of something approaching our modern system of pointing.

The system was formalized and codified by Aldus Manutius, the
great Italian scholar and printer (Aldo Manuzio: 1450–1515), who
founded the Aldine Press in Venice.

It was complicated by the Renaissance fashion of imitating the
style of Latin writers in English. Latin, which shows its grammatical
construction in the form of its words, uses punctuation to mark
rhythmical, or rhetorical, or dramatic, or elocutionary pauses.
English, being uninflected, needs punctuation to show the grammar, logic, and construction of a sentence.

Here is an example of the former sort of punctuation, to show
metrical pauses, and the rhythm of the final two lines of
Shakespeare's *Sonnet XXV*:

'Then happy I, that love and am beloved

> Where I may not remove, nor be removed.'

That was the punctuation in the original printings. Modern editions substitute punctuation to make plain the grammar and logic:

> 'Then happy I, that love and am belov'd,
> Where I may not remove nor be remov'd.'

This is not an improvement, giving the reader less help with his breathing and the rhythm than the original punctuation.

Here is an example of punctuation to point out grammar and logic, from the Authorized Version of *Mark* IV, 1:

> 'And he began again to teach by the sea side: and there was gathered unto him a great multitude, so that he entered into a ship and sat in the sea; and the whole multitude was by the sea, on the land.'

Punctuation is used both for rhythm, and for logic. You can observe the two kinds of punctuation wrestling together in such deliberately Latinate and aphoristic writing as Francis Bacon's essay on *Boldness*, printed in 1625 when punctuation was still inchoate and evolving:

> 'Mahomet made the people believe that he would call a hill to him, and from the top of it offer up his prayers for the observers of his law. The people assembled: Mahomet called the hill to come to him again and again; and when the hill stood still, he was never a whit abashed, but said, "If the hill will not come to Mahomet, Mahomet will go to the hill."'

Wrong punctuation or lack of punctuation can alter or destroy the sense of English. The school-child's puzzle, 'Charles the First walked and talked half an hour after his head was cut off', can be punctuated to make banal sense by the addition of a semi-colon and a comma.

Such jokes about the misunderstandings caused by mispunctuation have a long literary history, going back to the pristine points. The most famous is Quince's Prologue to the Pyramus and Thisby burlesque in *A Midsummer Night's Dream*:

> 'If we offend, it is with our good will.
> That you should think, we come not to offend,
> But with good will. To show our simple skill,
> That is the true beginning of our end . . .'

But we can trace it farther back than that. In *Ralph Roister Doister*, the earliest known English comedy, written by Nicholas Udall about 1553, Roister, the swaggering simpleton, had a love letter written by a scribe to Dame Custance, whom he is courting. Matthew Merygreek reads it out to her, punctuating it so that it is turned into a pasquinade:

> 'Sweet mistresse, whereas I love you – nothing at all;
> Regarding your substance and richesse chief of all,
> For your personage, beautie, demeanour and wit
> I commend me unto you never a whitte.
> Sorry to hear report of your good welfare . . .'

The catalogue of endearments turned into insults by false punctuating has a satisfactorily inflammatory effect on Dame Custance.

Our present, elaborate system of punctuation in English was developed for the pen, and perfected for the linotype-operator and printing-press. The new technologies of word-processors and photocomposition are developing a new and simpler system. This is part of the general simplification of English, and the smoothing away of nice distinctions, for the benefit of the vastly increased numbers of people who are using the language. If you are teaching a class of Philippine students, whose first language is not English, to programme computers, you may not want to spend time on the pretty distinction between the colon and the semi-colon.

The new technology itself is better at dashes than dots. You have only to watch a burly printer, with fingers like a bunch of over-ripe bananas, trying to cut out a full point with his scalpel and replace it with a semicolon, to know that you should not ask him to do it for a whim or passing elegance. We are perfecting pens that can mark the photocomposition paper with points that show up in print almost as faintly as if they had been put there in the first place by the VDU. But, in producing a daily newspaper at least, there is not the time to call back copy on the screen merely to correct punctuation. The consequence will be that punctuation will be increasingly simplified and standardized, with a preference for dashes and strokes rather than combinations of dots.

A small dot can make a big difference. At the time of the Jameson raid, Dr Leander Starr Jameson was sent a telegraphic invitation to attack the Transvaal, to coincide with a rising of 'uitlanders'. It ran, without punctuation: 'It is under these circumstances that we feel constrained to call upon you to come to our aid should a disturbance arise here the circumstances are so extreme that we cannot but believe that you and the men under you will not fail to come to the rescue of people who are so situated.' It all depends on where you put the stop. If you put it after 'aid', the telegram is a direct invitation to come at once. If you put it after 'here' it becomes a conditional invitation. Either way it was punctuated, it did not affect history, since the telegram was a put-up job. Jameson was going to lead his raid anyway.

The misunderstandings caused by mispunctuation or lack of punctuation are exemplified most vividly in newspaper headlines, which are our modern equivalent of carving on stone. A headline has to compress as much meaning into as little space as possible. If you have only twenty-four characters to express a summary of an article across two columns, you do not want to waste any space on punctuation, which will probably be misprinted anyway. G.K. Chesterton wrote about the inky art of headlines: 'If I choose to head an article An Inquiry into the Conditions of Mycenaean Civilization, with Special Reference to the Economic and Domestic Functions of Women Before and After the Conjectural Date of the Argive Expedition Against Troy, I really have no right to complain if (when I send it to the *Chicago Daily Scoop*) they alter the title to the headline HOW HELEN DID THE HOUSE-KEEPING.'

Compression and lack of punctuation can produce obscurity. Horace said it, twenty centuries ago:

> *brevis esse laboro,*
> *Obscurus fio . . .*

I try to be brief, and I end up being obscure. And so you get headlines such as PRIME MINISTER QUIZZED REFUSES BANK RATE RISE LEAK PROBE, the meaning of which does not leap out of the page at you. This is partly because the headline has used short general-purpose headline words, by which every inquiry becomes a probe, any kind of interrogation becomes a quiz, ban stands for any kind of restriction, and bid for any form of human effort; but the headline has also inspissated obscurity by dispensing with four prepositions and all punctuation. Even a comma would have shed a little light.

Headlines are a minor linguistic art form on which the Pun never Sets, but the punctuation gets left out. They remind us not to put all our begs in one ask-it.

The first and the one indispensable stop is the full stop or period.

Here is an eloquent example of its use to divide complete sentences: 'Honour all men. Love the brotherhood. Fear God. Honour the king.'

Within living memory narrow grammatical pedagogues have taught small boys that they could not write a complete sentence without at least one verb in it, and beaten them when they tried to do so. Like this. That was always nonsense. The definition of what a sentence is is a matter of dispute between the grammarians and the professors of structuralist linguistics. Is it a combination of words that contains at least one subject, one predicate, and a verb? Is it a group or set of words followed by a pause and revealing an intelligible purpose? In such a confusion of the authorities it is safer to define a sentence unhelpfully and circularly as what goes before a full stop; as the *OED* puts it: 'in popular use often, such a portion of a composition or utterance as extends from one full stop to another.'

One way that the language is changing is towards having shorter sentences and more full stops. The fashion for long sentences, structured from ranks of clauses into an elegant classical architecture, and exemplified in the journalism of Johnson and Gibbon, and, in our own day, Bernard Levin, is obsolete, or at any rate obsolescent; partly because short sentences are felt to be more readable and punchy, particularly in popular newspapers; partly because the new technologies of printing find short sentences handier to cope with (several printers may be setting the same article on their VDUs, and each one needs to have a new paragraph to start with); and partly because readers these days do not have the training or the patience to work their way through periods measureless to man, without losing the thread of the argument. Phew. There is a good, knock-down verbless sentence for you. As Richard Porson said of the majestic but occasionally verbose Gibbon: 'In some passages he drew the thread of his verbosity finer than the staple of his argument.'

One can use short verbless sentences for many effects and reasons ranging from arch comment, as in that 'Phew' above, to transition or summary comment on what has gone before, as in Sir Ronald Syme's favourite phrase, 'So far so good,' to dramatic climax. Alfred Jingle, the jaunty and self-possessed strolling actor in *The Posthumous Papers of the Pickwick Club*, is the patron saint of the verbless sentence for dramatic effect: 'Terrible place. Dangerous work. Other day – five children – mother. Tall lady, eating sandwiches. Forgot the arch. Crash. Knock. Children look round.

Mother's head off. Sandwich in her hand. No mouth to put it in. Head of a family off. Shocking, shocking.'

The opposite vice to the rolling Gibbonian and Gladstonian periods, where a full stop occurs as infrequently and as agreeably as an oasis in the Sahara, is a proliferation of full stops and short sentences. Fowler described this vice as the spot plague, and argued that it was tiring to the reader, on whom it imposed the task of supplying the connexion, and corrupting to the writer, whose craving for brevity persuades him that anything will pass for a sentence.

For example: 'He was a good man. He was a brave man. He was also a very kind man. He had a very kind wife. She was not brave but she was certainly very good. He and she formed an almost ideal couple. At least I think so. You may think differently.' Etc. *ad taedium*. Yawn.

The truth is that there are as many varieties of punctuation as there are varieties of English; and the prudent man uses the variety suited to his purpose. When writing for the newspapers, which are going to be read in a hurry and with incomplete concentration, or when giving instructions to a computer or a platoon of infantry, the prudent man will use short sentences and plenty of full stops. When writing a learned article or book for educated readers, the writer can afford to indulge in longer sentences and more elaborate punctuation, which will allow him finer distinctions and greater flexibility of meaning. The man who uses a variety of punctuation in the wrong context is liable to excite misunderstanding and derision.

Another modest little use of the full stop is to indicate an abbreviation. E.g., e.g. for *exempli gratia*, and Capt. for Captain. There is a useful distinction in this use, and it is widely ignored or misapprehended. There are two principal ways of abbreviating words. We can either give the first letter or few letters of a word, and then stop, as in Nov. for November; or we can drop out some portion of the middle of the word, as in Dr for Doctor. The logical and useful convention is to put a full stop after the first sort of abbreviation, but not after the second sort. Abbreviations are puzzling, but it is not their purpose to puzzle. Anything that we can do to help the reader elucidate them is worth doing. The punctuating convention is that a full stop after an abbreviation indicates that the word has been cut short; no full stop indicates that the word has been disembowelled, leaving some first and last letters. So, we write Bp (for Bishop) but Archdeac. (for Archdeacon, if we are impertinent enough); Capt. but Cpl; Mlle but Frl. (for Fraülein), doz. but cwt (for hundredweight). What we do about Ms, since it is an artificial abbreviation with no generally recognized longer form, I do not know. But the convention is not to put a stop after it, taking it to be related vaguely to Mistress or Missis. To put stops after abbreviations which retain the last letter of the original words, as in Mrs., Mr., Ld., etc., is useless and silly.

For abbreviations made by combining the initial letters of two or more words, the style of *The Times* used to be to put stops after each initial, as in B.B.C. and R.A.F. An exception was made for initials of organizations that had become words in their own right by reason of their pronounceability, in a word, acronyms. We were allowed to write NATO and UNESCO, because that was how we pronounced them; but we had to punctuate the E.E.C. and the U.S.A., which nobody pronounces Yousir. Because of the general modern tendency to simplify punctuation, and because of the difficulty that photocomposition and compositors have with small dots, we now say, 'Out, damned spot', wherever possible, and print BBC, RAF, UNO, and all the rest.

The modern world is infested with acronyms and organizations named by their initials, not all of which are immediately recognizable by those outside the speciality. The prudent writer sets out their names in full at first reference, before abbreviating, whether with or, more probably these days, without full stops.

For such a funny little slug, a comma can cause a lot of trouble, not just to compositors. Its misplacement can affect the meaning. Here is an example from a newspaper report of what somebody said about cannabis: 'There should be a government monopoly in pot. If it was sold at a controlled price, it would completely kill off the black market in other harmful drugs.' Thus punctuated the report means that the speaker considered pot a harmful drug. However, the earlier part of the report makes it clear that he considered pot harmless. What he said was 'other, harmful, drugs' (other drugs that, unlike cannabis, are harmful). For the want of commas his meaning has been reversed.

Occam's Razor should be applied to commas as well as to entities: *commata non sunt multiplicanda praeter necessitatem.* Commas ought not to be multiplied, except from necessity. It is not necessary to enclose adverbs and adverbial phrases in commas unless they are unwieldy or need special emphasis. Too many commas obscure the main outline of a sentence. 'He had not, previously, met the plaintiff, except when, in 1984, he had, unexpectedly, found himself in Paris.' Cut out all those commas with a razor, or a compositor's scalpel, except those before and after 'in 1984'. They obstruct the flow and therefore the understanding of the sentence. Omit the comma before 'if', 'unless', 'because', 'since', and 'when', unless the sense demands it. Commas are not usually needed before or after 'therefore' and 'accordingly'.

Words or phrases in apposition take a comma after as well as before. 'Trinity College, Oxford, is a nest of eagles and owls.' 'She, top of the best-seller list, has just published her seventy-third romance, *Love is the Enemy*, or *How She Came to Marry Him*, sentimental and maudlin, cloying and revolting, as usual.' In such cases commas hunt in pairs, although the second may be absorbed in a stronger stop.

The use of dashes for commas is deprecated. Dashes usually indicate that the sentence is badly constructed and needs rewriting. These bossy prescriptions to go easy on the commas and to avoid dashes like the Black Death were born in the age of steam-printing, and are being affected by the new technology. Photocomposition has trouble in distinguishing tiny points like commas, and much prefers dashes. In small ways it is changing the style of written English.

The use of commas in enumeration is a notorious debating-ground for punctuation pedants. Consider a list of three or more items; for example, *The Times*, the *Telegraph* and *The Guardian*. One school of punctuators, the logical, argues that the comma between *The Times* and the *Telegraph* takes the place of 'and', and that there is therefore no comma between the *Telegraph* and *The Guardian*, because it would be otiose and tautological. Those who are parsimonious about scattering commas across their pages support this school.

However, enumerations are not all as simple as that: life seldom is. Trouble comes with complex enumerations: for example, *The Times*, the *Telegraph*, and *The Morning Post and Advertiser*. I think that you need a comma before the first 'and' there to show that *The Morning Post and Advertiser* is one paper, not two. They drank beer, gin, vodka, whisky, vintage port, and tea. We need a comma after the vintage port to show that the vintage virtues go with the port but not the tea. Take-over bids were made for Shell, BP, Woolworths, and Marks and Spencer. We need the comma before the 'and' there to make clear that this rich chap was bidding for four companies, not five. The lucidity of Newman, the wit of Dr Johnson, and the prolific Gibbon. We need the comma after Dr Johnson, or we attribute wit to Gibbon – which indeed he had, particularly in the majestic impropriety of his footnotes, but which was not the point of the punctuation in the list.

The other school of punctuators argues that since you are going to need a final comma before the 'and' in some complex lists, to avoid ambiguity, you might as well put it in always, for the sake of uniformity. This uniform school has the virtue of giving one simple invariable rule. It is the one preferred by *Hart's Rules for Compositors and Readers at the University Press Oxford*.

The other vice with commas is mislocation or the intrusive comma, which puts asunder things that should not be put asunder. There is a temptation in a long sentence to bung in a comma or two to break things up, to give the reader a pause to draw breath, or merely to make it look pretty. Fowler called this vice 'separating inseparables'. You alter the meaning or make nonsense by putting a comma between a verb and its subject, or object, or complement, between a defining relative and its antecedent, or between an essential modification and what cannot stand without it. 'The prudent writer uses only commas, which have a logical or grammatical point' might suggest that you are recommending commas as the sole punctuation mark. You indicate that the relative clause is a defining one by omitting the comma. You could also help your readers by using 'that' instead of 'which' in defining relative clauses. 'The prudent writer puts a circle around his commas, which are the smallest punctuation marks and easily mistaken by a compositor in a hurry.' The comma is correct in that sentence, because the relative clause is non-defining.

There are pitfalls for commas at the end of long and complicated subjects. The temptation is to put in a comma to show that you have come to the end of the subject, or that some subsequent clause refers to the whole subject, not merely to the last leg of it.

For example: 'No punctuation marks are allowed to be used except full stops, commas, and dashes, that have secured the approval of the National Graphical Association and the new technology.' In this sentence the comma after 'dashes' removes the possibility that the NGA's certificate of approval is needed for dashes only; but only at the cost of separating the inseparable: the defining relative clause from its antecedent.

The only way out of this pitfall is to recast the sentence by breaking it in two. 'No punctuation marks are allowed to be used except full stops, commas, and dashes; and these must have secured the approval of the National Graphical Association and the new technology.'

'Spelling, grammar, and punctuation, in particular are tricky.' The comma after 'punctuation' is intended to show that 'in particular' refers to all three parts of the subject, not just to 'punctuation'. It is, nevertheless, a stumbling-block and a mistake. We can save the sense and restore logic by removing the 'in particular' from the tail of the procession to its head.

Misplaced commas can damage your sense. In the absolute construction there is a temptation to mistake the noun as the subject of the main verb, and separate it from its participle with a comma; 'The hack, having finished his piece, the sub-editor inserted an otiose comma and destroyed his meaning and equanimity.' 'These objections were overruled, and the compositor, having pleaded not guilty, the page was made up.' The absolute construction is not common in English, and is a pitfall full of sharp commas for the unwary.

When alternatives, or other pairs or series, finish their courses together, there is a tendency to omit the necessary comma after the second or third of them: 'As regards stops, many, if not most of the conventions are intended to make writing easier.' You need a comma after 'most' to make your sentence ship-shape and logical.

You can get in a right muddle of commas when lists include phrases in apposition, and the enumeration commas are confused with the apposition commas. 'Dr Johnson, the Great Cham of English Literature, Shakespeare, the Swan of Avon, Browning, Sir James Murray, Ivor Brown, editor of *The Observer*, and Eric Partridge were all logophiles and wordsmiths.' But how many were there going to St Ives? The way out of such Gadarene stampedes of commas is perhaps to use brackets.

In poetry and 'literary' writing a comma can make a huge difference in effect as well as meaning. Consider the opening sentence of *A la Recherche du Temps Perdu*: '*Longtemps je me suis couché de bonne heure*' and the effect that a comma after '*longtemps*' has on the rhythm and resonance of the sentence. Fortunately most of us do not have to write with as meticulous an eye on the resonances as Proust. Fortunately Proust did not have to compose on a word-processor and have his work set by a VDU; for otherwise the poor old boy would have been rolling around on the floor, chewing the cork in frustration, more than he did anyway.

The semi-colon is the most popular of the lesser points; but its popularity is diminished by the new technology. A dash is easier to see on a screen, and easier to correct or insert in a page than the small and finical semi-colon. It is, nevertheless, an elegant and useful stop in literary writing; less useful in popular journalism, which favours short sentences that do not demand much concentration from its strap-hanging readers.

It is often the best stop to use before 'but', as in the first sentence of the preceding paragraph. And there are certain contexts when a semi-colon is essential, not just a refined elegance. For example: you need it to separate principal clauses that are themselves separated by commas. The Prime Minister favours hanging, flogging, censorship, and the deportation of journalists; the Leader of the Opposition favours penal reform, abortion, and freedom for consenting adults. His books include *Words, Words, Words*; *Words in Your Ear*; and *Words in Time*. Without the semi-colons those enumerations would become tangled, and tax the reader's patience.

The danger in a long and complex period is that one uses a semi-colon to separate elements of a group that is separated by nothing more than a comma, if that, from the rest of the sentence. 'If you want to use stops logically, so that your sentence fits together shipshape and Bristol fashion; if you want your semi-colon to pull its proper weight, and not unbalance the structure, you should not scatter them like a man throwing crumbs to the birds; you could start by substituting a comma for the first semi-colon in this sentence.' This is the vice of making the less include the greater; which is absurd.

The colon is a stop preferred by self-conscious stylists in impressive contexts: sometimes, I suspect, for not much more purpose than to demonstrate that they are educated and rare *literati*, who have at their command punctuation beyond the ken of lesser men. The days when the colon was second in the hierarchy after the full stop have gone: though it will remain a familiar stop for as long as we read the Psalms in versions descended from King James rather than *Reader's Digest*.

Its principal use today is to introduce lists. 'The main punctuation stops are: full stop, colon, semi-colon, and comma.' It is a mark that expresses *viz*. There is a tendency in newspapers to start the enumeration after the colon with a capital letter: 'The chief genres of fiction are: Crime, science fiction, historical romance, fantasy, and bodice-rippers.' This would have been judged wrong by grammarians a generation ago: their rules stated that a capital was correct only after a full stop. Newspaper designers consider that a capital letter gives emphasis to the first item on a list. We do not have to conform to their style outside newspapers.

Whereas the semi-colon separates equal or balanced clauses

('There is tears for his love; joy for his fortune; honour for his valour; and death for his ambition.'), the colon marks a step forward: from introduction to main theme; from cause to effect; from premiss to conclusion; etc.

It stands for *scilicet*, that is to say, and i.e., as well as *viz*. It is the usual stop to introduce a quotation of any length, and in this case the case the quotation does start with a capital letter. He said: 'Who will rid me of this turbulent stop?' The colon is regularly used to introduce examples, antitheses, parallels, and other clauses that need a formal fanfare of trumpets to announce them. It is an eloquent little stop, somewhat threatened by the dash because of the imprecision of the new technology, in its present form at least, at handling small spots.

Those are the principal punctuation marks for the logical or rhetorical division of sentences. There is a modern tendency for the dash to replace them as a stop-of-all-work, partly because it shows up better on a screen, and partly because its use avoids discrimination and thought. On this subject Bernard Shaw, who sub-edited his own copy, and whose views on such matters are stimulating, though not necessarily authoritative, wrote to T.E. Lawrence: 'The Bible bars the dash, which is the great refuge of those who are too lazy to punctuate. I never use it when I can possibly substitute the colon, and I save up the colon jealously for certain effects which no other stop produces.'

There are few problems, logical or technical, with the question mark. It shows up quite well on the small screen. It is used with direct questions, such as: 'Is the question mark a proper stop?' It is not used with indirect questions, such as: 'He asked whether the question mark was a proper stop.' The only difficulty lies in not recognizing or in forgetting that some sentence is a question. 'Will you please remember to punctuate properly' is a question, and needs a question mark after it. It is easy to forget that a long and complex period started off as a question. 'Can it seriously be believed that, with all the resources of the English language and grammar, with punctuation elaborately developed over six centuries, and with every advantage of modern printing, I am going to plod to the end of this boring sentence, and forget that it started as an interrogative.' You're darned right it can, baby. To put a question mark between brackets as a sneer is as contemptible and amateur as using *sic* for the same purpose. 'The Minister of Education said that these were the benefits (?) (*sic*) of teaching children formal grammar.'

Male chauvinists call the exclamation mark a female punctuation stop, and animadvert on its frequency in the works of such as Barbara Cartland. It would be kinder and more accurate to say that excessive use of the exclamation mark is the sign of an uneducated or unpractised writer. It is usually possible to show the tone of the words by the words themselves rather than by a sign-post.

The exclamation mark, or gasp-mark, or screamer, is properly reserved for true exclamations such as 'Oh!', 'Great Balls of Fire!', 'Damn your impertinence!', and 'How you vex me!' It is sometimes necessary to use a gasp-mark with a sentence that is not a proper exclamation to indicate that the words have an unexpected tone, which is not evident from the words alone: 'You thought punctuation didn't matter!' 'And I was told he was a teetotaller!' 'He learnt at last that the solecist was – himself!' In these two categories of statement, exclamations and sentences that are not what they seem, the exclamation mark is not an unnecessary symbol, but a useful one. Elsewhere the prudent scribe will avoid it like the plague. And printers of both the old and the new technologies dislike it, because it is an unusual and easily mistaken mark.

We are in a state of confusion about the most insignificant of punctuation marks, the apostrophe. You cannot walk down your local high street without seeing signs exhorting you to ASK ONE OF OUR ASSISTANT'S FOR ADVICE, and not to TAKE PRAM'S INSIDE. We are bombarded with VIP'S, OAP'S, and MP'S. There was an ugly outbreak of 'bread and circus's' in the Letters Column of *The Times* recently, I regret to have to report. For-jolly-sooth, or not, as the case may be; at this rate we shall be printing *The Time's* on our mast-head. The most alarming instance of apostrophitis I have come across was on a stall at Oxford Circus, selling royal tat and junk, which appeared to advertise ROYAL WEDDING – SOUVENIR PENIS. What it actually had was SOUVENIR PEN'S; but that was bad enough.

What is to be done? I suppose we can help ourselves by remembering the origin of apostrophe. It comes from the Greek word *apostrophos*, which means 'turning away'. It is the accent of turning away, used to indicate that something has been turned away, *viz.* elided or omitted.

The apostrophe was introduced to mark the possessive case in genitives where an 'e' had originally been written, but was now left out, as in fox's, James's. The genitives used to be written foxes and Jameses.

Alternatively the apostrophe may indicate the abbreviation of the word 'his' which was introduced as a new way of saying the genitive in the sixteenth century. They started to say 'John his book'; soon pronounced 'Johns book', and written correspondingly 'John's book', to mark the elision that had been turned away. This was extended to Mary's book as well, written 'Mary's book', an absurd contraction for 'Mary his book'. The English cannot bear very much logic in their grammar.

This particular construction was confined to the English/Dutch/ Frisian part of the West Germanic tongue. Others carry on with the ancient genitive; but in Dutch one says 'Jan zijn boek', and writes it informally 'Jan z'n boek.' The Dutch, however, have not been able to stomack 'Marijke z'n boek', as English-speakers have done, and say 'Marijke der boek', literally 'Mary of her the book', and write it 'd'r'.

The apostrophe to indicate the genitive was gradually extended to all possessives, even where 'e' had not previously been written, as in man's, children's, conscience' sake. This was not yet established in 1725. But it is established now. And a lot of trouble it causes.

One difficulty peculiar to newspapers is the difficulty of transcribing dictated copy. Envisage the scene. Literary Editor fights his way to public telephone box that works, eventually makes contact, and starts dictating. What he wants to dictate is 'Dickens'', possessive. What he says is, perforce, 'Dickens'. The copy-taker, tap-tapping at full speed, transcribes 'Dicken's'. And there are another twenty sarcastic letters to answer.

One solution would be to put an apostrophe followed by 's' even after names ending with 's': thus, 'Dickens's', pronounced 'Dickenziz.' The trouble is that we cannot do that with some of the better known names, where custom has been hallowed by practice. We cannot start saying 'Achilleses' with four syllables, or 'Jesus's', 'Jesuses' with three syllables. Why not? Because.

I think that we just have to watch our apostrophes, as well as our ps and qs. One obvious solution to the apparently ubiquitous modern misuse of the apostrophe occurs: simply leave it out. Punctuation is intended to make it easier to read a written piece. In what way is it easier to read 'don't' than 'dont', or 'James'' than 'James'? It reflects no pronunciation difference; but only the desire of a more pernickety age to write correctly – by their standards.

This is already happening, especially in plural nouns, where the nouns are adjectival without any real possessive sense. 'Boys School'; the Womens Institute and Citizens Advice Bureau so write themselves. I suppose that MASTERS LODGE, which is written outside the appropriate stately building in Darwin College, Cambridge, might cause confusion; but only to the hopelessly ignorant or the mischievously pedantic.

The decay of the apostrophe has happened long ago in some place names. St Andrews, so written, probably refers to the monastery; St Neots comes from *villa sancti Neoti*; St Paul's from *monasterium sancti Pauli*. Usage rules in such matters; and usage is seldom wrong.

Punctuation marks are navigational aids, not scientific or moral laws. They change, as the language and the technology of printing changes. All of them pose little problems, some of which are insoluble. Photocomposition is particularly stupid at breaking words and hyphenating them in the wrong places. It is possible that we may be able to programme the computer to break them in the appropriate places. There is an interminable and insoluble disagreement about whether inverted commas always come after the other stops, or in their logical place, sometimes before, sometimes after. There is no universally accepted practice about capitalization, hyphenization, and brackets.

The dash, which used to be execrated by English teachers and Chief Sub-Editors as a mark of sloppy thinking and bad construction, is spreading because of slapdash modern ways and photographic modern printing. All we can do is hang on to our colons: punctuation is bound to change, like the rest of language; punctuation is made for man, not man for punctuation; a good sentence should be intelligible without the help of punctuation in most cases; and, if you get in a muddle with your dots and dashes, you may need to simplify your thoughts, and shorten your sentence.

# BIBLIOGRAPHY

A Dictionary of Australian Colloquialisms, edited by G.A. Wilkes, 1978
Aitchison, Jean, Language Change: Progress or Decay?, 1981
Barltrop, Robert, and Jim Wolveridge, The Muvver Tongue, 1980
Barnhart Dictionaries of New English, 1973 and 1980
BBC Pronouncing Dictionary of British Names, edited by G.E. Pointon, 1983
Berresford Ellis, P., The Cornish Language and its Literature, 1974
Bodmer, Frederick, The Loom of Language, 1981
Brewer's Dictionary of Phrase and Fable, edited by Ivor H. Evans, 1981
Brock, G.L., Words in Everyday Life, 1981
Burgess, Anthony, Language Made Plain, 1964
Chambers Twentieth Century Dictionary, edited by E.M. Kirkpatrick, 1983
Chomsky, Noam, Reflections on Language, 1976
Collins English Dictionary, edited by Patrick Hands, 1979
Cottle, Basil, The Plight of English, 1975
Cowie, A.P., R. Mackin, and I.R. McCaig, The Oxford Dictionaries of Current
    Idiomatic English, 1975 and 1983
Curme, George O., A Grammar of the English Language, two volumes, 1977
Donoghue, Denis, Ferocious Alphabets, 1981
Enright, D.J., A Mania for Sentences, 1983
Fowler's Modern English Usage, second edition revised by Sir Ernest Gowers, with
    corrections 1982
Gilman, Richard, Decadence, 1979
Green, Jonathon, Newspeak, A Dictionary of Jargon, 1984
Grose, Francis, A Dictionary of the Vulgar Tongue, 1811
Halliday, F.E., The Excellency of the English Tongue, 1975
Harris, Roy, The Language Makers, 1980
Harris, Roy, The Language Myth, 1981
Herbert, A.P., What A Word!, 1935
Hudson, Kenneth, The Dictionary of Diseased English, 1977
Hudson, Kenneth, The Dictionary of the Teenage Revolution and its Aftermath,
    1983
Hudson, Kenneth, The Jargon of the Professions, 1978
Hudson, Kenneth, The Language of the Teenage Revolution, 1983
In Honour of A.S. Hornby, edited by Peter Strevens, 1978
Kress, Gunther, and Robert Hodge, Language as Ideology, 1979
Language and Learning, The Debate between Jean Piaget and Noam Chomsky,
    edited by Massimo Piattelli-Palmarini, 1980
Longman New Universal Dictionary, 1982
Lyons, John, Language, Meaning and Context, 1981
Lyons, John, New Horizons in Linguistics, 1970
Maleska, Eugene T., A Pleasure in Words, 1983
Michaels, Leonard and Christopher Ricks, editors, The State of the Language, 1980
Migliorini, Bruno, The Italian Language, 1966

Miller, Casey and Kate Swift, The Handbook of Non-Sexist Writing, 1981

Nash, Walter, Designs in Prose, A Study of Compositional Problems and Methods, 1980

Neaman, Judith S., and Carole G. Silver, Kind Words, A Thesaurus of Euphemisms, 1983

Palmer, L.R., The Greek Language, 1980

Partridge, Eric, A Dictionary of Catch Phrases, 1977

Partridge, Eric, A Dictionary of Slang and Unconventional English, two volumes, 1937

Partridge, Eric, The Concise Usage and Abusage, 1954

Partridge, Eric, You Have A Point There, 1953

Pierssens, Michel, The Poer of Babel, 1980

Rawson, Hugh, A Dictionary of Euphemisms, 1983

Robinson, Ian, The New Grammarians' Funeral, 1975

Robinson, Ian, The Survival of English, 1973

Scragg, D.G., A History of English Spelling, 1975

Schur, Norman W., English English, 1980

Shenker, Israel, Harmless Drudges, 1979

Six Thousand Words, A Supplement to Webster's Third New International Dictionary, 1976

Studies in English Linguistics for Randolph Quirk, edited by Sidney Greenbaum, 1980

The Concise Oxford Dictionary of Proverbs, edited by J.A. Simpson, 1982

The Fontana Biographical Companion to Modern Thought, edited by Alan Bullock and R.B. Woodings, 1983

The Fontana Dictionary of Modern Thought, edited by Alan Bullock and Oliver Stallybrass, 1977

The Oxford Dictionary for Writers and Editors, 1981

The Oxford Dictionary of English Etymology, edited by C.T. Onions, 1966

The Oxford Dictionary of English Proverbs, compiled by William George Smith, third edition edited by F.P. Wilson, 1970

The Oxford English Dictionary, 1884–1928

The Oxford English Dictionary Supplements, 1972, 1976, and 1982

The Oxford Latin Dictionary, edited by Peter Glare, 1968–1982

Vetterling-Braggin, Mary, Sexist Language, 1981

Wakelin, Martyn F., English Dialects, 1972

Webster's Third New International Dictionary, 1971

Weiner, E.S.C., The Oxford Guide to English Usage, 1983

Williams, Raymond, Keywords, A Vocabulary to Culture and Society, 1976

Wright, Peter, Cockney Dialect and Slang, 1981

# INDEX